REVIEWS

D1373147

"… Templeton's tome may well become "the" book for actors. Whether you're just starting out, following a particular method, or are a seasoned professional, there are plenty of tips and tricks that can aid actors in their work.

For starters, this book is fairly comprehensive, focusing on the art of acting itself, proper technique, and how you can make it work for you as a business venture. That basically covers what you'd want to learn in a very advanced acting class, after studying the craft for years. But, this text is written in a way to try and enthuse, inspire, and enlighten, making sure to include all the pitfalls that can occur, as well as how you can avoid them. In short, it's probably today's new "Acting Bible", whether you're a student of Stanislavsky, Hagen, or any other method.

As you read it aloud in your head, Templeton's energetic voice comes through loud and clear. You'll feel like you have your own acting coach, leading you on your path to getting the roles you are best suited for, and can make your own. Simply put, this is a great reference book that will grow dog-eared from repeated readings.

Highly Recommended!!"

— Chris Gibson, Reviewer Broadway World.com

"Penny Templeton leaves no stone unturned in her examination of the craft and business of acting. It's a thoughtful and inspired look into an art which she presents as both a calling and a career, and is a must-read for both beginning and veteran actors. The book covers everything from the history of the craft, technique, development of the actor, and the application of all that artistry in today's world. She does a remarkable job of showing the evolution of technique from master teachers like Stanislavski and Stella Adler, or Lee Strasberg and Sanford Meisner to her own set of acting exercises that allow the actor to have a structure to their work and process; but to also be released and free within that structure. It's important because it's that structure that allows an actor to not only grow as artist, but to feel confident whether in an audition, rehearsal, or performance. It makes a fantastic addition to any actor's bookshelf."

— Reader Review, Barnes and Noble.com

"Out of all the many books I have purchased and read on acting this is the one I will not lend out! I have been highlighting it continuously since I bought it in October, and I refer back to it at least once every two weeks. The section about technique for the camera is just as useful and relevant to today's actor as are the sections for finding classes and choosing headshots. Penny has written an enjoyable to read book for the modern actor, helping to illuminate the path to becoming a successful working actor."

Reader review on Amazon.com

"Dear Mrs. Templeton,
We have never met, therefore never worked together — *however* — after "mauling" through your book — I now feel like a new "baby cub," I should say! (You should see my book with coffee stains, underlines, highlighter and um, pasta sauce & mayo)! Incredible material, hands down. Stunning new material by Penny Templeton! As an Actor, it doesn't matter if you're a Meisner guy/gal, Strasbergian, an Adlerite, a Hagenist — read this book! It's like sitting down to a good meal (with wine and dessert). Refreshing hands down! Things move rather quickly on set and on stage these days. Nice to know Penny "gets" it. She dives right in, no fluff. It doesn't matter if you only use one or more of the golden nuggets she gives you. Point is, what are you doing to up the ante'? Actors are well read and NEVER stop learning. Nobody's getting my copy!! … Okay maybe if they roar a lil.
Thank you Penny!
Respectfully, Always in the Art," **Shawn Michael, Email review**

"Very few books cover the art of making the right choices – the choices of how to approach one's character, it requires more planning than many would think. Finding the right choice in a performance is extremely important – how many young actors and actresses are aware of the importance of finding that choice before taking it to show?

Penny's book, aptly titled *Acting Lions* is the book for all actors, both acting and aspiring to use as their bibles. To read it is simply engaging – enough to make you want to follow your dreams, as you always should. The three keys in the book are Artistry, Technique and the Business of Artistry. These are all extremely important things to follow."

— Bryan Cain-Jackson, Technorati.com

TESTIMONIALS

"I've never seen anything like it. It's not limited to one technique; it has everything. It is going to become the actor's bible."
— Judy Henderson - Casting Director - *Homeland*

"Everyone should immediately read this book. Penny Templeton's passion for the craft and invaluable expertise makes it a must-read for today's actor!"
— Ronald Rand - Publisher -*The Soul of the American Actor*, Author of *Acting Teachers of America*

"The question always arises, 'Do we really need another acting book?' In this case the answer is yes. This book is really a complete course in the art, study, and business of becoming an actor."
— Bud Beyer - Professor Emeritus Northwestern University

"I'm thankful to have her in my corner. Training with her and her technique has allowed me to feel prepared for every job." — Ramon Rodriguez - Actor - *Charlie's Angels, Battle: Los Angeles, Transformers II, Taking of the Pelham 123*

"Acting Lions is truly a comprehensive guide for actors of all backgrounds."
— Andrea Haring - Associate Director of The Linklater Center for Voice and Language

"Penny made my work come alive." — Gina Tognoni - 3 Time Emmy Award Winner - *One Life to Live, Guiding Light*

"What I love about the prose is its simplicity and the pervasive optimism and joy in acting that comes through clearly … A book that adds to the canon of acting." — Sam Chwat - Dialect Coach

"What you have not written is 'An Idiot's Guide to Acting'. It is an encyclopedia of acting." — Darren Bevill - Screenwriter

"Penny teaches you how to get the job and what to do once you've got it."
—Tricia Helfer - Actress - *17th Precinct, Battlestar Galactica, Dark Blue, The Firm*

"Excellent. One only hopes that every actor will read this. A must read!"
— Joan D'Incecco - Casting Director

"Penny Templeton is THE lady to show you how to be an acting lion. Her classes are hands down the most creative, supportive and unique in the city. I've worked with her not only as a student, but also helping to guide her other students to be powerful business people too. I give her and Acting Lions a huge thumbs up!" — Leslie Becker - Broadway Actress, Author of *The Organized Actor®* - *Anything Goes, Bonnie & Clyde, Nine*

"I couldn't have done this without Penny's help." — Rochelle Aytes - Actress - *Mistresses, Work It, Madea's Family Reunion, Detroit 187, Desperate Housewives, White Chicks*

"A juicy steak! I am completely blown away by this book. I wish I had access to it a long time ago!" — Jody Litman - Actress - Playwright

"I credit Penny with every role I get." — Sarah Wynter - Actress - *The 6th Day, 24, Damages, Bride of the Wind*

"Penny makes you work harder, and at the end of the day you are a better actor because of that." — April Hernandez - Actress - *SAG Award Nominee, Dexter, Freedom Writers, Person of Interest*

ACTING LIONS

UNLEASHING YOUR CRAFT
IN TODAY'S LIGHTNING FAST WORLD
OF
FILM, TELEVISION & THEATRE

By

Penny Templeton

Penny Templeton Studio, Inc.

ACTING LIONS

Unleashing your craft in today's lightning
fast world of Film, Television & Theatre

Published by
Penny Templeton Studio, Inc.
New York, NY

All rights reserved
Copyright 2011 by Penny Templeton

ISBN
978-0-615-46569-2

$24.95 US
$27.95 Canada

Printed in the United States of America

www.ActingLions.com

THIS BOOK IS DEDICATED TO:

The "Eva Barringtons":
My great-grandmother, grandmother, and mother,
Whose theatrical DNA is inherited,
And indelibly imprinted in me.

And to God,
Who set me on the path,
And is with me every step of the way.

TABLE OF CONTENTS

16. You're Hired! Now What?
How to Prepare and Do the Job   251

Appendices

ACKNOWLEDGEMENTS

In appreciation to my assistant, Michele Athena Morgen, for all her dedication and hard work.

To my role models and teachers—Wynn Handman, Paul Sorvino, Patricia Grantham, and Diana Hauser—mentors who were always there to guide me and light the way.

To Sandra Hill, a dear friend who had the epiphany that I become an acting teacher.

To Freddy Bosche, whose paintings displayed in my studio, and ingenious art work for my book cover continue to inspire us all.

To Ronald Rand, whose kindness and generosity in asking me to write articles for *The Soul of the American Actor* lit the spark to write this book. His advice on the great Masters, Stella Adler, et.al. was invaluable.

And Maria Wolf, who made me face organizing this manuscript and getting rid of all those dangling participles.

To Staci Swedeen, whose editorial assistance, wisdom and encouragement brought me over the finish line.

To Charlene DelFico, who tracked down and researched all the wonderful photos included. And to Angelina Ticic, who enthusiastically climbed on board and final proofed everything.

To Dawn Botello, Robin Sanders, and his sons, Alex and Robin Jr. To Vincent Bagnall and Oliver Gray 2nd— who put themselves on the line to make my dream of the accompanying DVD come true.

To my dear children, Danielle and Chris, and daughter-in-law Kelly, whose talents, love and support make me so proud. And to my grandchildren Penelope, Julia, and twins Luke and Lily, who make my heart smile.

To Hank, my dear husband and teaching partner, who loved me enough to take my hand and say, "You can do this!"

Last but not least, to my actors who have provided a bottomless supply of curiosity, inspiration, and talent, including our working actors who generously share their experiences with our acting family, which helps keep my teaching meaningful and relevant.

A SPECIAL THANK YOU

To James Kiberd, where it all started. You inspired both of us to bring an artistry of craft to the fast-paced world of Daytime Television. We had so much fun in your dressing room, working on new scripts and Shakespeare. It was a privilege to witness the birth of the "Trevor Ties" which lead to fulfilling your dream of becoming a Unicef National Ambassador.

*   *   *

I had the great good fortune to begin my coaching career as a personal assistant to James, who at the time was playing the iconic "Trevor" on *All My Children.* Faced with the challenge of bringing enormous amounts of text to life each day, James sought to develop a new working process that would fuse Impulsive Physical Acting with Mindful Method Acting for a more fully engaged performance. He insisted that while the process be simple, specific, and true, it must also generate numerous choices that would work in the given scene. What he eventually came to was a structure of —"Scoring the Text" — giving each "Beat" a "Burning Question"; a "Physical Verb Action" to answer the Question; and a "Physical Verb Tactic" as to how that action was being accomplished—all in support of the script.

I was immediately drawn into the adventure. We spent many great hours battling over what worked and how the process should be applied to that day's script. It was like getting my Master's & Doctorate all in one. Working on the role of Macbeth for The Pennsylvania Shakespeare Festival, we ultimately discovered that this structure applied to any text whether classical or contemporary. After 4 years, I moved to teaching full-time. Continuing the spirit of adventure, I built Penny Templeton Studio. I have always thought of my mentor and friend, James Kiberd, as my cornerstone.

WHO AM I?

Where did this burning desire to be in the theatre come from? I was sitting in front of my computer in the early hours of the morning, typing into all the search engines, determined to find out the answers to these questions. I typed Eva Barrington actress, Eva Barrington *Wizard of Oz*, Eva Barrington Victor Herbert's *Babes in Toyland*. An image suddenly appeared on my screen! It was a picture of a young woman posing for a stage photo of the *Babes in Toyland* tour in Seattle. I had never seen an image of my grandmother, Eva Barrington, as a young woman or as an actress. Now I held my breath. I recognized grandmother at once, with her unique face, pale skin, black eyes, and dark hair fashioned in the "Gibson" style.

My discovery encouraged me to search for my great-grandmother, the "original" Eva Barrington. Her photos from the 1880's are housed in the Billy Rose collection at the New York Public Library and include a photo of Eva Barrington looking very young in a black dress in a dramatic pose of the day.

My great-grandmother was disinherited for eloping with her true love and fleeing to America on an ocean liner. She soon became a well-known concert singer and played Sacharissa in the Gilbert and Sullivan production of *Princess Ida*. She also appeared on Broadway, at the Star Theatre, in the play *Whose Are They?*

While riding in Central Park, she was thrown by her horse. Her foot caught in the stirrup and she was dragged, tragically resulting in her back being broken. Bedridden for a year, she finally died of pneumonia. My heartbroken great-grandfather sent his eight year old daughter, my grandmother, back to England to be raised by her grandmother, the stern matriarch of the family. As soon as

x

she was eighteen my grandmother, like her mother before her, escaped on an ocean liner to come "home" to America to pursue her dream of the stage. She toured the country with other shows such as *The Wizard of Oz*, and crossed paths with Buffalo Bill, Diamond Jim Brady and other luminaries of the day.

Barely two months after posing for the photos of *Babes in Toyland* in Seattle, the tour was brought to an abrupt end by the 1906 San Francisco earthquake. The walls of my grandmother's hotel room collapsed, crushing her roommate's little dog. Grandmother grabbed a suitcase and the porcelain Little Bo Peep prop doll and ran to the theatre to help save the production. To her dismay, the police had cordoned off the theatre. My grandmother headed down to the bay, where she was picked up by a lifeboat from a nearby ocean liner. A week later she was on her way back to New York City.

Her daughter, my mother, continued the Barrington tradition. She took to the stage, including playing a role in *Trilby* with the most famous singer of her day, Jeannette McDonald. My mother loved theatre

so much that at one point she was going to move us into a house that sat next door to the home of the famous actress, Helen Hayes. My mother, grandmother and I were ecstatic. "Helen Hayes!" My father didn't share our enthusiasm for the move, when he found out the house we would be moving to had no electricity or running water. Dad never knew what to think of us. He had one overriding plan for my life, "Anything but the stage!" However, my mother and grandmother's passion for the theatre was contagious and I was drawn into their world.

I am a fourth generation actress, descended from a line of strong women whose lives centered around the stage. The pattern was not to change. My parents were bewildered by a five year old who would sit in front of a tiny television and watch Shakespeare, a play about Abraham Lincoln, and a program called *You Are There* with Walter Cronkite interviewing historical characters such as Joan of Arc at the stake, played by Kim Stanley. At five years old I knew where I belonged. Unfortunately, I was not to inhabit that world for a long time.

Giving into my father's wishes, I went to college, married, had two marvelous children and lived in a beautiful house. But something was missing. The magnetic pull of three generations on the stage was undeniable. As my children grew older and went to school, I walked into the Little Firehouse Theatre, a beautiful small theatre in New Jersey, and thought, "I'm finally home." Now I had to learn the craft if I was really going to become an actress.

I was lucky enough to get in a class with the well-known actor, Paul Sorvino, Artistic Director of The American Stage Company in New Jersey. The first time I worked with Paul he observed me as I stood nervously waiting for several seconds. Then he quietly said, "You are an actress." Our classes were a dream come true as he expertly lead the actors through the techniques his master teachers had handed down to him. When the premiere production of *All the King's Men* was being mounted at the theatre, the casting director asked me to audition. I'll never forget my joy and the proud look on Paul's face when I was cast as his wife in the play. When Paul had to move to LA to do film work, I asked him, "Where do I go? I can't stop my training now!" He encouraged me to work with a master teacher in New York City.

I managed to get an audition with the legendary New York master teacher, Wynn Handman. After I finished a monologue from John Osbourne's play, *Look Back in Anger*, there was a pause. Wynn, carefully choosing his words, said, "I think you are a very talented actress but you have a family. I feel that the commitment would be too much for you to go back and forth from New Jersey." Devastated, shaking, I stood my ground. "You have to take me. I am here because I want to be a great actress! I will never let you down!" After seeing my fervor he said, "Oh, okay, okay," with a twinkle in his eye.

While studying with Wynn, one of my actress friends from class, Susan Keith, asked if I would like to work with her husband, actor James Kiberd. James was playing "Trevor" on the soap opera, *All My Children*. My job started as a rehearsal partner for his scenes. I played every character in "Pine Valley." James thought I had a good "eye" for observing the work, and decided to train me to be his coach. When we worked on scenes, we knew that the acting technique had to be adapted to work in the fast-paced world of Daytime Television. James came up with the idea that we should create a structure specifically tailored to allow actors to work faster, yet deeper in this environment. So for a year we put our heads down and hammered out a structure that worked. In the midst of all this, Wynn Handman called me into his office and cast me in Joyce Carol Oates' *I Stand Before You Naked*, a production he was directing at the American Place Theatre.

I soon found myself in demand to coach with other actors. I would spend half a day coaching with James on the set of *All My Children*, and the other half working with professional actors in my apartment, or on the sets of various shows. A studio then invited me to teach acting classes, at the same time that my agent contacted me about acting in a show out of town. The question, "Who am I, a teacher or an actress?" hit me. It wouldn't be fair to abandon the actors who were putting their faith in me as their teacher and coach. I knew I couldn't do both. I asked my husband, "What do I do?!" Hank responded, "This is an easy decision, I hear your passion for teaching coming through that door all day long." I turned down the show. I committed to becoming an acting teacher. It didn't take long to realize I had found myself, and my passion: Teaching actors the craft.

WHY I WROTE THIS BOOK

Acting has drastically changed from the days of Stanislavsky and the Group Theatre, when techniques were geared for the actor who would rehearse for 5 or 6 months, or more. Gradually, the business began speeding up, as television and film work increased and theatre rehearsals went from 8 weeks to 6 weeks, down to the current 4 weeks.

What didn't evolve was the way the techniques (the craft) were presented and used by the actor. I discovered that because of the fast paced industry, actors were increasingly abandoning their craft and acting by the "seat of their pants." This has led to "playing the words" and to work that, though real and believable, is in many cases uninspiring because it lacks depth, thought, and inspiration. I personally thought the craft needed to catch up!

One of the misconceptions is that the craft of acting is only for theatre. The fact is that today, actors go from theatre to film to television; therefore the craft has to go with them. Today's actor is under constant pressure to deliver the goods faster and faster. They are constantly under fire in what often seems like hostile conditions in enemy territory. What should be a collaborative effort can feel like a battle just to survive. How do actors make themselves totally vulnerable to access the deepest emotions while coming under fire from all over the set? Actors need a bulletproof vest — a strong and flexible acting technique that works for them, day in and day out, in this "act fast" world.

My entire career as an acting coach and teacher has been about developing and giving actors that technique. It began with my coaching Daytime actors on a 75 page full length "play" every day, and continues as I work with actors in Film, Television, and Theatre. I coach them and they keep me up date with good "intel" on what is happening in the trenches of the set. This helps keep me current and evolving. My actors are always ready to "act under fire." They can face the challenge of every acting situation without fear because they are armed with the bulletproof vest of their technique. In fact, they relish it!

SPECIAL NOTE

Throughout this book I have used true stories of working with real actors. My purpose is to use these experiences as "parables" for all of us to learn from. However, I regard the work I have done with these actors in class and coaching sessions as private and confidential, so these actors shall remain nameless. The point is not to impress the reader with "names," but to share insights, successful or challenging, that the actors and I have found together in working on the craft.

However, with their permission, I do use the first names of actors who have created and shared techniques with the classes over the years.

Two of the chapters in this book were contributed by my partner and husband, Hank Schob. He brings his many years of practical experience as an actor and stage manager to his classes on Stagecraft (blocking), Script Analysis and Beginning Technique. I have asked him to share that valuable knowledge by contributing the chapters on Blocking and Script Analysis found in this book.

PART I
ARTISTRY

1

HOW TO BE AN ARTIST
WITHOUT TAKING 20 YEARS TO DO IT!

My passion is developing actors into artists. Anyone can decide to be an actor, take an acting class, and start auditioning. But what makes performers like Leonardo DiCaprio, Sean Penn, Meryl Streep, or Johnny Depp stand out? They are first and foremost artists. They take their work seriously and love what they do. Their work has longevity. It's not a fad or a trend. It's a creation.

WHAT IS AN ARTIST?

Artistry chooses you. It's part of your soul, part of your DNA. You find ways to act, because you're not complete unless you do. You strive to be the best. Your motivation and drive come from within, you must do the work.

Being an artist means making a deep commitment to the craft, being consistent with the work, and knowing how to do what you do well. You live life fully and are affected and shaped by the events and people in your life. As much as an actor, at times, needs the quiet reflection of the lone mountaintop, conversely, the actor must come down off that mountain to engage in life. This is the well from which you will draw on to create your characters, and that well needs to be filled with life's experiences, good and bad, large and small, complex and simple. You need to continually keep that well full.

ACHIEVING ARTISTRY

When an actor works deeply and effectively, their work becomes consistent. They're complex on the inside with an energy that's clean and clear on the outside. I call that place "profound simplicity."

A great actor may be terrified when diving into the work, but will demand more of themselves than the material offers. They will reach to use their real feelings to illuminate the truth of the author's story. Then the artist trusts in all the work they've done, lets go, and rides the wave. The journey has a life of its own. The audience connects to that artist's personal truth, and goes on the journey with the actor.

THE "SUCCESSFUL" ARTIST

"Never confuse the size of your paycheck with the size of your talent."
—Marlon Brando

You can be a great artist and never be paid for your work. Although actors might take an occasional project for money, they understand that money does not equal artistry. The joy of doing the work is enough. This is a point that gets hotly debated amongst actors. How can you be a success if you're not being paid professionally? The key is that "success" and "artistry" are not the same. Many brilliant artists have never been discovered. Are you going to let that stop you?!

Being paid is doing a job. Yes, we would all like to support ourselves solely through acting. But is acting just about money? Is that why you put up with rejection after rejection? Actors who stay in this business year after year without earning a living have other passions driving them besides money.

Something aside from "fame" fuels you, and makes you come back time and time again to acting, even if you wonder, "Why do I keep doing this?!" It's your artistic voice speaking, the voice that says you have to act in order to live.

STEPS TO ARTISTRY

FIND INSPIRING ROLE MODELS

How do you start on the road to becoming an artist? One of the best ways is to find a role model, someone who inspires your creative soul, and sparks your inner fire to be the best you can be.

An actor, Richard Jenkins, desperately wanted to escape his family's legacy of working in the coal mines of Wales. Jenkins set out to get his teacher, Philip Burton, to mentor him. Finally, his teacher took Jenkins under his wing and into his home. Jenkins said, *"He didn't adopt me; I adopted him."*

He was a strong, disciplined force guiding the teenage Jenkins:

> Philip took Richard out on to the hills and up to the top of Welsh mountains like master and disciple in some in some biblical parable. The boy would speak, "say the chorus from Henry V and I would go further and further away from him, forcing him not to shout but to make certain I could hear him. He soon learned that it was distinctness not volume that mattered." The voice changed: darkened, soared over the valley.

Jenkins was so indebted to his mentor that he took on his surname to honor him. Richard Jenkins became the legendary Richard Burton.

You never know where you'll find inspiration. A mentor could be a grandparent, a teacher, or another actor. It could be a stranger who gives you words of wisdom in a challenging situation. If you don't have a mentor, set out to find one. Artists recognize other artists. Sometimes they are open to handing their experience and guidance down to newer artists who want it badly. They were once struggling too! Don't be afraid to connect with actors whose work you admire. If they seem open, approach and ask them about their craft. Who did they study and learn from? Many new actors are inspired by the response and guidance from another artist.

A former student went to see Dame Judi Dench in a Broadway show. After signing her autograph for my student, they began talking about acting. Ms. Dench invited the actress to her dressing room where she mentored the actress on her art and how to shape her future. How fortunate you are if an artist reaches out to you!

My first ballet teacher, Diana Hauser (aka Diana Turner), taught and mentored all her students as a ballet family. She trained her dancers to be professional, take care of themselves: "Sew your own ribbons on your ballet shoes. Learn to apply your own stage makeup. This way you'll be happier because you won't have to rely on someone else. Never just mark a performance, how will you do it full out when you're on stage?"

Diana, a former soloist for American Ballet Theatre, also opened the total world of ballet to us, filling in the important details about the choreographers, composers and famous ballet artists. We not only danced the steps, we knew every ballet term and what it meant, and how to apply it to ourselves. We were bused into New York City to see

American Ballet Theatre's opening nights, where we would sit way up in "heaven," to experience and breathe in the world we were studying. Diana didn't do "recitals." She would put on a full ballet. She worked with us as professionals with her company, Ballet Arts. We would all have to audition, and the dancers were carefully chosen for the roles. Every role was important. She learned to make all the costumes herself, and they were so magnificent, other ballet companies would line up to rent them for their productions.

We would perform in many venues, from the World Trade Center (where we changed in the boiler room) to a performance next to a lake in an outdoor park, where dragonflies alighted on our tutus and made our ballet, *A Midsummer's Night Dream* truly come to life. At one performance, on a stage that was surprisingly about the size of a postage stamp, I remember hearing encouraging words from Diana's lilting voice, "Dance under yourselves." It was an adventure!

I learned many lessons from Diana. Many of them still applied to me when I became an actress and all of them apply to my lessons of how to be an artist in the real world.

TAKE INVENTORY

- What do you want? What is your dream? What do you need to do in your life to make this happen?
- What kind of actor do you want to become? What actors are you drawn to? What makes them so compelling, and inspires you about them?
- There's only one you! Find out who you are and what makes you special. Go on the hunt to define your unique qualities and how you can build them into your strengths. (More about this later in Chapter Two).
- Use the guidance of your mentors to evaluate and plan the steps you will take in order to develop and build yourself into the kind of actor you want to be.

EXPAND YOUR KNOWLEDGE

Immerse yourself in art. Go see plays, films, dance, opera, concerts, and art exhibitions. Go to see shows first hand. Read reviews. Ask other artists whose judgment you trust, their insights about what you've seen. Use all this to develop your own opinions and artistic eye.

4

HOW TO BE AN ARTIST

Get to know who's who in entertainment: producers, directors, writers. Read newspapers or reputable news websites to know what's happening in the world. Be informed so you can connect and dialog with informed artists. Read plays, scripts, acting books, magazines, and the trades. Be involved in what is going on globally. Use Google and other search engines. The more information you have, the deeper your connection will be to who you are, your artistic voice, and what you want to express to the world.

Don't have tunnel vision, explore the world around you. One of my actors likes to get away from his professional environment and reconnect with nature. He camps on a beach, hikes through woods, climbs mountains, and allows the full spectrum of Mother Nature's power to rejuvenate his creative juices. There are many famous artists and actors who inspire their creativity through painting, playing an instrument or writing, etc. Some actors invigorate their art by traveling and immersing themselves in other cultures. So, discover what inspires you as a human being and artist outside of acting.

EVALUATE YOUR SKILL LEVEL

There are three main stages actors experience: Starting Out, Training, and Stretching as an Artist.

STARTING OUT

There are lots of ways to start. Are you just beginning? If you're still in school, audition to perform in school plays, or a local theatre. Educate yourself. Background or "extra" work can be a great way to see and experience what happens on a film or television set, until you know "the lay of the land." Ask to apprentice at a TV station, or observe on a film set. Join a theatre company. Look for well-run, established acting programs. Act in student films. Agents and managers will often use volunteer apprentice aids. Don't be afraid to ask. Search for ways to get involved and engaged.

TRAINING

Do you have serious training under your belt? Do you have a technique that works for you? Or are you still learning your craft and honing your process?

Where do you need to go next? Don't focus on one method to the exclusion of everything else. A good builder doesn't build an entire house with one power saw. Learn a core technique, but keep adding to that base. Develop your own long range vision. If you have studied Meisner or The Method as a foundation, then ask yourself, "What else do I need?" Perhaps vocal work, a movement or an on camera class. Nowadays, even if these sources are far away, you can video conference with teachers and coaches. Keep cultivating your strengths while eliminating your weaknesses. Develop a course of action that will fill your acting toolbox with the right skills and techniques.

STRETCHING AS AN ARTIST

Have you been working professionally, but feel that your technique needs to change or develop further? Have you entered another stage of your life, leading to a transition in the types of roles you want to play or could be cast as?

When you become a working actor, you have to continually stretch and inspire your work. A true artist always keeps raising the bar; there are no limits to artistry. To cultivate yourself, you need to be working consistently, whether on stage, on screen or in class. Don't allow yourself to become stagnant. Keep finding new outlets to work your acting muscles, and keep evolving.

HOW TO WORK SMART, RATHER THAN JUST WORKING HARD

CULTIVATING BUSINESS SENSE

Hard-working actors can make short-term investments that lead to "dead ends." Many actors spin their wheels worrying about things that ultimately don't matter in terms of they want or need. As I said before, sometimes actors focus too intently on one aspect of their craft to the exclusion of everything else. Or they fall for offers that make unrealistic promises to advance their careers. As earnest and sincere as they may be, actors can have blinders on with no vision or balance. Research, then set and follow through on your goals. Ask seasoned actors, or other professionals, to give you their guidance and honest input on the choices you're considering.

PERSONAL ISSUES

- Toxic relationships, drugs, alcohol and binge partying take their toll, destroying actors and their careers. That charming and dynamic party animal can turn into the "has been" that everyone avoids. What kind of roles do you want to be doing in your 50's or older? If you are constantly in an altered state, in turmoil with a partner, or only focusing on money, you could burn out like many artists who never survive a youthful career. Or you can evolve like Michael Caine, or Robert Duvall, or Meryl Streep. Look ahead! Develop yourself for your own future.

- Avoid actors who gripe about the business. Watch out for the actors always looking for "easy" shortcuts, who don't work on their craft. These dysfunctional types can quickly drag you down with them. Search for smart actors who are passionate and dedicated to their craft.

- "Acting cool." It's one thing to borrow and incorporate from another actor, but it's another thing to copy a quality. When you walk around like James Dean, you are a copy of James Dean. Or Marilyn Monroe, or Marlon Brando. Or any of the originals. All you are doing is creating this idea of who you are in your head. You're not being yourself: you're walking around as someone else. Art is about finding the truth. Great artists are not afraid to be who they are, whatever that is, good or bad. If you're not being truthful to yourself, how can you send your true voice out to the world?

- "Burn out." It's hard to remain an artist in the world. Some actors who work for a long period may lose their enthusiasm and joy. Not everyone can work at their highest level all the time. You may need to go away from acting and come back to it later, and that's okay. In fact, stepping away for a while can refocus what's important, refueling your passion for the work.

- Balancing artistry demands so much energy, work and time, that it's a challenge to always be fully involved with family or relationships. Figuring out a balance is not easy. Those close to you may experience rejection and feel you are putting acting ahead of them. At times, sacrifices in your personal life are necessary for your art. You have to have the vision and forethought to choose what's right for you.

KEEP YOURSELF AT THE TOP OF YOUR GAME

Auditioning is a skill, not a craft. It's completely different from creating a role in a play or film. Therefore, it's important to keep yourself at the top of your game in between jobs. If you don't work at your craft, what kind of shape will you be in to do a role when you do get cast?

One of my working actors in feature films and television has me take him through a twice weekly workout between projects. He is always raising the bar for himself, to keep his skills sharp and continue to grow in his craft.

ALWAYS GIVE 100 PERCENT

Don't be one of those actors you remember from a movie or a TV series and wonder, "Whatever happened to him? He was great in so-and-so, but I've never seen him again," or "Her work was so wonderful but now she keeps phoning in the same performance over and over."

This leads me to the torment of many acting teachers who have former well-trained actors, who leave their disciplines behind as they start working regularly. Why would you stop doing what made you stand out and get work in the first place?

An artist never stops growing. Ever. If they do, their work becomes their "job" rather than their passion.

2

CREATING YOU

"There is vitality, a life-force, a quickening that is translated through you into action, and because there is only one of you in all of time, this expression is unique. And if you block it, it will never exist through any other medium and be lost. The world will not have it. It is not your business to determine how good it is; nor how valuable it is; nor how it compares with other expressions. It is your business to keep it clearly and directly, to keep the channel open." —Martha Graham

TAKE OFF THE MASK

A vital part of the artist's journey is the path to finding yourself.

To discover and embrace who you really are.

To connect to your power by taking off your mask.

To let your core shine through to illuminate every part of your work.

How liberating to take the risk to be you!

EMBRACE YOUR VULNERABILITY

Often actors are embarrassed about what makes them unique. Many actors are afraid that they are not enough. They think they are "too nice" or "not nice enough" and try to hide themselves behind a "confident" cover or a "nice" cover or an "attitude" cover of what they think they should show, when in fact what they need to show is their truth. Insecurity, pain, sexuality, anger or remorse can be the actor's most effective tools. The things we regret or embarrass us most in our lives are often the most powerful and useful experiences we can draw on as actors.

DARE TO BARE YOUR TRUE SELF

One of my actors was cast as the lead in a feature film. The director chose him over well-known stars because he had an unbeatable combination of elegance and fierceness. When I went to see the film, I realized this actor had not revealed the powerful, unrelenting side of himself that is essential to his character. The reviews were mixed. The actor wanted to know what I honestly thought. I shared my wish that he had shown his fierceness in the role. He then revealed that his family didn't like that wild and out of control side of him. He wanted the audience to like him. But, the simple truth was that if he had auditioned with the performance that wound up in the film, he would never have been cast in the first place.

The embarrassing or uncomfortable qualities of actors are often what audiences connect with. When you bring the essence of you to a character, the audience thinks, "Wow! You're brave to show what you're really like! Fantastic!" Audiences love to see real behavior on the stage or screen—the craziness of Jack Nicholson, the self-deprecation of Ben Stiller, the painful shyness of Diane Keaton, the quirky intelligence of Sandra Bullock, the haunting quality of Benicio Del Toro, the private painful side of William H. Macy. These actors have great range, but they are cast repeatedly because they bring their uniqueness to every role.

WHO AM I?

How do you put your finger on the pulse of who you really are? Take the time to step outside yourself, search your soul, and examine this character you play in real life. Search the same way you would playing a character on stage or screen. Go on the hunt! Ask your closest friends to be brutally honest: "How would you describe me in three different words?" Be even braver and ask your family. Dig into yourself to ask, "Is there anything secret that I'm afraid to reveal?"

Here's a great exercise that I learned from casting director, Karen Kayser. Get together with other actors and record interviews with each other on a video camera. In the replay, stop tape as each person appears on the screen. Ask everyone's first thought when that person is seen on camera. In what kinds of professions could that person be cast? Nurse? Farmer? Doctor? Construction worker? Businessman? Mother? What about age range? What kind of person does this actor look like? The nice friend? A sleazy guy? An abused wife? The young heroine? Don't be afraid of being brutally honest. We categorize and evaluate people every day in real life, audiences do it from their seats and casting directors do it from behind the table.

CREATING YOU

In an interview in *Screen Actor*, the Screen Actors Guild magazine, Karl Malden illustrated the importance of knowing your type. He said, *"The biggest lesson I learned was that I wasn't a leading man, that I was a character actor..."* So I said, *"If I am going to stay in this thing, I'd better be the best character actor I can be."*

DEVELOP YOUR UNIQUE QUALITIES

"You've gotta be original, because if you're like someone else, what do they need you for?" —Bernadette Peters

Training to be your own best creation is an ongoing project. Look for teachers who not only work on strengthening your acting skills, but who help you to discover the individuality that makes you "You."

My Method teacher, Pat Grantham, used to make observations about the actors in our class; how we looked and what was special and singular about each of us. Even if it were a beginning actor, she would find something, but I observed that it was always truthful. When we walked into a room or performed, we knew who we were and what was unique about each of us.

ELIMINATE WEAKNESSES

You have a responsibility to the audience to illuminate truth. Your strengths affect people. Your weaknesses lessen the impact of your performance. Why would we want to watch anyone who mumbles or has sloppy speech? If you are from the American South, Europe, Long Island or elsewhere, and you do not have a good Standard American accent, then you have dramatically reduced the number of roles you might be considered for. If you have been told more than once that you have poor posture, can't be heard or have a speech problem, take it to heart and work to correct the issue.

THE IMPORTANCE OF YOUR APPEARANCE

"Acting is a tough business and you need to be in good shape mentally and physically" —Juliette Binoche

Actors who are fit and good-looking will always have opportunities but there have also been exceptions to that rule. These days it really seems that the exceptions are the rule. Now every "type" has the opportunity to be a star. But actors should consider being physically able to survive the rigors of work on stage or set.

For those of you who fit the beauty roles or handsome male type, your appearance is the first impression before your work is seen. How you take care of your body is an indication of how you feel about yourself, and many decisions to represent or hire an actor are based on that first impression. Agents and casting directors see so many actors, that even being slightly out of shape can be a strike against you. It's the unspoken rejection. Actors don't want to believe it, but it's the painful truth.

If your goal is to be a leading television or film actor, remember the camera adds weight. You should be slimmer, but eat wisely to be prepared to endure stressful working conditions and long hours of rehearsing and performing. Crash diets will only exhaust and age you. If you find that you need to drop some pounds find healthy, long-term ways to lose weight.

When you are out of shape, your appearance also reflects on those who represent you. An agent once critiqued a class that included an actress the agent represented. The actress had gained a few pounds and the agent, horrified, shared with me how upset he was. As talented as she was, she had to work hard to get herself back in the agent's good graces.

BRING YOURSELF TO THE ROLE

TYPECASTING

Most actors don't want to be typecast" or "pigeon-holed" by casting directors. However, if you bring too many qualities to an audition you will confuse the casting director, and lose the opportunity to do roles that are tailored to your core. Typecasting is about targeting your essence, the very things which make you special and different. Figure out which category of "type" you belong to.

If you figure this out in advance of stepping into interviews and auditions, you will have a distinct advantage. Yes, agents and casting directors may typecast you, but it is you who led them to your creation—you.

ALWAYS START WITH YOU

Some actors are afraid they may be just playing themselves and not being true to the character. When an actor brings their emotions to a role, it can actually expand their range into parts of themselves that they suppress in everyday life. If the character is much different than the actor, then the actor must find those parts of themselves that are like the character and stretch them until they have a complete human being. They become the character, and the character becomes them. But this must evolve from the actor. If you can't find the truth in yourself, how are you going to bring the truth to the character? Ask yourself, "How am I like this human being?"

Our feelings evolve from six primary emotions:

LOVE • HATE • JOY • SADNESS • POWER • FEAR

We all feel these emotions to a greater or lesser extent. You may feel rage at your boss, but you wouldn't act on that rage by committing murder. But you can do anything you choose in your imagination, including killing your boss. You have the capacity to play anything and must feel the fullest extent of the emotion that your character is feeling. Is it more inspiring for an audience to watch the actor "acting" like the character, or to believe the actor is the character in the moment?

FRAME YOURSELF

USE YOUR TOOLS WISELY

Use your headshot, resume, reel and monologues to frame yourself in interviews and auditions. If you use these tools skillfully, agents, casting directors and directors, will immediately "get" you when you step into the room. When a role appears in the breakdowns that is your core, they will call because they know who you are.

An actor shared his new headshots with me. His photographer had captured a wide range of different types, from "edgy and street smart" to "nice guy." The core of the actor happened to be the "nice guy," the cute, guy-next-door type. However, his manager loved the dark, raw shots and chose the most sexual and dangerous-looking picture to represent him. The actor was called in for many auditions from the new headshots, but he wasn't getting cast. Why? Because in an audition room full of "edgy" actors, he was at his weakest. In a room full of cute, nice guy types he had the advantage, because he really was the "nice guy."

LEAVE A LASTING IMPRESSION

An actor I worked with decided he was tired of being called in for the "good guy." With his agent's permission, he made a major decision to show his real core, which was unconventional, fearless and chauvinistic. His agent received a call from a major casting director saying, "Never send that horrible, disgusting actor to me again. How dare you!" But a few weeks later the same casting director called back and said, "Do you remember that actor you sent me a few weeks ago?" "You mean the actor you never wanted to see again?" the agent asked. The casting director hesitatingly responded, "Well ... yes. We have a role that we think he might be perfect for." She got him in a big way. He left a lasting impression, and when the perfect role came in, he was the first actor the casting director thought of. Even though she didn't like the guy personally, he was the one she needed for her to be successful. She had to have him.

Acting is a challenging profession. If actors can see themselves as industry professionals do, they can make themselves more castable without compromising their artistic ethics and ideals.

The power of knowing who you are. Isn't that a creative idea?

PART II
TECHNIQUE

3

A NEW REVOLUTION OF ACTING CHALLENGES:
EMBRACING THE PAST TO BUILD THE FUTURE

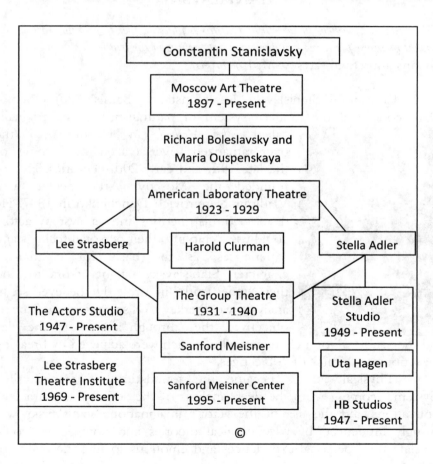

Every actor should educate themselves on the history of modern acting theory to understand the differences between the major schools of thought and how techniques evolved. The processes still widely taught and practiced today primarily come from Stanislavsky–"The System," Lee Strasberg–"The Method," Sanford Meisner–"The Meisner Technique," Stella Adler, and Uta Hagen. Richard Boleslavsky, Maria Ouspenskaya and Michael Chekhov also contributed to developing Stanislavsky's techniques for the Western world, especially in the United States. Familiarize yourself with the basics of each major school, then study and adapt the useful techniques and exercises for your process.

STANISLAVSKY

"The actor must believe in everything that takes place on the stage - and most of all - in what he himself is doing - and one can only believe in the truth."
—Constantin Stanislavsky, *My Life in Art*

Constantin Stanislavsky (or Konstantin Stanislavski) (1863 – 1938) conceived the modern system of naturalistic acting, originally called *The Method*, in response to the overdramatized, over-stylized performing of the late 19th and early 20th centuries. He co-founded the Moscow Art Theater with Vladimir Nemirovich Danchenko in 1897. He developed his theories into a system actors could use to tap into their personal feelings and experiences, as the basis for creating a character. Stanislavsky taught actors to find their "inner truth" in a role. He believed script analysis was the key to discovering the "super-objective," the "through action" of the play and the "subtext" of a character, all of which were achieved by breaking the script into "units" of "objectives."

Physical actions became the foundation of Stanislavsky's "System," coming from the deep analysis of the script, the character's motivations and the use of the actor's imagination. Stanislavsky was strongly influenced by psychological theories and how actors could translate their personal experiences and emotions to fuel the reality of their characters.

NOTABLE STANISLAVSKY TECHNIQUES

GIVEN CIRCUMSTANCES

Stanislavsky stressed that the actor begin with the script to investigate all the information the playwright provides about the actor's character, and what is occurring to his character in the play—the "given circumstances." From analyzing the given circumstances, the actor can use their imagination, actions and emotions to create a reality and history for their character. Stanislavsky began all rehearsals at the table with his actors. They would read the play and analyze the script in depth, often for several weeks before getting the play on its feet.

To put this technique into practice, the actor investigates specific questions about his character's environment, the year, the season, and the specific relationships with other characters, locations, objects, etc. What happened to this character before the play began? The actor answers the who, what, when, where, and why, of each circumstance in the script. Using the magic "if," the actor imagines the events that happen offstage when the character is not seen. The given circumstances can bring the actor closer to the character's world through asking, "What would I do if…?" or "What would I feel if…?"

PHYSICAL ACTIONS

The focus of Stanislavsky's use of physical actions was to create an action through mind and body, rather than "pretending" emotions. Stanislavsky said, "Whatever happens on stage must be for a purpose, even if you outwardly appear to be doing nothing." In his later years, Stanislavsky revised his system to focus even more on physical actions, and how emotion came from the physical action. This contrasted greatly to Lee Strasberg's methods of teaching actors to draw from their own emotions and memories.

Stanislavsky believed that before breaking down the character's individual beats, an actor needed to discover the driving force of the play, or the "super-objective." He asked, *"What is the core of the play, the thing without which it cannot exist?"* Once the actor finds that purpose, they then break down the super-objective into "units" (beats) and "objectives." The actor starts with the largest unit (i.e. the overall objective of an entire act of a play) and works down to the smallest (an individual character's objective in a single unit).

What obstacles are in the character's way? "Actions" are the different choices a character makes to overcome an obstacle in order to achieve the objective. The actor must believe in the purpose of the action, not just pretend. If the actor commits to the action, their physical movements will have intent and will be believable. The "through line of action" is a character's driving objective throughout the entire play. Each character's through line of action must lead to the super-objective.

SENSORY

Stanislavsky created exercises for actors to train their imaginations through all the senses. This was done in order to layer in the reality of sensory responses in the environment, and in the emotional life of the character. Stanislavsky's method taught that potent acting was as real as possible, including authentic sensory reactions. He believed acting was not just about "pretending," but believing.

One such exercise is to create an environment. The actor imagines it's snowing. What do they see? Hear? Smell? Taste? What do they feel on their skin or clothing? Another example would be for the director to pass a piece of crumpled paper to the actors, who are sitting in a circle. The actors are instructed to imagine that the crumpled paper is an injured baby bird. Using all their senses, they must pass the "bird" from one to the next around the circle and observe each other's responses.

THE MAGIC IF

In order for the actor to honestly connect to their character, Stanislavsky created the use of "if." The actor asks the question, "What if this situation is happening to me?" This allows the actor to not just pretend the given circumstances, but to experience and think "as if" they are the character. Stanislavsky said, "'If ' is the starting point, the given circumstance, the development. One cannot exist without the other.'" "If" establishes a conduit between the actor's life and the role. In each circumstance throughout the script, the actor should ask, "What if I…?" in order to connect to the character.

As mentioned above, the actor creates the life of the character that isn't shown on stage. They ask, "Where do I come from? What do I want? Where am I going? What will I do when I get there?" The actor writes a character biography, filling in all the blanks about their character's life, building on what is provided by the writer.

There are many ways for an actor to exercise their abilities with the magic "if." The actor can imagine they are packing their suitcase as if they are going on vacation. Then they can try it as if they are going to war, or to a funeral. Altering the given circumstance, but responding as if that circumstance is happening to them, will change how the actor reacts and feels.

EMOTION MEMORY

This technique allows an actor to recreate an event from their past to evoke feelings needed for their character in the present. Stanislavsky believed that the emotional content of events from the actor's distant past are filtered with time, making it easier for the actor to control intense feelings and not be overwhelmed. The actor rehearses the emotion memory to the point where it becomes a conditioned response. Stanislavsky worked emotions from the "outside in." To bring up an emotional response, actors first create their environment from a past memory in detail and interact with it intensely, triggering the emotional response. In *An Actor Prepares*, Stanislavsky states, *"Plan your role consciously at first, then play it truthfully...Never allow yourself externally to portray anything that you have not inwardly experienced."*

References and recommended reading on Stanislavsky: *An Actor Prepares*, *Building a Character*, *Creating a Role* and *My Life in Art*, all by Constantin Stanislavsky.

LEE STRASBERG AND THE METHOD

"The actor creates with his own flesh and blood all those things which all the arts try in some way to describe." —Lee Strasberg

Lee Strasberg (1901-1982) is credited with developing what is known as "The Method" in American acting training. Strasberg first studied at the American Laboratory Theatre with Richard Boleslavsky and Maria Ouspenskaya, Russian actors most responsible for bringing Stanislavsky's work to the U.S. In 1931, he co-founded The Group Theatre with Cheryl Crawford and director, Harold Clurman. In 1951 Strasberg became the Artistic Director of The Actors Studio. In 1969, he founded the Lee Strasberg Theatre Institute, where

he taught until his death.

Though The Method is based on Stanislavsky's techniques, Strasberg focused on "Affective Memory" as one of The Method's core teachings. Affective Memory, is reliving potent real-life memories, physical and personal, of intense past events to bring up emotions for the character.

Strasberg is famous for working with many great American actors such as Al Pacino, Julie Harris, Marlon Brando, Montgomery Clift, James Dean, Paul Newman, Anne Bancroft, Jane Fonda, Gene Hackman, Martin Landau and Marilyn Monroe at The Actors Studio.

NOTABLE STRASBERG TECHNIQUES

RELAXATION

Strasberg believed that *"When there is tension, one cannot think or feel."* He also believed the idea that the human being is *"naturally expressive."* Simple relaxation permits things locked in the instrument to come out. Strasberg recommended: *"Wherever the actor is, sitting or standing, that the actor find a position for the body in which they could go to sleep; a position in which the pressures are taken off the body, so that it can begin to relax naturally."*

After physically relaxing, the actor then proceeds to the second phase of dealing with the mental tension. The first of these is the temples. The actor simply becomes aware of this area and permits these nerves to relax. The actor is encouraged not to do anything with their hands, but to control relaxation through inner concentration. Then the actor works on relaxing from the bridge of the nose into the eyelids. Finally, they try to relax the whole mouth area. As the actor becomes responsive, his instrument gives forth a new depth of resonance. Emotion that has been habitually held back can suddenly rush forth. The actor becomes real—not merely simple or natural.

SENSE MEMORY

Sense memories are designed to hone, focus concentration, and to add layers of personal experience and physical reaction to a character. Beginning with an object, the actor learns to recall and explore, for instance, an orange or cup of coffee, through the five senses. As the actor gains experience, they move on to recall a sensory experience and the emotions that experience evokes. Eventually, an advanced actor can combine layers of sense memory simultaneously to create realism in his work.

Strasberg created a specific sequence of sensory exercises, all of which are cumulative. Actors let their reactions happen naturally and try not to focus on an end result. Once an actor discovers a consistent response to a particular object or sensation, it is believed they can then use that sensory to bring up the response when they need that specific emotion for a role. Strasberg's order of sensory exercises are: the breakfast drink, the mirror, putting on and removing shoes and socks, getting undressed, sunshine, sharp pain, sharp taste or smell, sound or sight, a place, overall sensations such as a bath, shower, wind, rain, sauna, etc., and a personal object. When the actor reaches this point, they are then instructed to combine two sensory, then three, then four, working their way to a "private moment." Sensory work is to be practiced daily by the actor for at least an hour to develop their abilities and sharpen their responses.

PRIVATE MOMENT

Strasberg recalled:

While reading Stanislavsky, I came across the discovery that, 'The problem of the actor is to learn to be private in public.' It struck me that there should be an exercise that deals with that particular problem, so I made up the exercise, developing my ideas from Stanislavsky's phraseology. The private moment exercise came from my effort to see whether I could help the actor learn to be as private in public, as he is in private. By private, we don't mean just being alone… It's not the deed that's private. It's the significance to the individual that makes it private.

Start with creating the place using the five senses. Bring in a few objects to remind you of the place… Now pick something you would never do in front of anyone. If someone interrupted you and asked what you were doing you would say, "Oh, nothing at all." Without losing the thread of the private moment, we eventually add all other exercises to it, overall sensations, personal objects, daily activities, monologues or songs.

One of the difficult things to fight against in the theatre is the idea of, "I want the audience to get it." The private moment exercise eliminates the presence of the public, shuts out the pull of the audience. A kind of ease is created. In the private moment, the audience disappears, and there's no "them."

AFFECTIVE MEMORY

Strasberg related:

Affective memory is memory that involves the actor so personally that deeply rooted emotional experiences begin to respond. His instrument awakens, and he becomes capable of the kind of living on the stage, which is essentially reliving. The original emotional experience can be happy or frightening or fearsome. It can be anything your mind immediately goes to when you ask yourself, 'Has anything strange, unusual or exciting happened to me?'... It is wise to go back at least seven years to find emotional experiences.... The older the pattern of conditioning, the greater its tendency to function continuously and without change.

The important thing in using affective memory is to maintain one's concentration, not on the emotion, but on the sensory objects or elements that form part of the memory of the original experience... In affective memory you try to see the people you saw, hear the things you heard, and touch now the things that you touched then. You try to remember through your senses, what your mouth tasted, what you wore, and the feeling of that garment against your body. The emotion you try not to remember at all... Out of a hundred affective memory experiments six may work, although all may work to some extent. But some emotional conditionings are permanent, and the conditioning strengthens with time.

References and recommended reading on Lee Strasberg and The Method: *A Dream of Passion* by Lee Strasberg, and *Strasberg at the Actors Studio*, tapes edited by Robert Hethmon, and *The Lee Strasberg Notes* by Lola Cohen, using Lee Strasberg's notes on teaching.

SANFORD MEISNER
THE MEISNER TECHNIQUE

"Acting is living under imaginary circumstances"—Sandy Meisner

Sanford Meisner (1909-1997) joined The Group Theatre (founded by friends Lee Strasberg, Harold Clurman, and Cheryl Crawford) in 1931. By 1933, Meisner found himself disagreeing with the way Strasberg taught The Method, finding it unhealthy to delve into an actor's past traumas. Around 1940, Meisner moved to  The Neighborhood Playhouse where he spent the great majority of his life developing his series of exercises based on the "reality of doing." In 1995, Meisner opened The Sanford Meisner Center for the Arts with James Carville and Martin Barter.

The Meisner approach is a blend of different acting techniques, including Stanislavsky. The main difference, however, is that emotion is not the goal, simply the by-product of acting. Much like behaviorists who were proposing new theories of human psychology in the 1940's and 50's, Meisner believed that emotions evolved from interactions with the environment and others. He felt behavior and actions formed the foundations of acting, not emotions. Meisner agreed with Stanislavsky that true emotion is to be found in the "given circumstances" and not from exploring personal trauma like Strasberg. He developed a series of exercises to train the actor to believe in the given circumstances of various situations by responding as themselves in the moment.

In terms of "affective memory," Meisner believed that the actor doesn't always have a relevant experience to relive, and that the meaning of past events changes over time. He stressed that the imagination can create a stronger reality, and creates a stronger emotional response, rather than actual past events. Meisner said, *"Don't be an actor. Be a human being who works off what exists under imaginary circumstances."* Some of Meisner's notable students include Robert Duvall, Grace Kelly, Diane Keaton, Joanne Woodward, Gregory Peck, James Caan, Sandra Bullock, David Mamet, James Gandolfini, Steve McQueen, Jeff Goldblum and Paul Sorvino.

NOTABLE MEISNER TECHNIQUES

Each exercise is thought of as a specific progression to the next, like building blocks.

STORYTELLING

A group of actors sit in a circle and tell a story one word at a time, listening without anticipating, planning or trying to control the story. The lesson of this exercise is to listen, give up control and respond to what you receive.

REPETITION

Two actors sit in opposite chairs, facing each other. Actor A makes an observation about Actor B. Actor B repeats it word for word, reacting from their own point of view. The goal is for each actor to stay true to their individual responses while listening and connecting to their partner.

WHAT IS HAPPENING

Building upon "Repetition," Actor A asks the partner whatever question first comes to their mind. Actor B repeats the question from their point of view. Actor A then notices something about Actor B's behavior. For example, A says to B, "You're fidgeting." The goal is to continue learning to focus on your partner and to begin to notice their behavior. In a more advanced version of this exercise, Actor B would begin to repeat the observation made about them by Actor A from their point of view.

WORKING OFF

In the next step, in the "What Is Happening?" exercise, Actor A and Actor B keep with the repetition, but allow it to change and evolve without going back to a previously asked question. The goal is to become available to what is happening with your partner "now."

PINCH AND OUCH

Then, after "Working Off," Actor B does not repeat what Actor A says, but responds with how they personally feel about what Actor A said. If you look at the exercise as if it were an action, Actor A "pinches" Actor B and Actor B articulates their "ouch" back to Actor A.

COMING TO THE DOOR

Building upon previous exercises and adding the element of imaginary circumstances, Actor A knocks on a door from outside. Actor B answers the door from inside in response to Actor A's knocking. Each actor must have no other intentions beside knocking and answering the door. The goal of this exercise is to learn to have no expectations.

ACTIVITY

Inside the room, Actor B chooses a challenging activity that has an achievable end. For example, building a house of cards is an activity that is both difficult and possible. Actor A comes to the door while Actor B is doing the activity. The repetition continues as before. The goal is for Actor B to focus on his activity at hand and their partner at the same time.

In the next step of this exercise, Actor A knocks at the door three times. Each knock should be different. Actor B, while continuing their activity, describes the three knocks out loud. The repetition continues. The goal is for Actor B to strengthen their focus on Actor A, regardless of their activity. Actors must remain acutely aware of each other and continue to notice their partner's behavior, regardless of what they are physically doing.

IN THE EXTREME

Actor A continues "Coming to the Door," Actor B is occupied with an "Activity," but this time, each actor must use their imagination to come up with three vital and urgent reasons why they are either coming to the door or doing the activity. The reasons must imply, "I must do this right now because I have no other options!" The more specific and truthful, the greater the actor's faith will be in support of the imaginary circumstances. Actors should continue with the repetition as usual, adding the conflict of the door being locked. Actor B (inside) must stop their activity in order to open it.

ELEMENTS OF TRUTH

After both actors have created specific and urgent reasons for doing their activities, they then add an element of truth. Meisner suggests the actors find something that they would do for the reasons they have given themselves. For example, you are trying to glue and repair your grandmother's prized antique serving bowl that she gave you, her favorite grandchild. You just dropped it, and it broke into a hundred pieces. In half an hour, she will be coming over to celebrate her 90th birthday. You told her you were serving the main dinner course in her bowl.

IN RELATIONSHIP

The last step in the Meisner exercises is to refocus attention back onto the other actor. Actor A and Actor B should decide on a specific relationship, i.e. mother-daughter, neighbors, co-workers. Don't do anything with this information, just know it. Actor A (the actor coming to the door) makes their reason for coming to the door: For example, something happened they must tell Actor B. The ultimate goal is to accept imaginary circumstances, make those circumstances both specific and crucial, and make everything in service to interacting with the other actor. In this last step, all the base techniques of the Meisner approach to acting are at work.

References and recommended reading on Sanford Meisner: *On Acting* by Sanford Meisner & Dennis Longwell, *The Actor's Art and Craft: William Esper Teaches the Meisner Technique* by William Esper and Damian DiMarco, and *The Sanford Meisner Approach* by Larry Silverberg.

STELLA ADLER

"When you stand on the stage you must have a sense that you are addressing the whole world, and that what you say is so important the whole world must listen."
—Stella Adler

Stella Adler (1901-1992) grew up as the youngest daughter of famous Yiddish actors Sara and Jacob Adler, and began acting in the Yiddish theatre at the age of four. She performed in more than a 100 plays and Yiddish theatre shows across the United States, Europe, and South America. While studying at the American Laboratory Theatre, Adler met Harold Clurman. In 1931, she was invited by Clurman to join the newly formed Group Theatre and starred in *Awake and Sing* and *Paradise Lost*. In 1934, Adler studied with Stanislavsky in Paris for five weeks, the only American actor to be taught by him personally. She came back to New York and had a bitter split with Strasberg over the role of "Affective Memory" in acting training. She left The Group Theatre for Hollywood in 1937, where she starred in a few films and became an associate producer for MGM. In 1949, she formed the Stella Adler Theatre Studio in New York City, later renamed The Stella Adler Conservatory of Acting, and then The Stella Adler Studio of Acting. During the McCarthy era, in 1950, after refusing to name names for the House Un-American Activities Committee, Adler was blacklisted in *Red Channels*. This was a book citing artists in the entertainment industry with alleged communist affiliations.

One of the most important aspects of her work was giving to the actor a sense of the nobility of themselves as artists and of their profession. She was quoted saying, *"You have to get beyond your own precious inner experiences."* Adler's techniques are more closely aligned to Stanislavsky's later system, *The Method of Physical Actions*. Adler placed emphasis on imagination, script interpretation and creating physical actions. Some of the prominent studio actors included: Marlon Brando, Robert De Niro, Warren Beatty, Elaine Stritch, Mark Ruffalo, Candice Bergen, and Benicio del Toro.

NOTABLE ADLER TECHNIQUES

ACTIONS

Actions are the heart of Adler's acting technique and show the direct influence of her Paris training with Stanislavsky. Her primary technique comes from what she learned from Stanislavsky and the chart he gave her in Paris, "The method of Physical Actions." Actions must be do-able verbs, such as to attack, to comfort, or to seduce. One of the most important elements in the Stella Adler technique is Justification— "why you are doing something every moment." Without the proper justification, an action is useless until the most believable and richest reason you can come up with leads you to the strongest action possible. The "justification" of the action should "agitate" the actor so they fully experience the action. The emotion will then come naturally. There is a "what," "where," "when," and "why" of each action. Actions can be completed or interrupted or turn into another action. These actions must also be clearly defined within the circumstances of the script.

Stella Adler fought her whole life against the idea of trying to activate emotions by recalling past experiences. She believed the action comes out of living truthfully in the given circumstances. The actor is so immersed in the action in the moment, the actual doing and living completely in the given circumstances, that honest emotions will occur. Nothing is recalled because it doesn't have to be. She never wanted an actor to work to get emotions from one's life. She always said most of our lives are too small, so you draw from the imagination and from the ages, and out of that "heightened doing" the emotions will come. Ms. Adler, unlike Strasberg, never wanted an actor to "draw" from their own emotion. She said, "You are not playing yourself, you're playing Hamlet. Find his reactions, his emotions." The entire point of Adler's technique is that by choosing the strongest possible action, your imagination will become so agitated that emotion will surface.

IMAGINATION

Adler believed that actors should create with their imagination, the life, emotions, and world of their characters, using one of Stanislavsky's tools from his chart, "as ifs." If the actor believes something is real, it is real for the actor and, therefore, real for the audience. One of Adler's exercises trained the actor to actively describe in highly expressive, detailed words, the imagined environment, object(s) and circumstance. The objective is to "fire your own imagination. Your own enthusiasm. And to communicate to the audience."

An example would be for the actor to describe, in as much detail as possible, the contents of his character's closet. Another would be to describe the view out his character's window so that when the actor imagines it in performance, the audience can "see" what he is experiencing. The circumstances of the script are to be explored in this kind of high detail and lived "as if" the actor exists in that world.

WORKING ON TEXT

A cornerstone of Adler's technique is script analysis. Adler believed that an actor needed to consistently go back to the text in order to truly understand their character, the circumstances, and the character's purpose in those circumstances. An actor should tell the story out loud in their own words before trying to create a character. Then they break down the script into "sequences" and then into "units," much like Stanislavsky taught. The actor chooses an action for each unit. Adler believed that actions came first, words second—it is more important for an audience to understand what is happening than to hear words telling them what is happening.

> References and recommended reading on Stella Adler: *The Art of Acting,
> Stella Adler on Ibsen, Strindberg, and Chekhov* and *The Technique of Acting* by
> Stella Adler, and *Acting with Adler by Joanna Rotté.*

UTA HAGEN

*"Talent is an amalgam of high sensitivity; easy vulnerability; high sensory equipment
(seeing, hearing, touching, smelling, tasting -- intensely); a vivid imagination as well as
a grip on reality; the desire to communicate one's own experience and sensations, to
make one's self heard and seen."* —Uta Hagen

Uta Hagen (1919-2004) was born in Germany then raised in the
United States. After high school, she studied
for a year at the Royal Academy of Dramatic
Arts (RADA) in London, and then spent a
year at the University of Wisconsin. She was
plucked out of university to play Ophelia in a
1937 production of *Hamlet* and this began her
long distinguished career as a stage actress.
Hagen was multiple Tony Award winner, for
Clifford Odets' *The Country Girl* and Edward
Albee's *Who's Afraid of Virginia Woolf.*

She began teaching at HB Studios in New York in 1947. In 1950
during the McCarthy anti Communist era, Hagen's name was given to
congressional committees by accusers who remained anonymous. She
was blacklisted and barred from TV and films, but her theatre career
remained largely intact since she was already performing on Broadway.
In 1957 she married HB Studios founder Herbert Berghof. Upon
Berghof's death in 1990, Hagen became chairperson of HB Studios.
Some famous students include Matthew Broderick, Christine Lahti,
Amanda Peet, Geraldine Page, Hal Holbrook, Sigourney Weaver, Jack
Lemmon and Whoopi Goldberg.

NOTABLE HAGEN TECHNIQUES

IDENTITY

Hagen's work begins with the actor learning who they are, and observing themselves in all of life's situations. The actor's identity and self-knowledge are the main source of the characters they will play. A person takes on different "roles," depending on who they are speaking to, where they are, the circumstances, etc. Once the actor understands who they are in as many varied circumstances as possible, they then have a starting point to begin working on crafting a character.

TRANSFERENCE/SUBSTITUTIONS

Hagen believed an actor wants to "find [him]self in the part" vs. "losing [him]self in the part." Instead of dragging up traumatic events from the past to recreate emotions, actors should use similar or recent personal experiences as substitutions. The actor places a similar experience they have had into the circumstance of the play to bring up the needed emotions, objectives, moods, locations, relationships, etc. The substitution is not an end all, but a tool to bring out justified character reactions, especially if the character's experiences are far from the actor's. In her second book, Hagen renames substitutions "transference," borrowing the term from Freudian psychotherapy.

RELEASE OBJECT/INNER OBJECT

The "release object" is a means for bringing up emotional responses that relate to the character's experience. An object or sensory recall from an event can release the emotions associated with that event. An exercise to find a release object is for the actor to tell the story of an unhappy event from their life in detail, including the surroundings, the weather, the sounds, the colors, the smells, etc. When they begin to describe the factor or object that brings up the unhappy emotion for example, describing the dark clouds overhead the day his father died, that factor becomes the release object that they can use in creating the emotional life of the character. When the actor's character is grieving, they can remember in detail the dark clouds the day their father died, to tap into their own grief. Actors can build a repertoire of release objects, or triggers to use for a variety of circumstances. One thing Hagen stressed was for actors to avoid examining experiences that are too emotionally volatile or secret—that acting wasn't psychotherapy.

THE OBJECT EXERCISES

Hagen created a series of six steps every actor should consistently practice when rehearsing or preparing for a role:

1. Who am I?
> What is my present state of being?
> How do I perceive myself?
> What am I wearing?

2. What are the circumstances?
> What time is it? (The year, the season, the day? At what time does my selected life begin?)
> Where am I (In what city, neighborhood, building, and room do I find myself? Or in what landscape?)
> What surrounds me? (The immediate landscape? The weather? The condition of the place and the nature of the objects in it?)
> What are the immediate circumstances? (What has just happened or is happening? What do I expect or want to happen next and later on?)

3. What are my relationships?
> How do I stand in relationship to the circumstances, the place, the objects, and the other people related to my circumstances?

4. What do I want?
> What is my main objective? My immediate need or objective?

5. What is my obstacle?
> What is in the way of what I want? How do I overcome it?

6. What do I do to get what I want?
> How can I achieve my objective? What's my behavior? What are my actions?

The object exercises are a practice to recreate two mundane minutes of the actor's life answering the six questions above. The actor identifies physical and psychological sensations. Then they recreate those two minutes as if they are happening for the first time. The actor rehearses with props in detail for an hour.

Answering the six questions allows an actor to recreate authentic behavior, leading to the achievement of objectives. It also allows the actor to work with the concept of the "fourth wall," seeing out over the audience without becoming distracted by the audience. Engaging with the fourth wall invites the audience fully into the action of the play.

ENDOWMENT

"Endowing the objects and the conditions prescribed by the playwright with imagined realities, he can produce sensations at will." Everything created by an actor must have meaning to the actor. All props used must have personal meaning. All relationships must have meaning. Giving meaning is what Hagen calls "endowing." People, places and things can be endowed with history, physical, and personal properties that cause the actor to respond as if they are their own. All endowment must tell a story that fits within the given circumstances. The actor is free to use their creativity as long as the endowment creates a personal response within, toward the person, object, or environment. Actors should ask themselves complex questions about what they are endowing and explore each detail through their imagination.

PARTICULARIZATION

Uta Hagen said:

> The making of each event, each person, and each place down to the smallest physical object as particular as possible, exploring these things in detail to discover in which way they are relevant to the character, in which way they are perceived, in which way they further or hinder the character's needs, and, consequently, how they will condition "your" behavior. Nothing should be left general or taken for granted. Everything must be made specific.

References and recommended reading on Uta Hagen: *A Challenge for the Actor* by Uta Hagen, and *Uta Hagen's Acting Class* on DVD.

4

TECHNIQUE UNDER PRESSURE
USING THE CRAFT IN TODAY'S WORLD

Traditional training doesn't address the demands placed on today's actor

The world is shrinking. American actors are in competition with international actors for fewer projects and roles. It seems an actor has to be a household name before they can get their first good role. Agents and casting directors complain about the diminishing number of movies, pilots, and productions. Reality TV has, for better or worse, become a reality. Producers have become so insecure about fewer projects that they only want stars with box office drawing power. Actors who are given their first roles are under tremendous pressure to deliver perfectly. Now!

How can the actor train and be sure that their training will come through for them? The truth is that, in most cases, it doesn't. The days of actors studying one technique for a long period of time, and then putting their toes slowly into the deep waters of the business are over. Now it's jumping into the roaring rapids. It's sink or swim. You can't just study one technique such as Meisner or The Method because the business is constantly changing. This is happening even as actors realize they also need vocal work, physical work, on camera classes, the business of acting, and more. The sad reality is that an actor generally has no clue of how to go about juggling and putting these pieces in place. Out of desperation, they often start to take separate classes to fill out their patchwork of technique, but that may be all they end up with— a patchwork of technique.

To understand how to build your craft, you have to comprehend the changing picture of the acting business. How do you get there directly in a way that will open your understanding and deepen your craft?

35

THE REALITY

Most actors think when they join the professional ranks they will be working with brilliant directors and first-rate actors who are committed to working as an ensemble. They will perform in theatres with great facilities, or on film sets that are organized with time to develop their characters and relationships.

The reality often is: if you get a good director, count yourself lucky. There may be many times you will be working with unprofessional, selfish, competitive, insecure and often less than brilliant actors and directors. Depending on the type of production, there could be conditions under which you are crammed with other actors into a dressing room with little room to change. Or on a set that's too big for the stage, with no wing space. Or lighting that gives you more shadows than light to work with, thanks to a designer who thinks mood is more important than seeing the actors.

As for film, rehearsals are rare or, for most television, nonexistent. Your first day's shoot may be the love scene at the end of the movie, with a leading man you've never met before. On location anything can happen, and most certainly will. When you're shooting exteriors, the day might start off with "Hurry up!" Then "Wait...!" as a technical detail needs to be resolved. But as the day nears its end, there will be frantic yells of "Hurry up! Let's get the shot, we're losing the light!" The pressure is now on the actor to get it in one take.

DIRECTORS

Although there are wonderful directors out there, there are also directors who are challenging to work with for variety of different reasons.

Many directors come to the job from the point of view of their first discipline. For example, a former cinematographer who is now a director will make sure the lighting is perfect, the right lens is on the camera and you're standing on the perfect mark for the perfect shot. However, they may offer very little direction. You're on your own, and you won't know whether your work is good or bad because they're mainly looking at the pictures.

Or you could have a director who was an actor and you'll think, "This is great!" They're going to give you wonderful insights and motivations for each scene, but when you go to see the movie, the shots are dark and the story line unintelligible because the director didn't know how to tell the story.

Lastly, there's the writer who becomes the director. They may insist the lines be delivered as "they" heard it in their head when it was written. The film may never take flight because the performances are stiff and wooden, since they never allowed the actors to be actors.

PRODUCERS

Then we have the producers. When you sign that first professional contract, you may think you've arrived and you are going to be treated with respect. Most producers are in the business because they too are artists. But there is always the "worst case scenario" — the producer who doesn't respect or appreciate the actor's contribution, hates the actors' unions, or wants to cut every corner, because they don't have enough funding to finish the project. Then, out of frustration, they start screaming at people and firing them. The first to go will be the director who loved your work, only to be replaced by a director who wants another cast. The only reason you've kept your job, might be because the producer couldn't afford to replace you.

THE REALITY OF THE UNEXPECTED

Sometimes, as soon as you start getting your part down, you're handed rewrites. One actor for instance, landed his first leading role on a television series. On the way to get a cup of coffee, he bumped into the producer who casually mentioned, "Oh by the way, we've made some changes in your character. He's not the nerdy computer geek anymore; he's now strong and heroic!" The producer added, "We should be ready to shoot your scenes in about forty-five minutes, here are your rewrites." The actor rushed back to his trailer to cram the new scenes and lines into his brain, while attempting to undo weeks of work on character development.

So if you were thinking this is an ideal profession and you'll have lots of time to create real "art," think again. Much of the time, the reality can be that you are frantically trying to use your artistry through a disorganized tornado of "Hurry up and wait," "rush, rush, rush," and "act fast, I want it now!"

So let's give you the advantage. Let's prepare you for getting through that hard reality by using your craft to thrive in that environment!

TAKING YOUR TRAINING TO WORK: SEAMLESSLY TRANSITIONING FROM ONE MEDIUM TO THE NEXT

Too much emphasis is put on the adjustments actors need to move between the mediums of theatre, film and television, when in reality, many of the acting skills and techniques are the same for all mediums. Most of the adjustments are with the technical demands of the space in which you are working. If you can adjust to these demands, you will be able to transition from one medium to the next with little difficulty. In order to understand how to use the tools you have developed for professional work, let's step back and look at the big picture.

THEATRE

Theatre requires the actor to have strong acting chops. It's almost impossible to become a great theatre actor without a solid base of technique, experience and understanding. Many talented film and television actors have made the choice to do a Broadway show, only to be devastated when they realize that they are in way over their heads. And the critics are generally not kind. Think about it. If you are a tap dancer and suddenly decide you could do a Balanchine ballet at Lincoln Center, it would be really tough, wouldn't it? In fact, it would be almost impossible without specific training and experience.

Theatre acting requires knowledge of plays, and the steps to bringing a play to fruition in an open space. It demands the understanding and experience of performing an entire piece from beginning to end, often eight performances a week. In theatre, the energy of live performance flows through the actor's body and releases into the audience. It requires a longer rehearsal process during which the actor puts the pieces in place that build and illuminate that character's entire journey through the play. There are no retakes. Performing in a large theatre without theatre training is like deciding to climb Mount Everest thinking it'll just be like hiking up a large hill.

The technical requirements for working in a theatre in the round are completely different from working in a proscenium stage. The technical requirements for working in a 99-seat theatre are different from working in a 2000-seat theatre. Actors can learn to adapt to the technical differences of these on-stage situations by adjusting the energy for projecting, and being aware of appropriate blocking for each kind of house.

Although stage mikes are commonly used today, especially on Broadway, theatre actors still need a trained voice able to project the playwright's words to the last row of the audience clearly and distinctly without strain. The actor's voice must be developed to have a range of emotional colors. The vocal power needs to be grounded in the body so the actor can be centered in their work, free from any encumbrances that might get in the way. Theatre actors are also required to be trained in stage movement, to develop stamina, and to build a relaxed, flexible and open body that can handle the rigors of all styles of performance.

FILM

The actor must always think in terms of the space they are performing in. In the case of on camera work, is it a wide-angled master shot or a tight close-up? Is there a boom for sound or is the actor wired with a remote microphone? Or are the filmmakers working with the camera's built-in mike?
How the sound is recorded will determine adjustments in volume the actors need to make when shooting.

Locations may prove challenging with different temperature and weather conditions. Sometimes an actor shoots their close-ups without having the other lead actors present. They must be able to create the same intimacy in their work as if the other actors were actually standing right next to them.

Continuity is also an issue. If the actor picks up their glass with their left hand in a certain way on a certain word, they need to do that movement exactly the same in every take, in every type of shot. Also, one of the greatest challenges in shooting on camera is that most movies and television shows shoot the scenes out of order. This is where the actor's process is most important. The actor must be flexible enough to be able to jump into difficult scenes without having the luxury of building up to the emotions and events in sequence as in theatre.

Once an actor learns to think in terms of the space within the camera frame, they will learn to naturally adjust their performance for the technical demands of the shot, just as they naturally adjust their performance when moving from a tiny Off-Broadway theatre to a Broadway stage. As a general rule, actors who have been doing theatre can make a quicker adjustment to the world in front of the camera because the main hurdle is adjusting to the spatial relationship and the level of energy required for working within the frame. The film actor shifting to theatre has a much more challenging job.

TELEVISION

Television acting requires an ability to read, understand, and bring a script to life within a shortened or non-existent rehearsal process. You are given your blocking rapidly, and expected to learn it immediately. It requires quickly understanding the scene, making choices, grounding those choices, and working them off the other character. This is usually done without ever having worked on the scene or rehearsed it with the other actor.

You also have the challenges of dealing with how the television program is being filmed or taped. Some television has a three-camera setup, such as most soap opera and sitcoms, whereas most nighttime dramas are shot on film with one or two cameras. So the actor has to be fully aware of where their camera is and how to adjust their gestures for the frame. The television actor has to come in with a fully fleshed-out character on their own. They must be prepared to move, adjust, and work that character off another actor they have never met. All this with little or no rehearsal.

To survive in these environments and working conditions, you have to know how to do all of this. The next chapters lay out a blueprint to lead you to success.

$$\boxed{5}$$

WHERE TO START - SCRIPT ANALYSIS

Contributed by Hank Schob

"The whole idea is to get yourself started on the part, and the basic start to me for working is: Why is the play written? ...What is this character about? Why is the character in it? How important is he to the play? What has he got to do to make the action go forward? And when you find that, then you start working on the truth of the character. To me, the truth is the most important thing in the whole character. And when you feel that you have accomplished the truth in a play, then comes the hard part: What can I do to make it interesting? Not to steal the scene but to make it interesting because I don't want them to go to sleep onstage."
—Karl Malden

Script analysis is one of the most important tools of the craft, yet it is largely ignored by many actors. Everything starts with the word. The better you understand the writer's words and intent, the greater your understanding of how to make effective choices. If a director asks why you made "that" choice, you can back it up with a solid analysis of the script. This will enable you to be confident and committed in your work.

This chapter is devoted to scenes, portions of scenes, and the audition sides you receive when you are hired as a principal or under-5. The principles of script analysis covered in this chapter are relevant to all the different styles and mediums. They apply to short audition sides used for auditions as well as full-length scripts such as *Hamlet*.

WORKING WITH THE SCRIPT

Research, research, research! With the Internet at your finger tips there is no excuse for not doing proper research on words you are unsure of and character terms you don't know. I coached an actor for an audition for a mini-series set in World War II. The character's name was John Basilone. From the audition sides, we knew he was a sergeant, a drill instructor and a hero. Basilone had fought in the "Battle of the

Ridge" at Guadalcanal, and he desperately wanted to get back to his old unit in the Pacific.

After Googling the character's name, I discovered this was a real person—the only Marine to receive both the Navy Cross and Congressional Medal of Honor. In the story, Basilone has been shipped back to the States to do bond tours with movie stars. Meanwhile, his army buddies were fighting and dying. After marrying a nurse named Lena, Sgt. Basilone got his wish to go back into action. He was killed by a mortar, leading his men on the charge up the beach at Iwo Jima. He was real hero. Research, research, research!

THE SCRIPT

Read the full script. However, for many auditions you won't have access to the full script. How do you find the information you need to bring the character to life in a three-page scene?

STEPS TO APPROACHING THE SCRIPT

Read the scene slowly when you first get your sides. Your goal is to get an objective point of view of the material, in the same way a director would read a script. Do not try to see yourself in the role immediately. This can be hard when your character's lines are right there staring you in the face.

Here's a great idea that works. Imagine a couple of your favorite actors playing the scene as you read it. This turns you into the audience, letting you understand the scene from their perspective.

Read through the material again to explore and magnify everything under the surface. Allow your sense memory to come through the words. Then go through the script again. This time look for hidden clues and information. Constantly ask, "Why? What does that mean? Why did he say that? Is it true?" Just because a character says something doesn't make it the truth. You want to discover what the writer is saying between the lines.

STAGE DIRECTIONS

Look at all of the stage directions: *She collapses in a heap, crying as her world caves in around her.* What are the questions you can ask yourself about this one line of stage direction? For example, what is her world? What things are caving in? If you only have three pages, those answers may not be there but as the actor, you need to find the answers to bring the scene alive. When we think of our world caving in, it usually refers to a series of bad things happening in quick succession. You'll need to find several substitutions you can use that will cause you to emotionally collapse in a heap. Later, after you've completed your analysis and chosen the purpose of the scene, you can begin making choices.

Based on your analysis, what choice could you make for this character in this situation? You could get angry. You could feel numb. You could even react with ironic humor—"God, why are you picking on me?" Or you could collapse crying. Whatever choice you make you have to believe in it for it to work effectively.

CHARACTER DESCRIPTIONS

It's dangerous for an actor to take character descriptions too literally. The descriptions are there to give you a sense of what type of person the character represents in the story. Read the character description thoroughly. Then put the description into the stock pile of all the information you discover in the script.

What is a "Perky Blond?" Reese Witherspoon? Kirsten Dunst? Cameron Diaz? Gwyneth Paltrow? These four completely different actresses have all portrayed "Perky Blonds."

A writer might include a supporting character's description with the stage directions: *The prissy clerk approaches the counter.* Why a "prissy" clerk? How does that impact the scene? Is it important to the scene that the character be "prissy?" These are the kinds of questions you need to constantly ask yourself.

WHAT YOUR CHARACTER AND OTHER CHARACTERS SAY

A basic teaching of script analysis is to look for everything that is said about your character. Also look for everything you say about yourself and other characters. This information can give solid clues into your character's background, personality, and views.

CAMERA SHOTS

Camera shots can be very informative: *Cut to John lurking in the corner.* What is John looking at? How does this affect the audience's perception and reaction to the events? At the end of a scene you will often see: *Off Stabler* or *Take Joan*. These are reaction shots that usually tell you something important has been revealed, that either stuns the character or confirms their suspicions. The camera shot tells you a definite reaction is required.

PUNCTUATION AND WORD EMPHASIS

As you study a scene carefully look at all the punctuation, which can help you discover the writer's actual intention for the line. However, just because there is a question mark does not mean your character must ask a question. If there is an exclamation point, you don't have to yell. Look for repeated words. If one character says, "Do you want to talk for a while?" and the other character responds, "I guess so, for a while." It's important that both characters actually say the words "for a while." A repeated phrase is often there for emphasis. Ask why?

ANSWERING THE QUESTIONS

Character analysis involves answering all of the questions presented by the script. Not all of the answers will come directly from the words you are given in a script. That does not mean there are no answers. The answers in this case are the choices you make to create your character. There is one cardinal rule—none of these choices may violate the script. All of your choices and answers must serve the purpose of the scene and total script. By this we mean, don't make a choice that is contradicted by something that is stated in the text or referred to in another scene. As long as you keep these principles in mind, every choice you make will be valid.

After you complete "mining the script for gold," and you put together all the information, it's time to answer the following questions:

1. WHAT'S THE PURPOSE?

The writer wrote this particular script for a reason. Why? In one short sentence, what does the writer want the audience to learn when the lights come up in the theatre? Examples could be, "Don't judge a book by its cover," or "We reap what we sow," or "Love conquers all." Finding the purpose is critical to focusing the scene so the audience "gets it." The purpose of the material becomes the path that leads the actor out of the woods. An actor can get lost if all they do is look at the trees. The trees are the words, and words can mean anything. You need to ask, "Where's the path?"

The great director, Sydney Lumet, delves into this subject in detail in his book on directing, *Making Movies*. He chose his lenses, depth of field, and placement of the actors and set pieces inside the frame, all to help the audience understand the scene.

2. WHAT IS MY JOB?

What do you need to do as an actor, to help the purpose of the scene be fulfilled? When you learn to define your job, your work becomes much easier. If you think about it, how can you do a job if you don't know what it is?

3. HOW DO I WANT TO DO IT?

This is where you get to use your creative side. As they say, "There's more than one way to skin a cat." How do you see this character coming to life? What would be an interesting way to accomplish your job? Most actors worry about what "they" are looking for. When you are able to make strong valid choices based on solid script analysis, you will bring the scene to life. As you study the following examples, look at how these questions are answered and how the final question is answered. Take control of your own work. How do you want to do it?

UNDER-5 SCENE

Do research when auditioning or filming a small role. Be familiar with every show on television. Record a couple of episodes or watch them on the internet. Familiarize yourself with the style of the show. The show's website will often give descriptions of the main characters and their relationships.

The following example is a typical under-5 scene from a soap opera. The character in the scene has only two lines. Apply your technique and craft to a small part, the same as you would for a leading role. Ask, "What is the purpose of the scene? What is my job? How do I want to do it?"

Look at the following scene as if you were asked to play the waitress. Read everything. Don't forget the writer's stage directions and camera shots.

<u>WILLOW TREE INN—DAYTIME</u>

ARLENE
Looking around, a bit troubled
When you showed up at the paper, and insisted on taking me to lunch...This was the last place I thought we'd go.

CORBIN
I wanted to surprise you. This was our favorite place when we first got married. I can't remember the last time we were here... Can you?

ARLENE
Fumbling for an answer.
The last time we were here together? I... can't remember, either.
She picks up the menu, trying to hide her discomfort. The waitress enters.

WAITRESS
Ready to order yet? *(To Arlene)* **Oh, nice to see you again so soon.**
Waitress exits.
CU (close-up) Arlene like a deer in headlights.

CORBIN
Arlene?
ARLENE
It's nothing. I was here a few days ago... for about two seconds.

CORBIN
Fighting a growing feeling of distrust. But I just asked you when you were last here, and you said you couldn't remember.

ARLENE
You're making too much out of nothing. I was just supposed to meet Kyle here to....

CORBIN
Keeping his voice low, with effort. Kyle! Right!

ARLENE
Overriding him. To talk about this stupid rivalry we've gotten ourselves into.

46

CORBIN
And in order to discuss this "professional" rivalry, you had to meet …here…in a secluded, out-of-the-way restaurant?

ARLENE
This place is <u>not</u> secluded!

CORBIN
And why did you keep this supposedly innocent meeting a secret?

ARLENE
Taking the offensive.
Because I knew you'd react like this.

CORBIN
That's bull, Arlene! *Cuts her off.* You can deny it all you want, but there's obviously something going on with you and Kyle!
Take Arlene.

WHAT DO WE KNOW?

We can tell from the dialogue that Arlene works with a man named Kyle. Corbin is extremely jealous of Kyle. Corbin also doesn't trust his wife. He is taking Arlene to a secluded, romantic restaurant that meant something special to them before they were married. Why? From the tone of the dialogue, we can assume that all is not well with their marriage. Imagine that Corbin is surprising Arlene and taking her to this particular restaurant to try to rekindle their relationship.

You can make some solid choices based on this. These are lead characters on the show. With research you would find out that Corbin is a high school principal in town. Arlene and Kyle work together at a newspaper and are not having an affair but there are "sparks" between them. Every soap opera has a core of good upstanding people surrounded by more outrageous characters, both good and bad, who stir things up.

WHY DID THE WRITER WRITE THE WAITRESS'S LINE?

By the end of the scene, has Kyle and Arlene's marriage gotten better or worse? Why did Arlene lie about being there with Kyle? It's likely their marriage is in serious trouble. Let's examine further. Arlene and Corbin are two of the good solid people on the show. The writers may want to split them up for more interesting story lines. However, if

Arlene were to actually cheat on Corbin, or Corbin's anger and mistrust of Arlene came from nowhere, these characters would cease to be sympathetic and the audience would no longer root for them.

In this scene, Corbin mistakenly draws the conclusion that his wife is having an affair with Kyle. His mistake is understandable. Their marriage is already struggling. He is already jealous of Kyle. His wife arranged to meet Kyle in a secluded and romantic restaurant. This isn't just any secluded restaurant. It is one that has special memories and meaning for Corbin and Arlene. The audience can understand Corbin's mistake.

Now, has Arlene really done anything bad? Stupid, yes. Bad? No. She never should have arranged to meet Kyle at this particular restaurant, and then compounded her error by lying to her husband. If they split up, it will be because of a silly and stupid misunderstanding, not because either of them did anything bad. Now the audience can continue to like and relate to both Corbin and Arlene, while feeling sorry for both of them. It becomes clear that without the waitress's line, this information would not have been revealed and the scene would never have taken place.

HOW DO THE WRITERS WANT THE AUDIENCE TO RESPOND TO THIS SCENE?

The clue is in the camera shot after the waitress's line. Arlene knows she is caught. Her marriage is in serious trouble. Loyal Daytime viewers know and follow these story lines closely. The writers probably wants a collective gasp of, "Oh no! Poor Arlene!" to the waitress's line "Oh, nice to see you again so soon." If that's the purpose of the scene, what is the job of the actor playing the waitress? Take a clue from the camera shot. The actor playing the waitress has to find a way to remember and interact with Arlene so strongly, that Arlene feels like a "deer caught in headlights."

BASED ON YOUR SCRIPT ANALYSIS, CREATE A CHARACTER

Now that you know your job as an actor, create a character, and come up with several interesting and contrasting ways to get the audience to gasp "Oh no!" and fulfill the purpose of the scene. Here are two examples to show how much room there is for creativity when you only have a couple of lines.

CHOICE 1

An obvious and safe choice is to be exceptionally attentive to Arlene. Start with your character. The character is not a "waitress," but a human being with a full life and dreams. Does the way you earn your living at this moment in time describe who you are? Of course not. Waitress, nurse, doctor, lawyer, cab driver, cop, salesman—these are jobs, not people. Don't play the "job."

Create a life for "the waitress." Make her an auditioning actor looking for her first big break. Why not? Now complicate your character's life. Make her a single parent who has a six year-old daughter to raise and support. Why are you being so nice to Arlene? You must create a reason.

What was Arlene like as a customer the night she came in with Kyle? Suppose she and Kyle had an expensive meal. She was very pleasant to you, paid the tab and left you a $50 tip on a $200 check. What would this reveal? Arlene has money. Also, her repeat visit might reveal that she's new to the neighborhood, liked the restaurant and your service and could become a regular customer. A regular who comes in several times a week and leaves $50 tips would really help you support your daughter and buy new headshots. You *want* her to remember your excellent service, so she will ask for you whenever she comes in. Now you have a reason to pay special attention to her.

Next, what kind of mood are you in on this particular evening? Choose being in a really good mood to help you be extra attentive. What would put you in a good mood? What about if you just found out you have a callback for a major supporting role in the new Tom Hanks movie? In fact, you are actually going to audition with Tom Hanks! Each of these choices supports the scene, and in no way violate the script.

CHOICE 2

Create a different choice. Make the waitress edgy. For this example, make only a few changes in the above scenario. What would cause you to be "edgy?" What if Arlene had been a lousy tipper? Create a back-story to support this. When she came in with Kyle, she was extremely demanding, complained about everything, and only left you a $10 tip on a $150 check.

Now enhance it by putting yourself in a really bad mood. You have the audition with Tom Hanks, but it is tonight. You worked the lunch shift and were getting ready to leave for your audition, when the owner said you had to stay and work because too many waiters had called in sick. He told you if you left you would be fired. If you weren't a single parent, you might quit. But this is a great job that helps you support your kid. So you are forced to work and will miss the audition. This puts you in a foul mood.

DON'T SHORTCHANGE YOURSELF

Through the creative use of script analysis, the same simple scene can be brought to life to enhance and illuminate the purpose for the audience in two completely different yet valid ways. Bring something bold and special to the table every time you work. If you are nervous about this when you have a small part, take the time to create two different ways of doing the scene. Don't take short cuts. Do the full process for both approaches. You could do the edgy waitress first and if they don't like it, you could then do the more conservative, pleasing waitress. If you look carefully, every choice follows the two principles— it doesn't violate the script and it serves the scene. The process is exactly the same when you are doing a leading role like Corbin or Arlene, but you have more material on which to base your choices.

• The main job for the actor playing Corbin is to react strongly to Arlene's lying and the mention of Kyle.

• The main job for the actress playing Arlene is to react and "take the hit" when the waitress recognizes her. She must then show she cares enough about her marriage, to scramble as hard she can to try and save it.

There is conflict between Arlene and Corbin, the two main characters. When all three actors in the scene do their job, they put the spotlight on Arlene to show she lied about being there. This brings home the purpose of the scene: <u>their marriage is in serious trouble</u>. In addition, the audience feels sorry for Arlene and Corbin because they are trapped in a big misunderstanding.

DAY PLAYER SCENE

The following scene is from a nighttime drama series about a mob family, *The Falcones*. Observe how the call sheet helps you figure out the purpose of the scene. Focus on the role of "Jimmy" while studying this example.

GEORGIE: (Contract Role) A Capo in the Falcone crime family. He is always feuding with his Boss, Carmine.
JIMMY SPANOWITZ: (Day player) 30's, non-descript
MRS. SPANOWITZ: (Day player) Jimmy's grandmother
EXTRAS (25) Doctors, Nurses and Patients
LOCATION SHOOT

EXTERIOR—HOSPITAL—PATIENT'S ENTRANCE

Jimmy, 30, is wheeling his grandmother, Dottie, into the hospital to be admitted for tests. Georgie is being wheeled out of the hospital after being discharged.

MRS. SPANOWITZ
Hey Georgie, what are you doing here?

GEORGIE
Had my gall bladder out last week. The quacks wanted to keep me another week but this place is driving me nuts.

MRS. SPANOWITZ
I know what you mean. They want me here for a few days for "tests." What are you gonna do? Hey, do you remember my grandson, Jimmy? He used to work for you at the butcher shop when he was about 12.

GEORGIE
How ya doin' kid?

JIMMY
Okay I guess. Grandma's been having her "spells" again.

GEORGIE
You take care of the old girl, ya hear.

MRS. SPANOWITZ
Georgie, you still got the old shop?

JIMMY
Hey grandma, I gotta go call Sylvia.

MRS. SPANOWITZ
You go ahead. I'm not going anywhere. (*Jimmy exits*) Kids these days. Always on the go.

GEORGIE
Yeah. No respect for their elders any more. But, what are you gonna do, huh? Look I gotta get outta here. You take care of yourself. (*Georgie motions his bodyguard to get going*)

HOW SHOULD AN ACTOR APPROACH THIS SCENE IF HE IS PLAYING JIMMY?

First, it is fairly obvious that the audience is supposed to learn that Georgie is getting out of the hospital. But what else can you learn by careful examination of all the material?

The scene is being shot on location at a hospital. The actor playing Georgie is under contract with the show, but Jimmy and Mrs. Spanowitz are Day Players. And there are 25 extras in the scene. With the exception of Georgie, all of these factors are expenses for the producer. The writers could add a line into another scene like, "Hey I heard Georgie got out of the hospital today." and save the producer $25,000. So it must be really important that the audience actually see Georgie getting out of the hospital.

Why? Who is Georgie? He is a Capo in Carmine Falcone's mob. You also know he and Carmine don't get along. You can reasonably infer that the writers want the audience to react strongly at the sight of Georgie. "Uh oh, Georgie's back. There's going to be trouble for Carmine!" The purpose of the scene is to get that strong audience reaction.

WHAT IS THE JOB OF THE ACTOR PLAYING JIMMY?

The actor must create a sense of danger. Something bad is going to happen. In this scene, Jimmy is a reflection of the audience's point of view.

Is it absolutely certain that this is what the writers intended? No. There is no way to be 100% certain. Sometimes it is necessary to make an educated guess and take a leap of faith. If your choice is off the mark, the director will give you an adjustment. But you must first make a choice!

Now how does the actor want to do the scene?

What kind of character and choices can you make that will convey the sense of danger? Make Sylvia Jimmy's wife. Since the writers don't tell us anything about Jimmy, you have carte blanche to make him anything you want. Make Jimmy a detective. To make it even more interesting, make him a crooked detective on the take from Carmine Falcone. This means he knows about Carmine's business and about Georgie.

Why would it be trouble for Carmine if Georgie is back in business? You don't know, but the character has to "know." While it is impossible to act emotions, you can make specific choices that will cause the desired reaction and emotions to happen. What is Jimmy feeling in this scene? Alarm, apprehension, fear and confusion might be some of his feelings. So make up a storyline that would cause Jimmy to feel those emotions such as:

Georgie was supposed to be in the hospital for two weeks. Carmine saw this as an opportunity to take over a piece of Georgie's territory. But the deal isn't finished and Georgie's early release could really screw things up. Since Jimmy is on Carmine's payroll, he knows about this takeover.

What happens when he hears his grandmother say, "Hey, Georgie, what are you doing here?"

Who does Jimmy have to call? Not Sylvia, but Carmine. And he better make that call fast. If Carmine found out that Jimmy knew and didn't call him, he could be in some serious trouble. On one hand, Jimmy has to get his grandmother admitted to the hospital. On the other hand, he must call Carmine before Georgie shows up on Carmine's doorstep. What does he do? Admit his grandmother, or call Carmine? Both of these choices cause conflict for Jimmy. Now he's "caught" and trying to decide what to do.

Jimmy is not going to call Sylvia. He's lying to his grandmother. He's torn. What would Carmine do to Jimmy if he found out Jimmy knew about Georgie but didn't call him? How sick is Jimmy's grandmother? These are specifics that can cause conflictive emotions and enrich the scene. Instead of just being real and believable, the actor has enhanced the scene and truly helped the audience to "get it." Once again, notice how answers to the important questions served the purpose of the scene and did not violate the script.

WHEN YOU DON'T HAVE THE ENTIRE SCRIPT

There may come a time when you will be auditioning or hired for a part that has only one line. All you may be given is that single page from the script. In this situation, whenever answering your questions, find the juiciest answer that won't violate the script you have in hand.

HOSPITAL—MIDNIGHT

NURSE PHILLIPS
I'm sorry! What do you think you're doing with that IV bag?!

Take trapped Debra. Fade out.

The key is the camera shot. *Take trapped Debra.* "Take" means a scene ending with a close up on trapped Debra for lots of tension.

WHERE AND WHY IS SHE TRAPPED?

When making choices from a short script like this, look for whatever facts you can find. Put them together to make the richest possible scenario.

Fact: Phillips is a nurse.
Fact: Debra is trapped.
Fact: Debra is up to something.

WHAT IS DEBRA DOING? YOU ADD THE JUICE.

What is the worst thing Debra could be doing?
Answer: Murdering someone!
Who?
Answer: A patient.

Where is this taking place?
Answer: In a hospital.

Why is that patient in the hospital?
Answer: Someone tried to murder him.

Does Nurse Phillips know this?
YES! It adds danger and conflict to the scene.

Debra is coming back to "finish the job." This makes her a threat to both the patient and to Phillips. Phillips must do two things with her lines—stop Debra to save the patient, and get help before Debra kills both of them.

Again, make creative and bold choices that serve the scene and do not violate the script.

SCRIPT ANALYSIS IS THE ACTOR'S BEST FRIEND

Script-analysis is the foundation on which to create all the facets of the character's life. Creating a compelling background for each character helps bring every line alive. This lets the audience witness a full human being struggling and trying to cope with all the problems that have been created by the writer.

Without script analysis you may always wonder if you have made a good choice for your character. It is difficult to fully trust your choices if you are constantly worrying about them. Script analysis will give you the confidence to make powerful choices you are fully committed to. Mining the script for "gold" allows you, the actor, to give the strongest performance possible and to soar to the heights. You will be a character living a life, not an actor performing a scene.

6

CREATING A CHARACTER

RECIPE

"Baking a cake is culinary magic. Nowhere else in cooking is the transformation of a few simple ingredients so profound and so appreciated...a great cake baker is attentive to technique, details and timing...because the same ingredients combined in a different order, mixed differently, or even used at different temperatures result in quite different cakes (or failures), good bakers are dedicated to the small things that produce beautiful cakes that taste heavenly."
—From *The Joy of Cooking*

Recipe for Creating a Character ©

Mix:　1 cup script analysis
　　　　1 cup structure
　　　　1 cup substitutions
　　　　1 cup feelings
　　　　Stir until well blended. Then add:
　　　　1 ½ cups improvisation
　　　　2 cups moment-to-moment discoveries

Sift all ingredients thoroughly to remove all "acting." Then beat in:
　　　　4 cups homework/preparation

Pour into a rehearsal pan and bake for as many rehearsals as you can get, until the character is well-formed and springs back to the touch.

Decorate your finished character with a frosting of:

　　　　1 tsp. accents and dialects
　　　　½ tsp. props
　　　　1 tsp. costume

Add a dash of hair and makeup

Place your finished character on a stage or set,
and let the audience enjoy!

I often use the analogy of baking a cake to illustrate the idea of how an actor can craft a character.

The first step in baking is to decide what kind of cake is wanted. Is it a deep devilish chocolate layer cake, a fluffy light angel food cake, or a dense fruit cake? Bakers choose the best recipe for their confections. Actors must also choose. What kind of character do you need to create, based on the demands of the script?

The chief components for making a cake are: flour, sugar, milk, and eggs, which are then beaten together in the right proportions. For an actor to begin creating a character, the main ingredients are: script analysis, structure, substitutions and feelings, blended together in the right proportions. These elements form the foundation for your character.

The baker's next step is to add secondary ingredients such as butter, salt, and baking powder. Under the supervision of the director (or head chef) the actor needs to "sift" the equivalent ingredients into their character. These ingredients include moment-to-moment discoveries and improvisation, which help ignite the character's feelings and imagination.

The baker then spreads the batter evenly into a pan. They place the cake on a rack in the center of the oven at a precise temperature. The "baking" and "rising" for the actor happens through homework, preparation, and if there is such a luxury, rehearsals.

The baker finishes their cake with decoration. It could be frosted, dusted with nuts and served on a silver-footed pedestal cake plate. The final accoutrements for the actor are the adding of accents, props, costumes, hair and makeup. Framed on a stage or screen and carefully lit, the character is then presented to an audience waiting to be transported by the perfection of your creation!

YOUR FIRST INGREDIENT—YOU!

Celebrated actress and acting teacher, Uta Hagen, credited director Harold Clurman with the initial turn-around in her perspective on acting in her best-selling text *Respect for Acting.* She sums up his approach in his demand for the human being within the character:

CREATING A CHARACTER

In 1947, I worked in a play under the direction of Harold Clurman. He opened a new world in the professional theatre for me. He took away my 'tricks.' He imposed no line readings, no gestures, no positions on the actors. At first I floundered badly because for many years I had become accustomed to using specific outer directions as the material from which to construct the mask for my character, the mask behind which I would hide throughout the performance. Mr. Clurman refused to accept a mask. He demanded ME in the role. My love of acting was slowly reawakened as I began to deal with a strange new technique of evolving in the character. I was not allowed to begin with, or concern myself at any time with, a preconceived form. I was assured that a form would result from the work we were doing.

START WITH YOURSELF

Too often we walk around concealing what we're actually thinking or feeling. We spend our lives editing, censoring, and hiding ourselves from the world. We believe if anyone knew what we were really like, no one would like us. We have all done things we have felt were hideous and horrible. We have fantasized things that are even worse.

We have to go in and find that little chest where we've buried these fears, fantasies and experiences, open it up, pull them out and go, "Here! Here's who I am!" And that is terrifying. But that's our job. So we connect into ourselves with substitutions, keep our emotions honest, and become that character. You don't "act" it. You become it.

Often actors read the material in a predictable fashion that I call "sheep" acting. The actors are earnestly saying the written words the way they think the writer wants them said. Take four different actresses—Mary Louise Parker, Cate Blanchett, Francis McDormand, and Reese Witherspoon—and give them all the same monologue. Each of these actresses' individual energy will uniquely color the words. There is no "one way" that's "right."

Character should be 90% you, 10% the difference. The key is to find that 90% that is you. Learn to "mine" yourself for every character you play. Think of a Rubik's Cube as the center of yourself. Each square of color is a part of you. The center of your cube is generally made up of a certain combination of core colors, but you want to rearrange those squares, so that your central colors match the primal emotions of the character.

If these colors are not familiar, you've got to bring them up, explore, and heighten them so they match what you need for the character. For example, say your center is made primarily of blues, greens, and a few squares of yellow. If you are playing a vampire whose center is made up of reds, purples and blacks, you need to find those reds, purples, and blacks within yourself to bring them to the center of the character.

"One of the pleasures of being an actor is quite simply taking a walk in someone else's shoes. And when I look at the roles I've played, I'm kind of amazed at all the wonderful adventures I've had and the different things I've learned."
—Willem Dafoe

While we each have our own individual truths, every one of those truths is also universal. When we "mine" our personal truths and connect them to the script, they touch and connect to the universal truth within us (the audience). We recognize ourselves. It's witnessing that expression that keeps us glued to our seats in the theatre. That's what great acting is about.

In 1969 Sir Ian McKellen was in Bratislava, the former communist Czechoslovakia, to give a performance of Shakespeare's *Richard II*. He was concerned the audience wouldn't be able to understand the depth of the story because they didn't speak English. Later, Sir Ian wrote about the experience of performing the section of the play where Richard stands weeping upon returning to his homeland:

> ... when it came; the gasps, the sniffles, the mewing...an audience, crying, I have never heard it since; They were grieving. I understood, fool that I had been, because Richard's words could have been their own, when their land was invaded so recently, when sticks and stones had been pelted at armored tanks, when the earth was their only symbol of a future freedom, of a continuing past.

Because Sir Ian brought his truth and core self to the performance, it didn't matter that the play was in a different language. The people of Batislava felt the truth that is universal, the language of heart and soul.

CREATE YOUR CHARACTER'S WORLD

The timespan of a story may be limitless, and often spans several months, if not years. Generally a script is limited—90 minutes to 3 hours. What is your character doing with all of this extra time where they are not seen? No writer can give you everything you need to create a full and rich character. It is this unseen life that can fill that character with rich, conflictive thoughts and emotions that add truth to a scene. It is important to give your character a strong vision that they are striving for. This need not come directly from the script but it must always serve the script. Let's look at how to mine a script to find everything possible to give you confidence in your strong choices to create a full and rich world for your character to inhabit.

In a *Political Action Thriller* you have been cast as the spouse of the star. He is a major spy for the US Government. It is 8 am, and your spouse has just gotten a call, and must leave immediately to stop terrorists from blowing up 5 major East Coast cities with atomic bombs. He has 10 days to accomplish this.

YOU ARE PLAYING "HONEY"

"Honey, can you drive Jimmy to his Little League batting practice Friday? His coach said he has to be there if he wants to start in the championship game Saturday. Oh, I forgot, I can't make Jill's dance recital after school next Tuesday. Yes, I know it's her first recital but I have to work. Oh, and can you take my tux to the cleaners. I need it for that state dinner in two weeks."

What facts are hidden in this dialogue that can help you make strong choices and create the character and the world that they live in?

WHAT WE KNOW

- The style of the film
- Why they were attracted to each other
- How old they were when they met
- Where they probably met
- Their education level
- What he does for a living

- How successful they are
- Their standing in the community
- Where they live
- What time of year it is
- How old each child is
- Who some of their friends or co-workers are
- The major life change "Honey" has had in the last year or so

HOW DO WE KNOW ALL THIS?

STYLE

It is a <u>political action thriller.</u> It is not a plain action film like a James Bond Film. Why? Bond doesn't have a wife. This is more like a "Jack Ryan" film (Harrison Ford) where the author wants the audience to think about good & evil, ethics & morality in the way our leaders act. You are a functionary character, the loving partner. For the audience to buy the moral and ethical premise of the film they must like the lead. If they meet him as a husband and father first, that bond is created.

The PURPOSE of the opening scenes is to get the audience to see what a great husband and father he is in spite of the conflict his leaving has on the family. Your job as the actress is creating that loving family.

HOW you want to do that is a choice you have to make.

All of this information is gleaned by using lateral thinking, and logic taken to its ultimate conclusion.

THE FACTS

How old is the son?

We know he plays Little League baseball. The ages for Little League are 8 to 12. He is playing in a championship game and he is 12.

How old is the daughter?

She is doing her first dance recital. When? After school. She must be in first grade so we know she is six or seven.

CREATING A CHARACTER

Where did they meet?

We know that they've known each other for at least 13 years, so they must be in their mid to early 30s. Therefore, when they met they must have been about 19. They probably met in college. They could've met many ways, but let's use what we can from the script to create your world and find your happiness. While we don't know much about you, we know a lot about your husband. Let's use that to create your character.

What does he do for a living? Who does he work for?

He works for the US government. He is a spy. This is a branch of the State Department which is a political function of government.

When he was in college, what courses might he have been taking?

He was probably taking courses in political science, law, and history.

What might have attracted these two to one another?

Again use what we know. When we are college age, "We are going to change the world." They were drawn together by an interest in the world, in making it a better place, perhaps through politics. Let's choose. They met in a political science class.

Now, what might she have wanted to do with her life in politics?

He became a spy. She could've run for office or become a consultant.

Now, what kind of advanced degree might she have gone for?

Most people in those professions have law degrees. So she would go to law school.

What kept her from going to law school?

She got pregnant. Her dreams of changing the world would have to be a put on hold.

Could she take a job outside of the house?

No, because he had to be able to travel at a moment's notice. So, we figured out how old they are, how many children they have, and how they met.

How do we know how successful they are?

Well he owns a tux, and very matter-of-factly, asks her to take it to the cleaners to get ready for a state dinner.

What is a state dinner? Where is it held?

State dinners are held at the White House to honor Heads of State, Kings, Premiers, etc.

So, who do you know?

The President. And, you've been to the White House before. We know that because he's so matter-of-factly asked you to get his tux cleaned. Now, we know you live in the Washington, DC area and you travel in very high circles. You're probably very well-educated yourself.

HOW DO WE USE THIS?

The purpose of all this is to choose a strong Happiness (Life Dream) for you, and create a life for your character based on that.

We said you had a major change in your life in the last year or so. What is that?

Well, how old is your daughter? Six or Seven. She is in first grade. You now have your days completely free!

What are you going to do with all that free time?

You could do anything, but let's stick with what we have already discovered. This way you will know you will be serving the script and on safe ground. You had a dream when you were in college. Why couldn't you now go back and get your law degree? Let's choose that. You went back to law school.

Now we really want this to be a heightened circumstance that has urgency for you. So let's add that you graduated law school six weeks ago. Why?

Because now what do you have to do?

Pass the bar! This would take every spare minute of your time. Every second of every day you are studying and studying. Very few law graduates pass the bar the first time.

ALWAYS GIVE YOUR CHARACTER A JOB

How much emotional turmoil does your job cause in your life? In this case she would have to work at home, perhaps something she could do with a computer. By using her "wanting to make the world a better place," we could make her a consultant for some environmental groups. Let's add urgency to that. Earth Day is coming up and you are busy preparing some PowerPoint presentations for a couple of big special events. You have to get this work done around your studying for the bar! You also have to give up studying to go to your daughter's recital and your son's baseball game. What other things are in your life that complicate your existence and interfere with your ability to study?

Your great dream is "To make the world a better place." Passing the bar is the next crucial step in reaching your goal, and achieving your dream.

We have created a life that began 13 years ago and everything in the script you have to do is a big interruption in your life. Actually the whole script gets in the way of your life. No matter what the writer has you doing in any given scene, you need to be studying for the bar. Now the writer is a pain in the neck. Everything the writer has you doing is keeping you from what you need to be doing. So now we see a human being living life, not an actor just playing a character in a scene.

How does this affect the script or this scene?
Use the life we just created.

How would this make you feel about the fact that your husband is leaving at this particular time?
Angry, hurt, frustrated. It's not fair! You put your dreams on hold for 13 years. It's your turn! But if your husband succeeds in defusing these bombs and catching the terrorists, it will make the world a better place.

Could he die doing this? Is it dangerous?
How does that make you feel?
Guilty.

The script merely had you loving your husband so that we would see this wonderful loving family. Creating a complete life around a powerful dream elevates the stakes of the work and puts everything in a context. It is so important because that allows you to live within the script. You must create a world in which your character lives apart from the script, but will serve the script. When you create strong and urgent needs, this world becomes easier to create. Then this world makes your acting much easier.

All of this emotional turmoil will help to paint interesting textures that will wrap the character and the scenes in a tapestry of truth coming from witnessing a real human being and not just a character. When taken to its logical conclusion you will develop a complete life for your character, that while independent of the script always completely serves the script.

CHARTING THE CHARACTERS EMOTIONAL JOURNEY

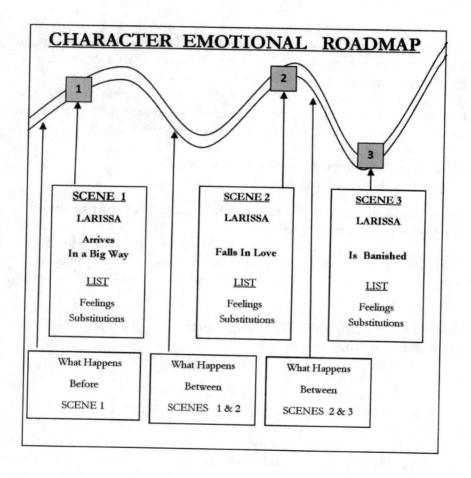

There are many different methods actors use to track the arc of a character. Here's one approach to mapping out an entire script, scene-by-scene:

- Along the bottom of an upright piece of 8x10 paper, make horizontal boxes across the lower half for each of the character's scenes. Head each scene box with a scene title that sums up the essence of the scene. For instance, in scene #1, the title, "Larissa Arrives in a Big Way" as her first scene.

- Then write what happened before that scene (her step mother kicked her out of the household and she had a daunting journey by stagecoach through a snowstorm, arriving unannounced, looking a mess, and creating upheaval to her grandmother's estate) to the left of that column.

- List the feelings your character experiences (fear, shame, apprehension and exhaustion) and the substitutions (see Page 89) you're using to feel those emotions (for instance the big audition you had the other day where you came in dressed inappropriately for the role) in the box itself under "Larissa Arrives in a Big Way."

- Then notate what happens after the "Larissa Arrives" scene (her room is freezing, she scorches the silk dress her grandmother has given her, standing in front of a fireplace, and has the realization her grandmother is in ill health) in the space before the next scene #2 box "Larissa Falls in Love" and so on.

Most of the before and after boxes are juicy and specific details you are creating with your imagination to flesh out and make your character more dimensional and interesting. The result is a map of the entire script with your character's history from the beginning of the story to the end.

- Using the top section of the paper, draw a roadmap to chart the peeks and valleys of your character's journey.

- Use different colored pencils to color in the center of your road to correspond for each emotion or blend of emotions for your character for each scene. The hues and their intensity will also be an instant visual reminder of what you need to bring to the scene.

- Change the colors chart the highs and lows (or **+** and **−** see page 90) of those feelings. It ends up looking something like the chart (but in color).
- Tape together and fold accordion style as many 8x10 sheets of paper as you need to track your character through the entire piece.

This type of map allows you to keep track of where your character is emotionally throughout the piece. This works when rehearsing a play or movie, but is also helpful when shooting a film or series out of chronological order or, when doing film, the shooting schedule changes, due to weather, location issues or other unexpected events. You will have substitutions at your fingertips, and will know with one glance where you came from and where your emotions need to be.

CREATING A CHARACTER BIO

A character bio is the life story an actor creates about his character that supports character details implied or spoken of in the script. The actor makes decisions about the past life of their character that may or may not be in the words or on the page. The purpose of a bio is to make choices and create a foundation that will flesh out and add conflict, dimension and depth to your character. The intention of a bio is not to give you added homework, or to make you feel that you will be a better actor by filling out a questionnaire.

How to decide what factors to use when creating a character bio?

- First, look at the playwright's descriptions.
- Search for what the character says about themselves.
- Find what other characters say about your character.
- Distill what important facts need to be explored in a bio.
- From these clues, deduce what pieces of your character's life and personality need to be fleshed out more fully.

How long is the play or film? Two or two and half hours? What time span does that cover? A couple of days, weeks, months, or a year? How many minutes of each day are we actually seeing your character? What are they doing all the rest of that time?

CREATING A CHARACTER

This is where the writer allows you to create a human being. You can paint bold strokes with creating your character's world. The more time you have, the more intricate it can be.

Appendix D outlines areas you might cover in a character bio.

AN EXAMPLE OF QUESTIONS TO EXPLORE IN A BIO

In the play *A Streetcar Named Desire*, the character of Blanche is a complex role. If you are creating a bio and foundation for Blanche here are some questions you might ask:

- What was the family estate, Belle Reeve, like when you were a child? Describe the estate in detail. What were your favorite places on the estate? What are your favorite memories of Belle Reeve, and where did they take place? Unhappy or troubled remembrances?

- Who were your beaus? How did they court you? What happened to them? Do you still have any of the mementoes that they gave you? If not, what happened to them?

- What set the downfall of Belle Reeve into motion? Remember in detail what happened to each member of your family. Do you have any physical keepsakes from Belle Reeve?

- Where and when, did you meet your husband? What was that first encounter like?

- Go through the hours of the last day of your marriage, from the discovery of your husband's male lover, leading up to your husband's suicide.

- Did you know in your heart of hearts that your husband was gay? Did anyone else know?

- How did you become a teacher? What did you teach? How did you feel about teaching? What led to your dismissal? How did it make you feel? Did you know it was coming? What did you do and where did you go?

- How did you feel about coming to live with your sister Stella? Their living quarters? Neighbors? What was your first impression of Stanley? How do you feel about him now? How do you feel about Stella having Stanley's baby?

- Who is your former beau, Shep Huntleigh, and what promises did he make to you? Where is he and why didn't you marry him? How do you believe he can save you?

Sometimes actors come in with a long character bio for an audition coaching session. They've been trained to do an extensive character bio, regardless of how much time they have to prepare the actual audition material. You will rarely have much time, considering how auditions are managed today. Learn to create an appropriate length bio, and choose key points to add conflict and dimension to your character in the audition scene.

YOU CANNOT PLAY A JOB

If we're going to see your character at work, try to get some on the job training and first-hand experience. This way you don't have to spend energy "acting" like a cop or a nurse. Your research and training will allow you to "be" a cop or a nurse, and allow you to focus your energy on your character and acting. Hospitals, stores, businesses, the FBI and government, are all places where you can contact the public relations department to arrange to observe professionals at their jobs. Some police departments will let you do a "ride-along" with an officer. By observing work environments first hand, you will be able to add specifics to your role that will make you feel and look real.

I worked with an actress who was cast as an FBI agent. She was coached at FBI Quantico headquarters for two weeks. She felt her time investment paid off in understanding what the job entailed, technically and emotionally. She was even inspired to base her character on the female agent who trained her.

When Dustin Hoffman played an advertising executive in *Kramer vs. Kramer*, he attended and observed an advertising conference. For several days he watched how executives talked, walked, and interacted with each other. Do you think he would waste his time and energy if he didn't know he would find acting gold?

Before Renee Zellweger filmed *Bridget Jones's Diary*, she was hired to work at a publishing company in London. They thought she was a regular applicant. They didn't even know she was American because she had perfected her British accent for the role. Working in, and observing the character's actual environment gives you real details for creating the job and character choices. It also adds a comfort level and familiarity that you don't get if you're just pretending. The experience also allows you to directly tap into feelings that resonate with your character, as you are in a similar environment.

Denzel Washington said he spent 15 months in physical training, for his role as the boxer, Hurricane Carter. He said, *"I mean, he is Rubin Hurricane Carter, so the Hurricane part of him I found and came to know in myself through the boxing training."*

One of my students used a technique to help merge himself with a character. The character had attended a university, so he went on the internet and took a virtual tour of the campus. He later explored the country online, where the character had been kidnapped and was being held.

He states: "I like to use pictures of people, places, and things to help build my character's background history. I find that just a quick peek at the photos on my phone helps me to refresh my background story, which for me makes the situation feel much more real. Sometimes I will even look at pictures of people I know if I'm using them as substitutions. I find this stirs up fresh natural feelings towards them right there on the spot, making the layering of them into the other character feel fresh as well."

CHARACTER INTERVIEW

My teacher, Wynn Handman, created a wonderful exercise called the "Character Interview." Wynn conducts interviews with actors "in character" in the character's own environment.

For instance, if you are playing Mary Queen of Scots, you might be interviewed in your chambers, in the castle where you are imprisoned by Queen Elizabeth. He might ask such questions as:

How do you feel about what's happening to you?
What do you think about your cousin, Elizabeth?
Did you plot to overthrow her?
Why is your religion the 'true' religion?
What is your strongest need right now?
What words would you want engraved on your headstone?

71

You answer the questions "in character." Some of your answers may be based on the script but you are also creating and improvising answers in the moment. What you create with your imagination becomes a part of your reality. Questions that are difficult to answer highlight areas of the character you need to fill in. Character interviews help to merge the actor with the character. Sometimes this exercise is referred to as "The Hot Seat." However, Wynn created the exercise to help the actor inhabit the character, not to feel the pressure of being on the spot.

REAL PEOPLE AS CHARACTERS

Researching a real person as a character is a challenge. Not only will you be compared to how that human being lived but also, how they moved or spoke. If you try to match the DNA only, you will lose the soul of the human being. For instance, look at all the "clones" of Marilyn Monroe, who was much more intelligent and complex than her sexual image.

Some important questions to ask are:

- How well-known is this person?
- What is so important that a play or screenplay is centered on this human being?
- What parts of their life affected this individual?
- What are the most important points that are needed to illuminate this person?   (see appendix D)

Do all the research on the individual that you can. Read the autobiography, biographies, newspaper and magazine articles. Dig on the Internet for more written information. Look for interviews, videos, and search on video sites like YouTube.

If the person is still alive, interview them or people who know them. Work on the physical specifics of how they look, move and speak. Work the social and psychological aspects of why they look, move, and speak the way they do.

You may want to work with a dialect or movement coach. When you have done all the homework and found out what makes this human being tick from the inside out, let the research go and work on the role. Trust that what is important from your investigation will stick. Do the work of finding yourself in the character of the human being. If you don't, you might end up with a character that has all the specifics of the real person, but no heart.

SOURCES FOR RESEARCH

- *Internet search.* Try different search engines like Google, Yahoo, Ask.com, etc., because each will bring up different results. Information sites like Wikipedia are also good places to start.

- *Video sites.* You'll be amazed what you can find on YouTube, Google Video, Hulu, Yahoo Video—acting performances, real life film of artists and famous people, interviews, entire films, footage of specific kinds of people, countries to study and research, and even how-to's like dialects, medical operations, etc.

- *Medical, professional and personal blogs.* If you are researching a character that has schizophrenia, blogs can give you insights about physical attributes, feelings, difficulties and the day-to-day life of a person with severe mental illness.

- *Newspapers and periodicals.* Online and in libraries.

- *Biographies and autobiographies.* Autobiographies help you understand the character from their personal point-of view. Biographies can give you a perspective of how this human being is/was perceived, and may delve deeper into the person's background and social issues.

- *Museums.* Look at artwork and sculpture for historical individuals as interpreted by artists. Research a period in history for costume, military uniforms, posture, daily life, etc. A good example is Van Der Meer's 17th century Dutch painting that inspired the film, *Girl With A Pearl Earring.*

- *Historical periods.* Historical documents, the National Archives in D.C., historical societies and archives, museums, national parks and monuments, (i.e., Independence Hall in Philadelphia or Manzanar War Relocation Center in California) as well as books and literature of the period.

7

STRUCTURE

Just as Michelangelo didn't start impulsively painting the Sistine Chapel, you also don't want to recklessly jump into a script. Think of every acting role as a commission. As an artist who is a creator, step back from your role and ask, "What do I need to create? What is my vision?"

Understanding how to structure a script gives you a streamlined and specific approach to the material. The structure you create will provide a blueprint for your work, that allows your acting to leap off the page. This blueprint frees you from the indecision that can paralyze you, or lead to vague choices. The following technique provides you with the flexibility to follow the suggestions of the director without getting lost.

ELEMENTS OF THE STRUCTURE

Purpose
Job
Style
Scene Type
Core
Happiness
Feelings
Driving Question
Beats
Inner Actions
Outer Tactics
Substitutions-As ifs
Putting it All Together
Preparation and Lift-off

BREAKING DOWN THE SCRIPT

PURPOSE

As previously spoken of in Chapter 5, Script Analysis, the first step in creating your structure is finding the purpose of the scene or script.

As an actor, your job is to: *Make the material come alive within the purpose of why it was written.* Therefore deciding on that purpose is essential. Investigate your role the same way that a forensic expert investigates a crime scene. Explore the material. Do your script analysis. Figure out the requirements of the material and your job as an actor within that purpose:

JOB

Once you have identified the purpose of the scene in is important to define your job. Why is my character in the script? Why are they in this scene. What is their function? How do they move they action.? What is it you have to do as an actor, to help the audience get the information necessary to fulfill the purpose of the scene? This is one of the most important steps towards making strong choices. How can you go about doing a job if you don't know what it is?

- What should the audience think at the end of the scene or script? Every scene in a play or script is written to bring the audience to a conclusion or thought: "Their marriage is in trouble!" or "They secretly like each other."

- Also all the scenes should add up to a moral or conclusion at the end of the script: For Shakespeare's *Romeo and Juliet* it could be "The tragedy of a family feud."

- What should the audience feel at the end of the scene or script? The audience connects to the characters' feelings. Understanding what the audience should feel at the end of a scene and conclusion of the story helps the actor hone in on what the audience needs for the point of the material to hit home.

- Again, in *Romeo and Juliet*, in the earlier scenes the audience might feel: charmed and delighted. Then empathetic towards the lovers as they come together against all odds, and devastated by the end, when Romeo and Juliet die for each other. When the lights come up in the theater, the audience might be so profoundly affected, they make a personal decision to end a dispute in their own family.

STYLES

Your next task is to identify and understand the style of the script. "If the scene's not working, you're probably playing against the rhythms and style of the material," my teacher Wynn Handman would say, so finding that style is essential. What follows is a representative list of styles that are found in plays, movies, and television shows:

Drama	Comedy	Period	Author
Tragedy	Romantic Comedy	Victorian	Shaw
Melodrama	Sitcom	Film Noir	Mamet
Realism	Camp	WWII	Pinter
Docudrama	Satire	Civil War	Williams
Dramedy	Farce	1970's	O'Neill
Thriller	Slapstick	Western	Shakespeare
Biopic	Black Comedy	Renaissance	Chekhov

OTHER STYLES

Action Adventure	Mockumentary	Reality
Science Fiction	Horror	Fantasy

TYPES OF SCENES

In my experience coaching, I discovered there are approximately 12 different types of scenes. When you understand what kind of a scene you are working on, you begin to be more precise in creating a journey that will carry the audience along with you.

1. *Meet Cute:* An age old literary device. Two characters generate sparks that turn into a bonfire of attraction. The predominate dynamic is "I can't stand you!" much like Katherine and Petruchio's relationship in Shakespeare's *The Taming of the Shrew.* Many male/female relationships are established this way. Contemporary examples might be, Jack Nicholson and Diane Keaton in the movie *Something's Gotta Give,* or Tom Cruise and Kelly McGillis in *Top Gun.* However, be aware, a "meet cute" scene can also be a male/male scene such as: Danny Glover and Mel Gibson in *Lethal Weapon,* or female/female—Susan Sarandon and Geena Davis in *Thelma & Louise.* Your job in a "meet cute" scene is to create chemistry, chemistry, chemistry.

Many talented actors build brilliant characters with interesting choices but forget to create chemistry. If there are no "sparks" with your leading man or lady, it won't matter how exceptional you are. For great Chemistry think of Brad Pitt and Angelina Jolie in *Mr. & Mrs. Smith* or Ryan Gosling and Rachel McAdams in *The Notebook.*

2. *Romantic:* Chemistry, especially sexual chemistry, is important in the romantic style. The dynamic is immediate attraction without combativeness, such as *Romeo and Juliet* or *Twilight.*

3. *Confrontation:* One character confronts or challenges the other character, like Tom Cruise and Jack Nicholson in *A Few Good Men,* or Russell Crowe and Joaquin Phoenix in *Gladiator.*

4. *Power Play:* One character exerts their power to try to manipulate the other character. Heath Ledger in *Batman Returns,* or Michael Douglas in the *Wall Street* movies, where many scenes exemplify this.

5. *Sales Job:* One character tries to win approval and/or convince the other character to their point-of-view. *Glengarry Glen Ross* (play and film) portrays the ultimate sales job to perfection.

6. *Seduction:* A form of sales job or power play in which sexuality or sexual chemistry can be part of the end result, such as the interplay between Glenn Close and John Malkovich in *Dangerous Liaisons.*

7. *Decision:* The character makes a climatic decision that causes them to reverse their current direction or pursue a different path. Sylvester Stallone in *Rocky,* Will Smith in *The Pursuit of Happiness,* or Mark Wahlberg in *The Fighter.*

8. *Uncovering:* A character opens up to disclose a vital piece of information, which results in a human revelation. Robert Shaw, as the character Quint, in *Jaws* gives a riveting monologue revealing his horrific experience in WWII. His true motives for relentlessly hunting the shark are uncovered. However, uncoverings do not have to be revelations. So while the uncovering could be a revelation for the character or to other characters, it is not necessarily a revelation to the audience.

9. *Revelation:* Revelations are often surprises suddenly revealed by a character. Revelations are the "aha" moments that drive the story. Sometimes a revelation is an uncovering, like the kind of scene performed in a courtroom drama, in which a murderer is revealed. Revelations can take both character and audience by surprise. An iconic example is the movie *Chinatown*, when Faye Dunaway blurts out to Jack Nicholson, "My sister and my daughter!" (meaning her father raped and impregnated her).

For an example to help you determine the difference between an uncovering and a revelation scene, look at the film *The Sixth Sense*. Bruce Willis plays Dr. Malcolm Crowe, a child psychologist who is uncovering clues in his attempt to help a young boy who "sees dead people." Dr. Crowe also wants to figure out what went wrong with his marriage. Each scene uncovers a different piece of the puzzle. Neither the audience nor Dr. Crowe has enough pieces to put it all together. The revelation comes at the end of the movie when the audience and Dr. Crowe learn that Crowe is the one that is actually dead. We have the "aha" moment and it's the climax of the film.

10. *Intrigue:* Tactics that are used to pull the audience into the character. A good example is Liam Neeson's first appearance as Oskar Schindler in *Schindler's List.* Before the audience sees his face, we see him getting dressed, putting on expensive clothes and cufflinks. This build-up intrigues us. We're eager to learn more about this man.

In the opening scene of *Raiders of the Lost Ark*, Indiana Jones is going deeper and deeper into a cave. As he descends he must avoid the dead bodies of everyone who attempted this quest before him. Why have so many men given up their lives for what's in this cave? Intrigue.

11. *Exposition:* The primary purpose is to give the audience necessary facts or background information. Exposition scenes abound in soap opera, science fiction, medical, legal and crime dramas. Your job is to make the information interesting so it's not just dry facts. To be able to do so requires using substitutions for the information you are conveying. You want to give these lines resonance, different levels, and at times, humor.

Exposition scenes are most successful when the actor can turn the exposition into a different type of scene. Julia Roberts takes a recitation of pollution facts and turns it into a sales job in *Erin Brockovitch*, convincing Albert Finney to take on the case. Susan Sarandon's voice-over monologue about baseball at the start of *Bull Durham* film becomes a seduction scene to entice the audience into the story.

12. *Tension:* This is a scene in which the characters are facing imminent danger, such as diffusing a bomb. *24* was an entire television show about the style of tension, utilizing cliffhanger endings. Soap operas employ cliffhangers to entice the audience to tune in to the next episode. The challenge with tension scenes is to find a range of different colors and feelings, so that the scenes are not all one level of energy.

MULTIPLE SCENE TYPES

Scenes can be more than one type but one style will be predominant. *Million Dollar Baby* starts with a "meet cute" scene as Hillary Swank first encounters Clint Eastwood at his gym. She also does a sales job when she tries to convince him to coach her. The primary focus is the meet cute, since chemistry is needed between them, but the sales job is an essential part of the scene.

Another example is the film *Memento*. The movie starts by telling the story backwards, creating an intrigue scene. However, the scene is primarily a decision scene. Guy Pearce makes the choice to follow the clues to his lost memory and it is this decision that drives the action of the entire movie.

THE CORE

The Core is the emotional center, the main motor that propels a character.

COMPLETE CORE LIST

CONTROL • LOVE • POWER • SECURITY
FREEDOM • PASSION • RESPECT • TRUTH

While we each have aspects of the various Cores within us, everyone has only one central Core that is the driving force in our lives. Your core is who you are despite everything that happens to you. The Core never changes.

Donald Trump's Core is power. Even if he went into a monastery and tried to change or cover it up, that would still be his Core. Bill Clinton's Core is passion.

Even if you perform on a series or soap opera for years, your character's Core will always remain the same. For example, in the long-running sitcom *I Love Lucy*, Lucy's Core remained passion throughout, Ricky's Core was respect and Ethel's Core was security.

There is a story about the legendary actress Uta Hagen. She was asked to play a comedic role, but because she didn't think she was funny she turned down the role. She changed her mind when she realized she could be as silly as the character by tapping into the part of herself that came out when she was feeding her poodles. You should be able to play each of the different Cores by asking, "When am I like this?"

CHOOSE THE CORE FOR THE CHARACTER

When we walk into a room, we size people up by their aura or "vibe." This aura comes from their Core, their emotional center, in the same way an audience sizes up a character as they come onto the stage or screen.

Though there is always more than one choice for a Core, decide on just one. You water the choice down if you choose more than one. If that choice doesn't work, you can change it. Select a Core that adds conflict, while also resonating with the script's purpose. Which Core is going to add life and depth to your character?

Let's say you're playing a husband and wife scene. In the scene your husband is being very disrespectful to you. Respect is a great choice for your Core because it adds tremendous conflict. In addition, other choices like control or truth might be effective. You also might want to think about picking a different Core than you've played in a previous role, to expand your range as an actor.

British actress Janet McTeer, made a great artistic choice for a Core in the 1997 Broadway production of *A Doll's House*. In an interview with television journalist Charlie Rose in 1997, she said, *"...the whole point about the character I've made is that I've created somebody who's acting."* She went on to say that she looked on *A Doll's House* as a humanist drama, not a feminist drama. She did not take the traditional view that the play is about a woman coming into her own. Instead, she viewed the play as being about the destruction of a marriage by betrayal. By approaching Nora as a person "full of doubt" who truly loved and was attracted to her husband, McTeer chose a core of security that completely changed the dynamic of the role from previous incarnations. The role of Nora is generally cast with petite actresses that look doll-like. Janet MeTeer is 6 feet tall, but no one who saw this production doubted that they saw Nora on that stage.

If you're looking at the character of Juliet from *Romeo and Juliet* you might think, "Other actors always play Juliet's core about love or passion. It might work to choose freedom or control." Or perhaps a light bulb goes off and you say, "Wait a minute! Let me make her about truth. How interesting that Juliet could be!"

Always ask, "What's my concept of this piece? Which core choice is going to inspire me and make my acting come alive?" You're given the tools and the writing, but it's you that makes the character come to life within the purpose.

You don't want to "act" a Core. You want to "be" that Core. For instance, you can't act insecure—you must feel insecure to be insecure. To do this you must find the essence of that particular Core within yourself. The Core guides you in determining the specific feelings your character is experiencing in the scene. The Core is the keystone to the map of your character.

CONNECT TO THE CORE'S ENERGY

The Core is like the first stroke on the canvas–it affects and colors all your choices. The Core also helps you say your lines with specificity. Say you're playing a bartender and your line is "What can I get you?" If your Core is power, you are going to say that line with a different energy than if your Core is respect or security.

THE HAPPINESS

The Happiness (or super objective) is the next big stroke on the canvas. My teacher Wynn used to say liltingly, "What is your character's Happiness?" The Happiness is not about what the character wants in the scene, but their ultimate dream. Stanislavsky called it the "super-objective."

The Happiness is probably one of the most vital parts of the actor's craft. Knowing how to use the Happiness in creating your characters will bring them to life.

You can boil it down quickly if you ask yourself, "If my character's fairy godmother could grant one wish, what would that wish be?" The Happiness should add dimension and conflict to your character. It does not necessarily have to come from the script but it shouldn't be at odds with the writer's purpose.

The Happiness you choose should charge and excite you. This choice should resonate through the material. It should turn you on and it should sound like your character's Core.

One of my students came up with an example for a character whose Core was power: "I want to be King of the gypsy cabdrivers on 42nd Street between 9th and 10th Avenues!" That's a specific Happiness that's primal and juicy.

Every scene is only a sliver of the entire world of the character. So create this world starting with the Happiness. The character should react to what's occurring in the script in the context of his entire "life." It is important to give your character an interesting and imaginative Happiness that will provide a rich and conflictive emotional life.

HAPPINESS CHANGES

Often a play or movie is about a life-altering event changing the Happiness. In *Victor/Victoria*, Julie Andrews' Happiness starts off as wanting to be a famous singer in Paris. After meeting James Garner, her Happiness shifts to wanting to marry him and live happily ever after. In *Blood Diamond*, Leonardo DiCaprio wants to make easy money through the illegal diamond trade. After meeting Djimon Hounsou's character, his "Happiness" changes to "save this family from certain destruction."

A character's Happiness affects almost every scene. While the Happiness can change during the story, it rarely changes more than once and never changes scene-to-scene.

CONNECT YOURSELF TO THE ROLE EMOTIONALLY

One important aspect when you break down the script is uncovering what your character is feeling—not just what the words are saying. Words can cover up many of these feelings, so we want to isolate the emotions to put your finger on the pulse of the specific feelings that your character is experiencing.

THE "EMOTIONAL BLEND" OF FEELINGS

A good writer has written an emotional arc for each character. Locate the major emotions in each scene. There are emotions dictated by the script. List the additional emotions you want to bring to the text. Be sure to write them down. (See Appendix A for a list of emotions).

Consider the different groups of feelings your character has throughout the scene. This is your "emotional blend." Start off with a group of 4 or 5 feelings at the beginning of the scene. When did you recently feel most of these emotions? Who made you feel these feelings? Find substitutions (see page 89) for the other characters and situations, to ground the material to yourself emotionally and bring your feelings to life.

Characters are most interesting when layered with conflicting emotions. The more emotions "bump up" against each other, the more inner conflict, heightened reality, and loaded thoughts you will have. If you are playing Hamlet you may simultaneously experience anger, and sadness, as you recite "To be or not to be." The choice of Core will narrow the group of emotions. If you've chosen a Core of "truth," you may experience a more specific blend of anguish, regret, revenge, and dread.

Another example is that of Stanley in *A Streetcar Named Desire*. When Blanche finally reveals she has lost the family plantation, Stanley's primal emotion may be anger. If you make Stanley's Core "power," you can find a more specific emotional blend of fury, loss of control, and revenge. However, if the Core chosen is "respect," the emotional blend could be betrayal, torment, feeling used or like a chump.

THE DRIVING QUESTION

(The Objective) What your character wants in the scene

The driving question usually begins with "How can I...?" You refer to yourself in the first person. The driving question gives you an objective for the scene. The question should sound like the character and come from their Core. By evolving the question from their Core, you remain in the energy of your character which fuels your choices.

Pose the driving question to the other character in the second person. Instead of, "How can I force him to hear me?" ask "How can I force you to hear me?" Stating the question in the second person keeps you personally engaged with the other character. It removes the invisible barrier, "the pane of glass" between you and that character/actor. Instead of "How can I freeze out this loudmouth?" personally challenge the person with, "How can I freeze you out?" Staying active and present makes your driving question potent and real. The concept of phrasing the objective as a question came a from a discussion with director Christopher Goutman of *All My Children*, who felt stating it as a question created an active need for that question to be answered.

CHANGES TO THE OBJECTIVE

The driving question changes when you either achieve or don't achieve your objective. In a scene from *A Streetcar Named Desire*, Stanley's driving question toward his sister-in-law Blanche might be, "How can I get you the hell outta here?" If Stanley can't get Blanche to leave, the driving question may change to "How can I destroy you?"

Suppose you're playing a scene in which you are a teacher working with a problem student. Here are some examples of driving questions reflecting different choices of Cores for the character of the teacher:

- If the Core is truth—"How can I get you to understand that these aren't just words? This is real."

- If the Core is power—"How can I force this asshole to learn this crap?"

- If the Core is passion—"How can I get you to embrace this amazing stuff?!"

BEATS

In music, a beat is a unit of time. In acting, a beat is the length of time it takes for you to play an objective from beginning to end. A beat can switch to a new beat if your character experiences a shift in feeling. A beat can also become a new beat when you achieve or don't achieve your driving question.

If your driving question is "How can I get you to love me?" and the other character confesses they committed a murder, that would signal a beat change. Your driving question might change to "How can I escape from you?!"

In music, beats add up to measures, which add up to stanzas that create a song. In acting, individual beats create moments that add up to a character's journey through a scene. Use your beats to create different levels and colors in your character's journey through the scene.

Anything that creates a change in the progress of achieving your driving question qualifies as a beat change. Beats for one character do not have to match beats for another character. You only need to be concerned with your character's beats. Beats vary depending on the material.

Beats in Shakespeare are much longer than beats in slapstick, where the pace is quick and physical happenings change frequently. Emotional interplay between characters or internal emotional changes can provoke beat changes. A revelation from one character to another would result in a beat change. A beat can also be a unit of action like a doorbell ringing, a character's entrance, or an explosion.

As you work through the material, you will decide on an inner action and outer tactic for each beat. Secret inner actions generally change with each new beat. Occasionally, the inner action will last for more than one beat. Usually each beat has a different secret inner action and outer tactic.

STYLE OF MATERIAL AND BEATS

If it's soap opera, you don't change the actions and tactics quite as much because it's written loosely. Because of time constraints, a soap script's not boiled down like a movie script or play

In a movie script, scenes are shorter, and there's usually more time and space around each line. Practically every line has a different action and tactic, because the camera is also showing what you're feeling under the words. Keep in mind scenes can be tweaked and tightened, because more time is invested editing a movie.

Plays have more dialogue, because the audience is further away from the actors. The audience often has to hear in the writing what might be shown in a movie, where the camera actually shows the characters thoughts and feelings. You can't take as much time with each line as you would on camera. A few lines tend to be grouped into actions and tactics.

SECRET INNER ACTIONS

Secret inner actions are your path to achieving your driving question. Because you may not want the other character to know what your real objective is, the inner actions are "secret." Actions are always active verbs that are as physical as possible. For instance to "snare" or "corral" are stronger verbs than to "ask." Actions always begin "to…"

If your driving question is "How can I crush you?" the journey of your secret inner actions could be: to bait you, to hook you, to reel you in, to corner you, and to annihilate you. The inner actions must lead to the driving question, or they are wrong. This creates a check and balance. Appendix B is a starter list of active verbs.

Say your Core is passion, and your Happiness is to live with your lover 24/7. Your driving question is, "How can I get Mom to give me the money for rent and two months down payment so I can be with Leonardo day and night?" This scene is a "sales job" on your mother, but you might not want your mother to know that you're doing a sales job on her.

It is easier to think of the journey to achieve inner actions, if you imagine your mother being physically far away from you. What's the first stepping stone on the path to your driving question? Since she's far away, your first inner action might be to grab her attention. Then you have to pull her in, then maybe intrigue her, melt her, hook her, and then finally mobilize her into writing that check! That's your journey. Inner actions are what we do on the inside. Outer tactics are how we do this on the outside.

OUTER TACTICS

If the secret inner action is what you're doing, the outer tactic is the how; it is specifically how you reveal or mask your inner action. The outer tactic is also an active verb, but ends in "ing." This dance between what you want (secret inner action) and how you go after it (outer tactic) is what many people unconsciously do in real life. With acting, you have to figure it out first.

If your character's Core is respect or truth, your inner actions and outer tactics will often have similarities and be aligned. This is because you choose to reveal your inner truth to the outside world. But if your Core is power or control, your outer tactic may be entirely different than your inner action. That would be the kind of person who often disguises or covers their true motives. For instance, if a person is insincere in complimenting you, the inner action might be to "cut you down" by "honeying." It can be more real and interesting when the actions and tactics don't match. Appendix C provides a starter list of outer tactics.

GIVE SPECIFICITY TO YOUR INNER ACTIONS

Inner actions by themselves are too general. You've chosen the inner action, "To seduce." Okay, but how to seduce? There are a thousand different ways. By daring? By befriending? By tickling? Each of these choices has a different energy. Inner actions by themselves are not specific enough. If you've only chosen a general action, chances are you will still be in your mind wondering, "Oh, I'm going to seduce...but how am I going to do that?" Outer tactics create the external mask of what the character is doing. Combinations of inner actions and outer tactics create tension, dimension, and layers. Choosing the outer tactics is a way of getting focused with your choices. You separate yourself from the general "I'm supposed to seduce," by deciding specifically how you're going to seduce. Your choices will make the material resonate in a more distinctive and inimitable way. The outer tactics are like having an artist's palette, and you get to choose from many different colors. You're the artist.

PERSONAL ACTIONS AND TACTICS LIST

Create your own personal list of verbs (inner and outer) just as you have created your own personal wardrobe. Take the starter lists from Appendices B and C, and explore them. Replace verbs that don't work with ones that do. Carry a little notebook and write down new verbs. Keep updating. You can also create your own verbs such as "to seduce by James Bond-ing" Or "to vent by what-the-hell-ing!" The actions list is like a starter set of tools. Generally, the list should be single words. If a phrase like "How could you-ing?" works better for you, then use that. It's more important to know what you're doing with the line than its being one word.

When you're nervous and under pressure at an audition, and trying to think of what choices to make, take out your notebook and choose a verb from your list. It's so simple when it's right there in front of you.

"You jot down ideas, memories, whatever, concerning your real life that somehow parallels the character you're playing, and you incorporate that in your scene work."
—Chris Cooper

SUBSTITUTIONS

You must connect the role to yourself to make the character come alive. You want to genuinely marry your emotions with that of the character to connect the role to you.

Recast every character in the script with people you know—friends and family, co-workers, girlfriends and boyfriends, etc. To do this, ask yourself "How does my character feel about the other character? Who in my life makes me feel like this"? This person is your substitution.

UNCOVERING SUBSTITUTIONS

Actor and teacher Paul Sorvino once said to me, "You need to go into a private room and think about what affects you. Your mother may not affect you as much as diamonds. It doesn't matter. Whatever it is, it is."

How do you find great substitutions? Trial and error. You have to try out different substitutions until you find the right ones. It's like uncovering jewels. You will use those substitutions as a springboard into the feelings of your character. If you are performing the role of the son, Jamie, in O'Neill's *Long Day's Journey Into Night*, you may start with a substitution of something recent that happened in your family—a divorce, a fight with your father, your tormented feelings that your family thinks you should get a 9-5 job. Once the substitution is anchored in and affecting you in rehearsals or performance and you now closely identify with the character and their feelings, then you may no longer need to consciously use the substitution. If your emotional reactions start to slip, then reuse the substitution or plug in a new one.

(More on Substitutions in Chapter 8)

OTHER ELEMENTS TO ADD INTO YOUR BASIC STRUCTURE

THE PLUS/MINUS FACTOR

I invited Screen Writing expert Robert McKee to give a seminar for my actors. One of the more interesting concepts he introduced was the plus/minus factor. If a scene ends on a positive note (a plus+) try to begin the scene with a negative note (a minus–). For example, you're an attorney and the scene ends with you winning a case. That's definitely a plus+. What could you create that just happened on a negative note – that you could begin the scene with? Maybe you received a phone call from your assistant informing you that they're bringing in a surprise witness. Because of that phone call you're late and you forgot a brief, all in the minus category.

If a scene is written in an angry and confrontational style you don't have to play the whole scene that way. Strong emotions are like aces. Anger is an ace. Sexuality is an ace. Crying is an ace. You don't want to play your aces over and over, because the audience gets their fill. When you keep repeating your strongest choices, it will lessen their impact.

Save your anger for the end. Come in with the attitude of, "This is going to work!" Use your sense of humor, a little flirtation or love, and play against the anger. When you do choose to play the anger card, it will then be effective. The audience will have a greater response to it.

SYMBOLS

There are times when you are performing that you must stop and "take in" a particular moment. It is very useful to have symbols and mark in your script where such a moment occurs. You don't want to rush through them. I use a couple of symbols as shorthand for reaction moments.

A forward slash, / is often used in scripts to mark a beat change. I use a double slash, // to note a longer or major "transition." The symbol for a "take-in" is a spiral ◉. A take-in is something unexpected that makes you stop and think. For instance, you notice your son shivering and have a moment to absorb it ◉, before you think, "Are you coming down with something?" or someone says something that makes you react ◉ and then think. There are times when something has to hit you even harder. That's an emotional "bomb." 💣 A bomb can be wonderful or horrific. Some examples might be your husband saying, "I'm leaving you." 💣 Or your boyfriend saying, "Will you marry me?" 💣 Draw a little bomb with a fuse in the script. 💣 If somebody lands a bomb on you, include that in your structure. And if you're landing a bomb you also need to include that in your structure. You must be aware that you're landing something that has an impact, even when you choose to land it in a gentle way.

Other symbols are a capital "**D**" for a discovery. For instance, your character has an epiphany or "**D**" discovery that leads to an answer.

A triangle ▲ stands for a decision. Your character has the moment where they make the ▲ decision to quit their job. As you go through your script, you should mark the discoveries and decisions because you want to illuminate them to the audience. These symbols are important because they help the actor uncover and create important moments, and moments move the audience.

You can also indicate on your script when your character is leading or driving the scene. For instance: after the character of your husband unleashes his anger at you, your character takes the reins and makes a decision ▲ to leave her husband. If you're not conscious of these energy changes you'll be missing levels in your work.

FINDING THE "CRACKING" POINT

A character comes in fighting for an objective. They win or they lose. The moment in the scene when they achieve or don't achieve what they want is where the scene cracks and goes to a different place. One of my students takes a pencil and draws a line across the entire page where the scene "cracks" to highlight this moment.

The crack is built into the scene.

CHOOSING THE MOMENT BEFORE

Be inventive with the moment before a scene opens. Make a precise choice that illuminates something about your character, and helps your acting as you enter into the scene. In a scene in which you are alone in your boss' office, don't simply wait for the other character to walk through the door. Your driving question might be, "I wonder if my boss is happily married?" With this question you pick up his wedding picture from his desk and look at his wife. Your inner action is "to gauge" and your outer tactic is by "lasering" her. You think, "Wow, she looks like a bitch!" Then the door opens. The boss enters adding conflict to the scene. You then have a reaction ◐, and your driving question has to change to: "How can I hide this?"

SETTING CHOICES

Reasons to make a choice:

- If the choice makes the next line make sense.
- Adds conflict to the other character/actor.
- Illuminates insights into the character.
- Adds emotional range.
- Adds interesting colors
- Works in a unique way.
- Resonates and deepens your connection to the character.

WRITE DOWN YOUR CHOICES!

Next? Put it down in "black and white." Use pencil to write all of your choices and blocking on your script, because there will always be changes. Write the choice down clearly and boldly. Seeing your choice written boldly in black and white makes that choice real. Russell Crowe once said in an interview, that he doesn't just make *a* choice; he makes *the* choice until a better one comes along.

Your choices, along with the stage directions and blocking, become the blueprint of the script itself. Since you have made every choice for a reason, you will remember the lines more easily. You understand why you're saying and doing the action.

PUTTING IT ALL TOGETHER

Write your Core on the top left of the script, or first page of your audition. Write your Happiness on the top right. Place your Driving Question just before the dialog begins at the top of the scene. Write the feelings or groups of feelings in a column down the left margin. The secret inner actions and outer tactics are noted in the right margin next to each line or beat. Separate the inner action from the outer tactic with a /slash line, i.e. uncover/peeling.

In class, my students take a short scene and complete this process in 15-20 minutes every week. Then I take the script away from them and film the scene as if they were auditioning. The more you practice this technique, the faster and better you will become until cold copy no longer threatens you. You'll know exactly what to do with it.

One of my students was perfect for a role in a feature film. The casting director encouraged her to fly out to LA for the audition. I encouraged her to go, since she was trained, prepared, and right for the role. It was intimidating for her, because there were many recognizable actresses sitting in the waiting room. What saved her from nerves was having a clear structure for her scene. She was able to focus on her choices and substitutions and "let go" when she was in front of the famous writer/director. She nailed the audition and was offered the role that started her career.

GETTING THE WORDS INTO YOUR BONES

I've seen many actors whose acting result was flat and lifeless because they memorized the words by rote. Never memorize lines by rote. Instead, learn the scene. An interesting way to physically get your lines into your body is to memorize your plan for the scene. Don't worry about your lines. Read the other person's lines out loud. Instead of saying your line, say and "physically do" your action and tactic as you are looking at your line. For instance, "When she (the other character) says her line, I'm going to 'put her down' by 'mocking,' and then when she responds with this line, I'm going to 'dismiss' her by 'queening.'"

Go through the whole script a few times this way, looking at what your line is, then saying and doing your action and tactic instead of your line. By not only saying, but also physically doing the action and tactic, you ingrain each line into your body. Now when you release into the moment as you do the scene, your choice will be triggered organically as you respond to the other characters. Because they're so deeply implanted, your actions and tactics will occur naturally as you respond to the other characters in the moment.

When you go back, plug in your substitutions and connect to them through improvisation. You take all the words that were just words and connect them to your life. You are now talking about things that you understand, and care about, in complete concepts. You know how you're feeling, what you're going to do and how you're going to do every beat. You've pretty much memorized the scene, not by trying to memorize words, but by applying your craft. In doing the work, the scene gets into your system on its own because you know what it's about in your gut, not just the words you are saying.

Your script is prepared. Your choices are made. Now it's time to put it all together for lift-off!

PREPARATION AND LIFT-OFF WITH STRUCTURE

Actors sometimes get confused and try to bring the structure into performing the scene. The structure has to be there before you do the scene. It's your homework. It becomes the circuitry you've created which will automatically trigger the impulses you need as you perform in the moment.

Think of the structure as a springboard and your performance as a dive. Divers who achieve perfect dives allow their bodies to take over and let go. They trust that they will know what to do in the moment they leave the diving board. Trust your preparation the same way.

Get the structure in your bones so then you can forget about it. Start with your head and your intelligence to work out your driving questions, actions and tactics for your scene. Then move this work into your heart and gut. Improvise your emotions to fuel the structure, prepare for the moment before, and then let it go! The structure and the preparation become strong instincts that will make the scene come alive. But you must jump off of them.

I coached with an actor who played Meryl Streep's husband in a movie. It was a fun process, as he shared with me how they were communicating ideas back and forth for their characters and their marital relationship. They took such joy in the homework of creating their roles. One day when they arrived on set, the director decided to film their scene in one continuous shot. This was nerve-wracking for the actor playing the husband. Meryl said, "Let's not worry about it. Let's just have fun!" That's why you want to do all the hard work beforehand. Because then you can "let go" and have an adventure being in the moment!

Some actors try to make every action and tactic stick. If you do that you won't be honestly responding in the moment. Actions and tactics depend on the energy the other actor is sending to you. It is like a game or a dance. If you don't work it off the other person, the returned energy won't make sense.

PREPARING

If you're preparing offstage or on set, it's important to fully amplify your feelings. In the opening scene of the movie *The Illusionist*, Ed Norton is simply sitting on a chair on a stage with tremendous sensory resonating through his relaxed face. He is so filled; he's like "a container that can be barely held." That takes a powerful preparation.

When you're preparing, think hot thoughts. Talk to yourself. When you start to feel yourself vibrating with emotions, jump up and down a few times to stoke those emotions to get them blazing. You don't want to start at the lowest level, because it takes too long to get to the height of emotion you need, and your energy can dissipate quickly. Keep that fire burning in your gut as you move to hit your mark or enter the stage. (If it's for camera work, relax your face as you approach your mark.) If you've prepared at home, you only need a 10-second preparation most of the time; you just need to concentrate on your trigger to help you bring up the heat.

One technique is to imagine the scene in your mind. Mentally go through the beats and quickly check that the feelings are awake. If you come to an emotional beat, don't delve too deeply into the feeling because you will diffuse it. Just touch on it to see if you're feeling the emotions and then back off, then go to preparing the moment before.

Sometimes you won't have the opportunity to go to a corner and prepare. Maybe you're playing a character that is incapacitated or unable to move. Don't just lie or sit, keep breathing and keep your energy moving until you're ready. When you prepare, breathe into the preparation, breathe into the feelings, and fuel the furnace. Create extraordinary thoughts for yourself. Make primal sounds out loud, or internally if that's not possible. You can also imagine a strong character gesture to bring the primal feelings to the forefront.

EXAMPLES OF A STRUCTURED SCENE

The following are two examples of how to break down a scene using script analysis and the structure. The results are two unique choices, grounded in the script, that don't violate the script.

Imagine you are playing the role of Brown, who is a defense attorney. Sabatino is a crooked judge. The following could be choices for structuring the role of Brown:

To view a video of the following scenes being played out go to:

http://pennytempletonstudio.com/acting-lions/the-acting-barre-videos/

CHOICE 1

CORE: Respect

HAPPINESS: To keep the powerful from trampling on the rights of the individual .

DRIVING QUESTION: How can I get you to live up to your oath of office?

EMOTIONS

ACTIONS / TACTICS

+ (Plus)

JUDGE SABATINO
It's a damn trap.

🌀 (Take In)

Frustrated
Annoyed
Determined

BROWN
It's only a trap if
Arnie Cox can hurt you.

Crack Open / Careful
Leash Pulling

JUDGE SABATINO
He's a little mouse. But you see what's happening. They're closing ranks around Blakemore.

Disbelief

BROWN
Russell...

Guiltify / What are you
doing? !

JUDGE SABATINO
The fact that I'm even a suspect – you have any idea what this could do to my chances with the Appellate court? I am this close. And they can't stand it, Henry.

BROWN
You're right about that.

🌀

Exasperated

JUDGE SABATINO
I didn't fill the party coffers, Henry. I didn't kiss ass. All I ever did was work hard.

Trap / I've got your
numbering

===============

▲ (Decision)
New Driving Question

How can I catch you at your own game?

Pissed
Tormented
— (Minus)

BROWN
Russell. If Arnie Cox really can't hurt you, all you'd be doing is locking up a defendant on a probation violation. .....No big deal. // Right...Russell?

Nail/ In your facing
💣 (Bomb)
Guiltify /Disappointed
Fathering

97

CHOICE 2

CORE: Power   **HAPPINESS:** To be the King of criminal attorneys in NYC
DRIVING QUESTION: How can I get you to tell me the truth, asshole?

EMOTIONS		ACTIONS / TACTICS

JUDGE SABATINO
It's a damn trap.

— (Minus)
Betrayed
On the Hunt
Determined

BROWN
It's only a trap if
Arnie Cox can hurt you.

⊚ (Take In)
Probe / No Big Dealing

JUDGE SABATINO
He's a little mouse. But you see
what's happening. They're closing
ranks around Blakemore.

Steamed

BROWN
Russell...

Shake up / Yanking

JUDGE SABATINO
The fact that I'm even a suspect –
you have any idea what this could do
to my chances with the Appellate
court? I am this close. And they can't
stand it, Henry.

⊚

BROWN
You're right about that.

Enraged

Rattle/Strangling

JUDGE SABATINO
I didn't fill the party coffers, Henry. I
didn't kiss ass. All I ever did was work
hard.

BROWN
Russell. If Arnie Cox really can't hurt
you, all you'd be doing is locking up a
defendant on a probation violation.

Trap / Buddying

=================

▲ (Decision)
New Driving Question

💣 (Bomb)

Vengeful
✚ (Plus)

*How can I let you know you're
screwed!?*
No big deal, Right...Russell.

Split-Open/Punching

STRUCTURE

Now that you have completely structured your script—be it an entire script or a three-page audition scene—it's now time to fully develop your character into a complete human being. Whenever you work on a role, this is your homework. The amount of time you can devote to this homework will vary. Having 24 hours before an audition won't give you the same amount of time as a three-week rehearsal period. You must prioritize your time wisely.

MAKE YOUR STRUCTURE FLEXIBLE

Your structure is your plan for how you want to perform the scene. By building the structure into the character it will become part of your impulses. You won't have to think about it when you're performing. When you've done your homework, broken your script down and made your initial choices, you will see what works and what doesn't clearly and quickly. Instead of guessing, you'll know what you did to get your result, so that you can be consistently great. You will also have a depth to your work that actors who are only work in the moment often will not be able to achieve.

TAILOR YOUR PROCESS TO FIT EACH PROJECT

So why do all this work if elements are going to change once you start working with the director and other actors? First, you will have a foundation from which to change your choices. If you go into a shoot or rehearsal just "winging it," it will be incredibly difficult to know where to start if you are asked to make new choices on the spot. Making changes after you have already worked your structure is often like rearranging a room. The architecture of the room and many of the pieces of furniture remain the same. You're just changing the placement to give a different feel to the space.

WORDS OF ADVICE: NEVER STOP DOING THE WORK

Unfortunately, some actors think structure is "boring." Or they get complacent and let their acting process fall away because they think, "I'm working. I don't have time," or "I don't need to do that anymore." When you begin to work regularly, that is the time to continue with your process. It's working for you!

Sometimes another actor might question why you just don't "go with the flow and be in the moment, man." Don't pay attention. An actor who is preoccupied with your process may feel threatened when they see you putting effort and preparation into your role. After all, you might make that actor look lazy or blow them out of the water. Focus on what you need to do. One of the greatest tools is your structure.

REMEMBER:

UNDERSTAND THE PURPOSE

KNOW HOW TO BRING THE SCENE ALIVE

FILL IT WITH REAL EMOTION

THEN LIVE IT!

8

ESSENTIALS OF AN ACTOR'S TOOLBOX

"With any part you play, there is a certain amount of yourself in it. There has to be, otherwise it's just not acting. It's lying." —Johnny Depp

FRESH SUBSTITUTIONS

From my teaching experience, the use of recent events in a person's life can have a powerful outcome for the actor in their work. It has a duel effect: First, it's effective because the feelings are fresh and personal. Sometimes all it takes is choosing a recent real event. Secondly, because it's personal, when you plug in a fresh substitution effectively, it makes the work extremely specific.

For instance, you've probably worked yourself up over an incident as minor as: someone taking your parking space this morning, or a coworker snubbing you at work. Also, when you use a recent, minor event for a substitution, your subconscious often responds, "Okay, that feels safe. I'll go on that ride!" Then you ignite these smaller sparks of emotion through improvisation and your preparation to achieve the heightened level you need.

Train yourself to recognize events as possible substitutions. Explore what happens to you in the course of a day. Note your experiences large and small, and your reactions to them. You want to develop the ability to recall these happenings quickly. Then when you need a substitution for something recent that angered or excited you, in other words, affected you, that person or event will immediately come to mind.

SUBSTITUTION/SENSORY JOURNAL

Keep a journal listing the substitutions and sense memory that affect you, so that you can have current "hot button" triggers at your fingertips. For example, if your mother-in-law criticizes you and makes you feel "belittled," list her as a substitution in your journal for that particular blend of feelings. Perhaps the scent of chocolate chip cookies baking consistently brings up feelings of togetherness and family for you. List it in your journal. This way, if you're at an audition, in rehearsal or on set and you need to shift gears to another substitution, you can look up a replacement in your journal to bring up those particular feelings and replace that substitution on the spot.

SAMPLE SUBSTITUTION CHART

EMOTIONS	PEOPLE	PLACES	THINGS	EVENTS	ANIMALS
LOVE	Julia/ Penelope	Central Park	New Sunglasses	Christmas	Blackie
HATE	IRS	Post Office	Pot Holes	Tax Audit	Rats
JOY	The Twins	Farm House	Pay raise	Reunion	Fawn
POWER	My Employees	Mountain Top	Black Sports car	Graduation	Hamster
FEAR	My Father	World Trade Center	Airplanes	Surgery	Bobcat
BETRAYAL	Boss who didn't give me a raise	Ex Spouses House	Car (lemon)	Foreclosure	Stolen cat
SADNESS	Grandma's Death	Haiti after Earthquake	Grandpa's Watch	Funeral	Old Dog
JEALOUSY	My Brother	Spa	Hi Tech Stuff	Alice's Wedding	Black Stallion

FINDING THE RIGHT SUBSTITUTION MATCH

If you're guest starring on a primetime drama and your "husband" is being arrested for murder, you can't "act" like you're in love with him. You have to "be" in love with him—even if you are meeting your "husband" for the first time the day of shooting. You will need to substitute someone from your life that you can layer into that that character, *someone who did something that cost you dearly in your relationship*. Someone who will trigger the emotions you need.

When you choose a substitution, don't worry about matching the identical situation to the circumstance of the material you've been given. Ideally, the situation will have a similar dynamic to the scene, but it doesn't have to be an exact match. In most cases, gender is not important. Imagine that your other person is there with you. Improvise out loud to see if this substitution stirs your feelings and makes you react the way the character would.

When you're performing, you're not just doing a scene with a character—you're also interacting with this other human being from your life. Your past experiences and your memories, all the good and bad, are hotwired into your response. When working with an affective memory or past substitution, bring it into the reality of the present by transferring it and working it off the other actor/character.

Find substitutions for the internal elements of the scene. Using the same primetime drama example, if your husband refers to an item or an event, how does that make your character feel? Let's suppose you have a line, "How could you do that to me?!" You need a substitution for "me," but you also need a substitution for the word, "that." What is your husband doing to you? You can't say the line truthfully unless you are affected by what he is doing. These substitutions bring home the emotional truth to your work.

Stay flexible. Substitutions are a starting point, part of your preparation. If another actor gives you an unexpected twist, or the director adds an adjustment, use the substitution as a foundation but don't cling to it. Substitutions are tools to connect your truths to your character, but the moment-to-moment discoveries bring the preparation to life.

One way to bonfire those feelings is to use the 10-Second preparation which is discussed in Chapter 9.

AFFECTIVE MEMORIES.

Time often heals; perhaps you've used past traumatic events in your work that don't have the same potent effect. If you decide to go back to an incident from your past, your subconscious might recoil against reliving that disturbing episode. Even though the trauma is still stored deep in your cognitive and muscle memories, your subconscious might do everything possible not to feel those feelings again. There are techniques to retrieving these memories, but they can be difficult and draining, and take time to resurface.

If you are currently feeling stressed or overwhelmed in your life, bringing up old emotional traumas may not be healthy; those unsettled emotions can start seeping into your everyday life. Recalling disturbing events can be dangerous. Lee Strasberg taught actors to generally use these kinds of memories after at least seven years, when the event was more removed, and would work more consistently. Maybe you still have a lot of anger or emotion about an occurrence in your life. For instance, a divorce, because of residual pain and frustration, may work for years. A death in the family or a broken engagement could be powerful triggers for a long time. Sometimes, however, the memory is too much and can overwhelm the work. The scene becomes about your personal recall, and not about the present reality in the scene—which is imperative. Emotional recall can fire you up, but it also can shut or break you down.

Be healthy. Take care of yourself. If you've had a traumatic event that you have not addressed, get professional help. Acting is a craft; it's not about being crazy.

LESS EFFECTIVE SUBSTITUTIONS

A common substitution actors often use in scenes is a best friend. This is often a weaker choice. Why? This close friend may make you feel too comfortable, not triggering the heightened emotions that are needed. It might be more effective to use a substitution that will provoke a stronger response.

Decide to use a friend if the choice will stir up a strong reaction. I once used the substitution of a dear friend, who would have been shocked at the affair my character had with a young student. All I had to do was imagine Rosemary, knowing she would have been stunned and upset at what I had done. The effect was so powerful for me every performance—the scene practically played itself.

EFFECTIVE USE OF "AS IFS"

An actress was working on a scene from *The West Wing*. The "given" of the scene was that she was on the phone in mid conversation, waiting for a co-worker who had upset her to arrive.

This actress used an "as if" to stir her feelings up towards the co-worker. She imagined the co-worker "as if" it were her boyfriend, who had just flirted with another woman.

But what is she doing on the phone before the "colleague" appears? What could heighten the conflict and raise the stakes of the scene? Here's the "as if" I suggested: "Iran just test-detonated a nuclear bomb, and you have a press conference in five minutes." This "as if" worked. Why? It was specific and based on a recent real news event. The "as if" allowed the actress to feel busy, engaged, and involved. She felt out of control, tormented, and angry. Just what her character needed.

Physical adjustments can also be helpful. With a longer rehearsal period for, say, a comedy, exploring an "as if" you're a bee in search of a flower could lead you to fun, new discoveries. Rehearsing a dramatic scene "as if" there are shards of glass on the floor, or "as if" the walls are closing in
on you, or "as if" a buzz saw is cutting through your brain can affect the material in interesting, and sometimes profound ways.

ENDOWING

ENDOWING YOUR CHARACTER'S WORLD

Endowing means to project emotional values onto people, places, and things. When you endow an object or a place, you add layers that help deepen your character. It's important that everything has significance, so that your whole creation has meaning. Every object in each scene should have a purpose.

For instance, if you're performing Martha in Edward Albee's play, *Who's Afraid of Virginia Woolf?* As an actor, when you come onto the set, imagine you were in this space dating George before you were married. That was thirty years ago. Was your father living with you? Focus on the couch. Did you make love on the couch? Did your father die on the couch?

There's a framed etching on the wall. Did George buy it for you on your honeymoon? Is it a drawing of a little town square in northern Italy where you stayed? Or, did you inherit it from your father? In other words, where did it come from, and what does it mean to you?

Did you paint the room together? Did you have a fight with George because he wasn't painting neatly? In the present you might cross the room, turn away from George, look at the wall, and notice a spot that he missed. That could be a trigger.

Taking the time to fill all these details is like putting little finishing brush strokes in an oil painting. You will have a detailed color canvas of memories affecting you, which constantly feed and nurture your acting.

ENDOWING A COSTUME

An actress I worked with was cast as a character in a play that takes place during WWII. She had some great 1940s vintage costumes that made the character look perfect. At least that's what she thought. However, the director said, "I think your character should be more voluptuous." When she got used to the extra padding that was added, her character did feel sexier, yet vulnerable. His insightful choice made a difference in how she felt about herself in playing the role.

Clothing has certain "energies"—dashing, cold and unforgiving, sensual, warm and fuzzy. One of my actresses playing Viola in Shakespeare's *Twelfth Night* "found" her character when the costumer gave a charming, funny little hat to wear as her character.

On a series, one of my actors was playing the "gang leader," whose introduction to the audience came up in an important scene. What did he want to say in that first moment about his character? The actor had done detailed work and broken down his script, but was still searching. Finally, he chose to wear a cross. He wanted to bring the complexity of his character being God-driven and having a relationship with God, even though he was "the bad guy."

Sometimes you might be forced to wear a costume that doesn't feel right for your character. If your costume can't be changed, endow it. What if your lover bought you the dress and thinks you look beautiful in it? Or a wonderful tailor created this suit especially for you. Use your creative imagination to find a way.

RELAXATION

My acting teacher, Paul Sorvino, used to put it this way, "If you're a boxer, you can't hit out of tightening up. Like in sports, the energy has to have a relaxed follow-through." As in many art forms, too much tension impedes creativity.

Relax! How many times do actors hear that word? At auditions you have no idea what to expect. It is nerve wracking to perform material, often for the first time, and be held up to every other actor auditioning for the same role. The pressure's on, because only one actor will be cast.

Then, if you are hired, the job might only be for a short period of time. Actors have many first days on the job, meeting a new set of bosses and co-workers every time. You'd be crazy not to be nervous!

And what do nerves do to the actor? They make you hold your breath. Holding your breath makes you scared, which shuts you down. Being shut down makes you stop hearing the director's adjustments, and cuts off receiving moment-to-moment responses from other actors. Sensory impulses are also blocked. Nerves even make actors freeze and forget lines.

Okay, now breathe. You're thinking, "Great advice, but how?" Adrenaline and nerves are a given. Therefore learning how to use your adrenaline and nerves is an important part of the craft of acting. Learn to embrace and channel them. You are always more relaxed when you know what you are doing. Training and technique give you confidence. So be sure to do all the work every time you approach a script. Nerves are transformed from a paralyzing fear into a positive energy when you are fully prepared. and know how to use them.

There are some additional methods to control the effect that nerves have on your system. Here are some ways to help you control your nervous energy:

THE RAG DOLL

Take three long, deep breaths, letting yourself flop over from the waist, while bending your knees slightly. Let your head hang straight down like a heavy weight, fully releasing your arms, shoulders and chest– everything hanging freely. After a few seconds very slowly rise back up from your waist, one vertebra at a time, allowing your arms and chest to freely hang while naturally falling into place as your spine straightens. The final part of the exercise is feeling your head drop into position as you finish straightening your body. While going through this process it's important to keep your breathing slow, rhythmic, relaxed and, even.

TENSE AND RELEASE

One method of relaxation that can be effective before performing is to tense each part of your body and then release it. Tense the muscle hard and then let go. Tense your feet, your calves, your thighs, and your entire leg on upward through your whole body. This helps release physical stress and tension.

INTERNAL RELEASE

Another way to control nerves that my method teacher, Pat Grantham used to teach us, is to internally release when you're in performance. If you feel a part of your body, like your jaw, get tense in the middle of a scene, say to yourself, "Relax my jaw" (or neck, forehead, or whatever body part is tensing). You don't have to switch gears to do it; you let your subconscious take care of it, similar to bio feedback. You can then move on with your performance.

In order for techniques to be at your fingertips, you need to work them in a class and as part of your regular acting exercise workout. Concentrate on breathing deeply from your diaphragm. Focus on the stream of breath as it enters and leaves your body. Don't hold your breath. You can gauge your level of relaxation by watching your work on a video camera. Turn down the volume and observe. You should see a steady but almost imperceptible rising and falling of the breath. Watch to see that you're breathing not only in your chest, but that the breath is dropping all the way down into your diaphragm.

When tension starts to take control of the scene, let your character do what you would do in the same situation. Stop; take a breath, regroup and exhale, releasing tension from your body.

SENSORY

Acting is divided into two parts, the things you can do and the things you can't "do." For the things you can't do, you must create an environment that allows them to happen to you.

Aristotle stated that there are five basic forms of sensations:

SOUND · SMELL · TOUCH · TASTE · SIGHT

Sensory work can bring up emotions for the actor that can affect and involve the audience. An actor has to feel from their soul, but the sense memory has to come through the face for all to see.

As she brings her eyes up to the camera in the climactic scene of *La Vie en Rose*, Marion Cotillard communicates her agony as she runs through the hallway grieving for her dead lover. Because we see her pain, we feel her pain. Words are not needed. Her sensory alone communicates her feelings.

There are some actors who can cry, but they're not really feeling the emotion, so we may not be affected by their show of emotion. Thoughts trigger feelings. Feelings trigger a physical response. When we are moved by that physical response, we know it's true.

SOUND

Does the ringing of a classroom bell bring back feelings of being out of place and alienated, as you felt in junior high? Perhaps the tinkle of chimes make you feel joyful. Does the sound of an ambulance siren scare you, causing you to remember the day that your grandmother died? The sound of a brook running might make you feel peaceful. Remembering these sounds can help to access the emotions they made you feel.

MUSIC

The primal and sensual rhythms that come through music can connect an actor to their character in a profound way. Try rehearsing with music to get the feel or style of a piece. For instance, the rhythmic banging of a drum in Greek theatre can be both stirring and unsettling. The soothing melodies of Paganini can offer a feeling of solace.

In the documentary about the making of *The Shining*, Director, Stanley Kubrick played the film's score while the actors were shooting the final scene running through the snowy maze. The music gave the actors the heightened energy, rhythms, and feelings they needed for the scene. That's an appropriate use of music. Music also stirs the audience, which is why a film score is often an essential piece of the audience's experience of a movie.

Some actors use music in their dressing room to relax and prepare themselves for the transformation into their character. Music can also help you immerse yourself in the character's world, and feelings.

Be careful though, you don't want the music to diffuse the emotional steam you need for your performance. Many an actor has been dry onstage after marinating in soulful emotion in the dressing room. Use music as a starting off point, but know when to use music and when to leave it behind.

SMELLS

Adding a smell or taste can help open up the personal emotions you need to feel. If you're supposed to feel sad and wistful, you might recall the aroma of an apple pie that was baking in the oven the moment when your parents told you they were getting divorced. The stench of garbage might make you feel nauseous. Perhaps the fragrance of lilacs or roses could make you feel the first stirrings of romance.

TOUCH-PHYSICAL SENSATIONS

Does the feel of sand transport you to a beach? The touch of fur make you feel sexy? Maybe a cool breeze blowing through your hair reminds you of when your husband proposed marriage to you. If your character is experiencing an emotion that you can bring up with the addition of a physical sensation, layer that into the piece and see what happens.

TASTE

Imagining the taste of a bitter pill, rancid milk, or liver might make you physically want to throw up. Perhaps the taste of vanilla icing makes you feel loved and special, as you did when your mother would make a birthday cake just for you, with her special vanilla icing. Or maybe the sensation of a dark piece of chocolate melting in your mouth creates primal, sensual feelings.

SIGHT

COLORS

Suppose you're doing a scene in which you're tormented. If the color of olive green really grates on your nerves, imagine painting that color right into the environment with you. If you're performing the role of a character that's in love, perhaps envisioning the colors of peach, sunny yellow or scarlet red help create the romantic glow your character is feeling.

An actress I work with was screen testing for the role of a gallery owner who lured an artist into murdering people. The character of the artist would go on a killing rampage when exposed to the color red, so the actress decided to carry a red scarf on her. When the actress had an impulse during the test, she suddenly pulled out the red scarf. She felt a surge of power. The actor playing the artist stopped in his tracks, stunned. He had a visceral response to the red scarf. It worked.

IMAGES

A Hawaiian sunset, an abandoned house, a dead carcass on the highway, an intimate candlelit room or a flag-draped coffin. What visuals create a response in you? Explore different images to see which ones move you. Write them down in your acting journal to have them on hand to layer in when you need them. Go online to explore pictures and films.

Some actors go on the internet to search for powerful images that can affect them. Pictures and videos of animals melt their heart, so this can be an area that is powerful for sense memory and substitutions—everything from an orangutan playing with a hound dog to disturbing images of dolphins being slaughtered. Actors can also look at videos or pictures of things that give them a strong emotional response just before warming up/preparing a character for a performance.

PLAYING ALTERED STATES

No two human beings are the same in experiencing "altered states"—drinking, drugs, mental illness, etc. You have to do research on your own.

When I was cast in the role of writer Carson McCullers who had several impairing strokes, I knew I couldn't just "act" my idea of a stroke survivor. In researching her condition, I went to an institution where the staff let me speak with three different patients who had suffered strokes.

Each of these patients shared their personal experience of the physical and emotional impact of a stroke. Their generosity in bringing me into their world helped me to develop a personalized approach to my character.

Avoid the temptation to "play" drunk or stoned. Whatever altered state is needed for the scene, you need to research what the effects are of that state. What are the obstacles created of being in that condition? What is your character doing to deal with and overcome those obstacles? How does your character cope with the altered state? Your character might let it all hang out if they're at a party with friends, smoking a joint. But, if they arrive home and their parents are standing there saying, "Where've you been?" then they have to mask the effects.

Drinking affects people in a range of ways. A sweet old maid, who is not used to anything stronger than a cup of tea, will certainly have a very different reaction to a shot of tequila than a seasoned Hell's Angel motorcycle gang member. A young teen taking their first hit of marijuana will be affected differently than the hardened drug dealer who smokes it frequently.

CHEMISTRY

"The meeting of two personalities is like the contact of two chemical substances: if there is any reaction, both are transformed." —Carl Gustav Jung

HOW TO CREATE CHEMISTRY

No matter how wonderful your choices are or how great your acting is, it won't go anywhere if you don't have chemistry with your love interest or partner. Movies, series, and plays have been made or broken by the chemistry, or lack of, between actors. There is much talk about chemistry, but how do you create the mysterious alchemy of attraction between two people? Here are some ideas to help you generate that special dynamic:

- Start with the truth. Find something real you love about that person: His beautiful voice. How hard she tries in rehearsal, etc.

- Substitution—Layer a person from your life into the other character/actor that makes you feel sexual, or alive and attracted.

- Endowment—Give them secret qualities that turn you on and make you react. Imagine he's a poet, and you know he's writing love poems about you. Or, create a scenario that she stood up for you to someone who criticized your acting. Or you know a secret about them. He's uncomfortable around other people because his father abandoned his family. You can add that you understand that because you went through this too, so you both have gone through a traumatic experience together.

- Use the negatives—if one or both of you don't like each other, use it. Hate is close to love, and being agitated means there are strong feelings involved and affecting you. Just know that many romances have started that way. You could think to yourself, "You don't seem to like me, but you're certainly feeling emotions about me!"

- Fight the chemistry—"I shouldn't be feeling attracted to you. You make me feel out of control. I shouldn't be doing this!" Holding back the feelings can actually have the opposite effect of stoking romantic feelings.

- Think bold, extraordinary hot and sexual thoughts— "Oh! This is naughty!"

- If it's appropriate, you could give your partner a little something thoughtful to open you up to each other—he loves fishing, give him a hand tied lure. Or give her a photocopy of an article about an actor she loves. Katherine Hepburn gave Henry Fonda one of Spencer Tracy's hats when they started filming *On Golden Pond.*

- If you're playing buddies in a comedy, keep the meet-cute teasing going—maybe even plan a few fun surprises. (again if it's appropriate)

113

- Build romance and history through your detailed and enhanced back-story or bio. Create how you met, and very specifically build the background of the other character to enhance your feelings about them.

"Acting is also working with people who invite you into their dreams and trust you with their innermost being." —Catherine Deneuve

Sara Krulwich/Times Redux

In the Broadway revival of August Wilson's Pulitzer Prize-winning drama, *Fences,* two actors who barely knew each other had to create the iconic characters of Troy and Rose, husband and wife. Much of the play is about Troy and Rose's sexual and romantic love. To accomplish that feat, Denzel Washington and Viola Davis had to forge a strong and palpable chemistry between them. They had to fulfill the actor's job of helping the audience to not only believe, but also feel, their passion. Through long discussions, they came together to weave a richly woven tapestry, to create a back-story that would enhance their chemistry.

To accomplish this they spent many hours outside of rehearsal both alone and together, finding the love and passion that brought Troy and Rose together long before the play begins. In a May 2010 *New York Times* article by Patrick Healy, they talked about their re-created first date, *"We talked until dawn, and he was the perfect gentleman. He kissed my hand and walked away."* Ms. Davis recalls, *"Part of me knew that he'd want to do more than kiss my hand,"*... *"The fact that he did murder someone—I didn't want to marry someone with that kind of past, but I fell into it because my loins were on fire."*

This is a great example of how you must use your creative mind to create the world and memories your character is experiencing. Your creative energy gives life to the spark that triggers your emotions organically, and allows the bonfire of that chemistry to engulf the characters in the flames of a passionate relationship. A relationship that causes Troy to proclaim about Rose, "I love her so much, I done run out of ways of loving her" ... "We go upstairs in that room at night, and I fall down on you and try to blast a hole into forever." Ms. Davis and Mr. Washington came together to enrich the author's words, because as director, Kenny Leon said, *"Rose and Troy—needed to seem inseparable in their bones if Fences is to truly work."*

MOMENT-TO-MOMENT

Moment-to-moment describes what happens when you and your partner work off what you're giving each other in the present moment. Unfortunately, some actors who have only worked on moment-to-moment technique may not always have a concept or appreciation of structure and script analysis.

There are some actors who negate preparation. They may wait for something to happen instead of being prepared. They might not know how to rehearse or what to look for in a script. There's nothing that says you can't create a structure and still be open to responding in the moment. It's certainly preferable if the other actor understands the acting job and you can create together. However, what if the other actor's performance is not up to speed?

This is why you must understand the script and all the aspects of the craft in a creating a character. You want to know, understand and be prepared; because in the professional world, you have to deliver consistently.

EMOTION ON DEMAND

When you're on set filming take after take, you don't always start at the beginning of a scene. Or, for instance, if a director is now shooting a close-up, you may have to go back and do additional takes of the same scene. If it's a student or low budget film, there may only be a couple of takes. Some major directors like Clint Eastwood shoot entire scenes in only one or two takes. Most films shoot out of sequence. In this case, you must be emotionally prepared, whatever the circumstance.

Occasionally, a director might direct you to bring in a different tone or feel to the scene. The director might even say, "Give me something else."

Sometimes actors freeze and don't know how to take their emotions to a different place. Actors think if they're crying they can't switch over to laughing. There is a beautiful example in the movie *Sunshine Cleaning*, where Emily Blunt's character goes to her special secret place (on a raised railroad trestle) to vent her emotions, from joy to despair. Emotions are like burners on a gas stove. If the flame of joy is lit, you can easily switch it over to the flame of tragedy and grief. Though you don't realize it, you may already be experiencing that emotion.

For example, in class I can give an adjustment for an actor to be angry. The actor personally gets pissed that they have to make an adjustment. Then they start doing an angry preparation. I say, "You're already there! Go!" Take the real feelings you are experiencing in that moment. Make them work for you instead of working against yourself. Getting stubborn or defensive drives directors crazy! Work on the script beforehand with different emotions so you are fully prepared. Then be flexible enough that you can switch to another feeling or adjustment on the spot.

REHEARSE THE EMOTIONS BEFOREHAND

Work at developing the highest level of the six primal emotions of: hate, love fear, power, joy, and sadness that were introduced earlier. Then start adding in variations of the feelings, such as: jealousy, curiosity, confusion etc.

Once you achieve the highest elevation of intensity of a great range of feelings, you can modulate your emotions to any version in between. Keep working on building and enriching your emotional library.

THREE LEVELS OF THINKING

There are three levels of thoughts:

- Character-to-character
- Actor-to-actor
- Outside thoughts

These different levels of thoughts give a character complexity and dimension.

CHARACTER-TO-CHARACTER THOUGHTS

These are the thoughts you're thinking as your character. You can have good and bad thoughts simultaneously. Keep your character's thoughts alive, moving and interesting.

In *Romeo and Juliet,* if Juliet is only thinking surface thoughts such as "I love you," that can be very one-dimensional. However, if Juliet is thinking a blend of different thoughts like, "My father's going to come in and he'll kill you! What are we going to do?!" or, "Romeo looks so hot. I wish my hair looked better!" then you have created a Juliet that is complicated in the way that real teenagers are complicated. What juicy thoughts would your character really be thinking?

ACTOR-TO-ACTOR THOUGHTS

In reality, when you are acting, you're doing a scene with another actor. Don't eliminate all the thoughts you have about that person. If the actor were late to rehearsal, it would be natural to have angry thoughts. That might bring the material to life in unexpected and exciting ways. Opposite thinking adds texture to the text.

I coached an actor on a show, who had great chemistry with his leading lady. As I watched this actress I wondered, "What is going on with her? What is she really thinking?" I couldn't figure out her mysterious thoughts. Turns out that she couldn't stand her leading man! Hot secret thoughts create fire, which ignites the scene.

OUTSIDE THOUGHTS

"I'm dying for a slice of pizza."
"I have to go to the bathroom!"
"Did Tony get theatre tickets for tonight?"

These little outside flashes of reality will crop up as you work. These enigmatic sparks also draw the audience to you because the audience is intrigued. Don't fixate on them and don't try to eliminate them. Think them. Then let them go.

An appropriate percentage of the three kinds of thoughts might be 60% character-to-character, 30% actor-to-actor and 10% outside thoughts. That's an approximation, of course, and you can accept or deny the thoughts. Keep in mind that blending these three levels creates a more truthful mix of how human beings really process thinking.

CONFLICT

Conflict is the foundation of all good acting. Creating conflict in the world of the character will ignite your work. A basic rule—the more conflict the better. Conflict redoubles your actions. When you add great conflict to your character, instead of climbing up a hill, you find yourself climbing up a mountain! That's more interesting to your audience.

The more ways you can find to layer-in conflict, the more interesting your character becomes. Your choices for conflict affect the other actors. That energy will bounce back to you and enrich your reactions. There are many ways to add conflict to your work. Here are some suggestions.

USING THE STRUCTURE TO ADD CONFLICT

Choose the Core that adds conflict. If your character is threatened with foreclosure on their home and you choose the Core of security, you are layering conflict into your choices.

Make your selection of The Happiness "To put down permanent roots in a perfect home for your family." That choice of Happiness will add conflict that makes it impossible for you to risk losing your home!

ADDING SECRETS

One of my Method teachers, Jack Garfein taught me that secrets can load your conflict. He illustrated putting little talismans on or near you that have personal meaning. Perhaps the scene calls for you to argue with your mother. You have a picture of your mom holding you as a baby, in your pocket. You put your hand in your pocket and touch it. How does that affect you?

118

Conflicted secrets must make sense within the purpose of the story. Your secret can't be that you're the axe murderer if the script has you as the good person in the story.

An actress in class was performing a scene with a partner, in which their characters, now both doctors, had been teenage lovers. Now they're just having a cup of coffee together in the hospital cafeteria. The actress added the secret that she'd secretly had an abortion when they were together in high school. This choice added weight to the scene. Her choice of conflict deepened the relationship.

In the television show *The Closer,* Kyra Sedgwick's character is a closet eater, sneaking food in private. Adding this human flaw helps the audience to relate to her because she's not perfect. We connect to her real feelings behind closed doors.

CONFLICT IN THE ENVIRONMENT

Add the element of conflict to your environment. You're in a scene in which the setting is outdoors. Your character is supposed to be calm, cool, and collected, but you've created the conflict that that the temperature is 95 degrees, so you're sweating. Or the opposite, maybe it's freezing and you're cold. Choose the moments, or places where this sensory choice could enhance or add an interesting texture to your performance. Just make sure your sensory work with the environment is appropriate and doesn't overpower the whole scene.

The more conflict the better, especially in comedy. Adding more obstacles when something isn't that funny can make it funnier. I was coaching an actress for the comedic role of a "bad girl" in a major feature film. In the scene, she was outdoors in the snow. To add conflict, I kept telling her to imagine the temperature was getting colder and colder. Her reactions, growing more and more extreme, became hilarious. Although she didn't get the role, the director was so impressed with her audition he recommended her to another director. This led to her first feature film.

COSTUME CONFLICT

If you're playing a passionate Victorian character but you are constrained by a corset and bustle, you are adding a conflict that feeds the reality of the script. Think of Kate Winslet as Rose, in *Titanic.* Rose argues with her mother, telling her that she feels trapped into marriage.

Her controlling mother then laces up Rose's corset so tight she can barely breathe.

In the film *Jefferson In Paris*, Nick Nolte's character, Thomas Jefferson, starts scratching his scalp under his wig. This interesting reaction came out of wearing an authentic wool wig from the period, which made his character have a very specific and real moment.

If you're playing a character with a limp like Frida Kahlo, try putting a stone in your shoe to create a real limp. Look for ways to physically create obstacles for your character.

ADDING CONFLICT TO THE MOMENT BEFORE

Some actors think that "the moment before" is literally what they were doing before coming onstage. That may be true but the moment before should be something that puts you in the emotional state of your character. You have to invent it. It needs to be something that you can repeat. The moment before you come into your scene is a great place to add conflict.

You're cast as Yelena in Chekhov's play *Uncle Vanya*. Yelena is married to an old professor. Her first scene is having tea in the garden after returning from an afternoon walk. Now add the invented secret that you've just discovered you're pregnant. It means you're trapped forever with your ailing, old husband. Having this secret for your moment before creates inner torment that you must cover up. As you enter, you have to try to put a mask on that "everything's fine."

Creating potent conflict will help you bring to life a complex character without "acting."

STAKES

A stake is what's at risk in a play or a movie—the event. When events look normal, you have to heighten the stakes even more. As I've said before, "Acting isn't reality, it's heightened reality." Knowing how to raise the stakes is important. If your character is buttering the toast in the kitchen, what is that symbolic of? Nurturing the family? The actor is aware that it's important to put a high beam on the family love. Then later on in the film when the family is destroyed, that moment of a cozy breakfast with mother buttering the toast will have weight.

Some actors focus only on the climactic moment of the story, but there are stakes that go on all throughout each scene, smaller pieces that lead up to that climax. If you don't pay attention to the smaller stakes, the stepping-stones along the path, then the big climatic moment doesn't have the depth and emotional punch it could have.

ENVIRONMENT

On stage and in film the audience expects the environment to enhance the scene. The environment gives the audience clues about the character. They look for those clues to be detailed and real. When the environment isn't exactly what is expected, it makes the audience start wondering, "Who is this person really?"

As an actor, if you want to study an interesting specific environment, go see Julia Child's kitchen in the Smithsonian. It looks like a normal, middle class kitchen. The pots are old. They're not spotless. It's definitely not a Martha Stewart kind of kitchen, but a homey, lived-in kind of kitchen. There is an old wall phone with a long, tangled chord and the refrigerator has scribbled bits of notes on it.

Maybe you're playing an uptight accountant, but your kitchen is like Julia Child's because that's where your heart is. The environment could highlight a different side of your character and their journey to finding and embracing who they really are.

THE ENVIRONMENT AS A CHARACTER

There are certain plays or screenplays in which the environment is so important it becomes an added character in the story. Think of the hot summer heat in *Cat on a Hot Tin Roof,* or the ice and snow in *Dr. Zhivago.* The characters are profoundly affected by their surroundings in these films. It informs their behavior. When Daniel Day-Lewis filmed *The Last of the Mohicans,* he slept in the woods and carried his gun with him all the time to actually experience life in his character's environment, as a frontiersman in the mid-1700s.

Casting directors and directors respond when an actor creates a specific environment. If the audition scene is in a diner and you're breaking up with your husband, who's at the next table? You can't whisper through the whole piece, but in an appropriate moment, you can choose where to lower your voice so other characters in the diner won't "hear" your conversation. Even though you might not have had much time to prepare the material, a choice to have the environment affect you makes the scene much more real.

Adding sensory to the environment will bring more feelings. If you're outside, where is the sun? Is the wind blowing? The sun shining in your eyes will produce a different reaction and feelings than a cold wind. How does the environment physically touch you? Get specific, and don't forget to add the layers of emotion that the environment can bring into your work. The actor's job is to decide when, and to what degree, the environment informs their behavior.

CHARACTER BEHAVIOR INSPIRED BY THE ENVIRONMENT

Perhaps you are performing a scene that takes place on a beach. Suddenly you get a bit of sand in your eye. In that organic moment, the bare stage becomes the real beach for the audience.

Be open to making unexpected discoveries by letting your character interact fully with their environment. You will find "gems" in your performance. Once, when I was rehearsing as the character Blanche in *A Streetcar Named Desire,* I went to drink out of a glass. There was an actual piece of dust in the glass, so I reached in and removed it. The director loved the moment and added it into the scene.

CHARACTER GESTURE COMING FROM THE ENVIRONMENT

In *The Shawshank Redemption,* Tim Robbins as Andy Dufresne crawls through a sewer tunnel to escape from his years of false imprisonment. As he climbs out of the filthy drain pipe he stands free in the rain with his arms outstretched, washed clean. This is a wonderful example of a character's gesture coming from the environment. Alternatively, picture Willem Dafoe as Sgt. Elias in *Platoon* as he is shot standing in an open field, a sacrificial lamb his arms outstretched like Jesus on the cross.

COMEDY—FINDING YOUR INNER FUNNY

The actress, Christine Baranski, added a conflictive choice to her character in the Neil Simon comedy *Rumors.* Baranski created the idea that her character was trying to give up smoking, and would hide cigarettes all around the set. When upset, her character would frantically search for the hidden cigarettes, which raised the stakes for her character. It also increased the laughter, because you knew if something stressful happened, this character was going to find the cigarettes, come hell or high water!

DISCOVER HOW AND WHEN YOU ARE FUNNY

Here are some different ideas you can use to discover the tools that help you on your personal path to finding how to be funny.

Ask those closest to you, "When am I funny? What's funny about me?" You may be surprised what they tell you. Everyone's funny at times, but no two people are funny in the exact same way.

Work in front of an audience. This can be in an Acting or Improv class, at an open mike night, or with your friends. When you perform comedy in front of an audience, you learn a lot about whether your choices are working.

When I was in Wynn Handman's class with John Leguizamo, he would work on character pieces that eventually became produced as the one-man show, *Mambo Mouth*. John used our responses to help build his material. After bringing in different male relatives as characters, we asked, "Don't you have any women relatives? Do a female!" The next week John came on stage in a mini dress with heels, sheer stockings and a long black straight wig down to his rear end. He was hysterically funny. The class audience helped him find a completely new side to his concept, one he hadn't thought of on his own.

Sometimes finding how you're funny is simply a matter of asking, "When am I silly?" A charming actress I know was late for taping a show and found herself memorizing her lines in the shower with her script hanging on the inside of the shower curtain. Isn't that cute and quirky? When you begin to discover amusing and funny things about yourself, you start to get a sense of how to bring "you" to the material.

Find your own way of doing things. When adding a costume or a prop avoid clichés, like guys who turn their caps backwards or women who file their nails and chew gum. If the audition sides say, "She takes out a compact and powders her nose," bring in a better idea they never thought of! Maybe you choose to brush one eyebrow with a tiny eyebrow brush. Make it humorous in your way.

An actress who didn't think she was comedic had an audition for the Christopher Durang play *Baby With The Bathwater*. To help her look funny I put her hair up in a crazy ponytail and had her wear bobby socks. Not only did the actress look funny, she also felt off-center—an element she needed for the character.

THE FORMULA OF COMEDY

Comedy is much more difficult than drama. Even with no acting experience, if you have a sense of reality, you'll probably be okay in a drama. With comedy, however, you have to put together timing, rhythms, and understanding, while being grounded in the moment.

There is a traditional mathematical equation that makes comedy work—the "setup," and the "punch line" or "pay off." You have to understand this equation.

Additionally there are certain key words that you have to hit. If a character is repeating a line with a specific word, you have to hit the right word so that the comedy works. A definitive example is the Abbott and Costello routine:

Abbott: "<u>Who</u> is on first!"

Costello: "I'm asking <u>you</u> who's on first."

Abbott: "<u>That's</u> the man's name."

Costello: "That's <u>who's</u> name?"

Abbott: "<u>Yes.</u>"

Much of comedy is like math. There are formulas where the structure of comedy becomes the foundation for being funny. Once you learn the 2+2=4 of these equations, they work with all kinds of humorous material.

WORKING WITH LAUGHTER

In working with comedy, you must factor in audience laughter. You may have an idea of what's working when you're rehearsing, but you don't know what the audience will laugh at "for sure." Having an audience at a dress rehearsal or previews will give you a better idea of when to pause and when to continue.

You don't put yourself in the position of shouting over the laughter, but you have to be ahead of the audience—you can't wait until the laughter dies down completely before coming in with your next line.

Then there's the art of picking up cues—what we call "no busses, no trains." At the end of the other character's line, come in immediately with the beginning of your line. That doesn't mean rush, but no pregnant pauses, unless there's one written into the formula for that particular comedic equation or bit.

If the material is funny and the audience is laughing away, you might have the urge to laugh yourself. Don't. Stay in character. Otherwise, the comedic tension you've built will be broken! In extremely rare cases, you will see the actors struggling to stay in character as they "crack up laughing," like the actors occasionally did on *The Carol Burnett Show*. However, if that had happened all the time it wouldn't have been so funny.

IMPROVISATION IN COMEDY

A mainstay of comedy is improvisation. There's a section on improvisation in Chapter 9, as it is an important tool in all kinds of acting. Comedy can go flat if you say the same lines repeatedly. You have to find the rhythms and pacing and also keep it alive and vibrant. Some comedians make a different choice or will change the energy of what they're doing with the lines in one or two spots, just to keep it fresh. Comedy has to have a feeling of spontaneity.

PROPS

PROPS MUST HAVE A PURPOSE

Props should not be used unless necessary. There should always be a reason for using a prop. You don't want the scene to become about "stuff." Props can be distracting, taking away the focus from what's important in the scene. Some actors get prop-heavy or wave props around to diffuse their nervous energy. It's not a good enough justification if the only reason you have for using a prop is that it makes you comfortable. Never use props as a crutch.

An actress performing as the maid in a scene from *Wuthering Heights* chose to show her apprehensive feelings through polishing the silver. As she's questioning the main character, Cathy, "Why did you make this choice to marry him?" she's trying to cover her feelings as she conveys her emotions with the props. Her choice enhanced the scene for a reason.

CONTINUITY AND PROPS

If you pick up and sip a glass of wine for a scene on camera, you have to do the exact move at the exact time in every take, or the editor will have a difficult time editing the scenes. This is one reason not to overuse props—continuity. You must physically do the exact same move in the master or establishing shot, which then has to match the two-shot, which then has to match the close-up.

In his book, *Acting In Film,* Michael Caine stresses the importance of planning your actions and rehearsing with props ahead of time. You want to work out the timing and be able to create the same action repeatedly.

How you use your props can convey much about your character. If you're drinking a martini and you take one sip, you're a social drinker. If you drink two sips, you're a heavy drinker. If you take three sips, you're a drunk. So don't just "drink" to make yourself (the actor) comfortable. Drinking out of your character's wine glass to avoid answering a pointed question, or setting a beer can down in a way that underscores your point are good examples of using props to "accent" behavior. In a wonderful scene from one of my favorite movies, *All About Eve,* Bette Davis picks at the hors d'oeuvres before a dinner party, using the food to show us how she's feeling about her female competition—"Eve."

ACCENTS, DIALECTS & VOCAL WORK

ACCENTS AND DIALECTS

Many actors are confused as to what the difference is between an "accent" and a "dialect." Accents are the pronunciation of words in specific ways determined by the region or social background of the speaker. For example, the United States is made up of many regions and socio-economic backgrounds, which cause accents to vary geographically. Midwesterners, Louisianans and New Yorkers speak the same language, but have different ways of pronouncing the same words. Those differences are accents.

Dialects, on the other hand, are not just accents but are distinct varieties in pronunciation, grammar and/or vocabulary. People who have immigrated often have dialects made up of the new country's language mixed with words and expressions from their country of origin. Accents and dialects require consistent practice. If you say you're skilled at recreating an accent on your resume, you must be able to do it on the spot in an audition.

RESEARCHING ACCENTS & DIALECTS

You can find excellent tools at arts libraries, acting bookstores or online. Find recordings that use native speakers to illustrate the accent and/or dialect. The International Dialects of English Archive (IDEA) is an excellent online tool. IDEA provides sound samples and accompanying text files of hundreds of accents and dialects from America and all around the world. YouTube is also a great resource.

If you need a specific Irish accent, go to the local Irish bar, buy a bloke a pint, and get him to say words into a tape recorder. If you need an accent from Peoria, Illinois, call the library in Peoria, tell the librarian that you're researching a Peoria accent and talk with her for a while. Ask her if you can tape some of her expressions and words over the telephone. Don't listen to accents or dialects from a movie unless it's filmed with actors from the region. A dialect coach worked with that actor so it's once removed, and the accent is not the actor's native speech.

You can also work also with a reputable accent and dialect coach in a classroom setting, or privately, in person or online.

AUDITIONING WITH ACCENTS AND DIALECTS

Your acting can go "right out the window" if you prepare an audition with a "full" accent. You can easily get so caught up in the accent that you neglect to connect to the character. Pick several important words that give a sense or flavor of the dialect. In other words, Just a touch of the accent or dialect will show the casting director and director that you can do it. If you have an important call back, screen test or are cast in the role, then work with a coach to get the dialect or accent perfected.

SPEECH PROBLEMS

If you are a foreign actor working in the United States, you must be able to speak Standard American. Otherwise, you will be pigeonholed as an actor with that specific accent. Even if you are a native-born American, if you speak with anything other than a Standard American accent you may end up playing the same stereotyped roles over and over again.

Problems like articulation and stuttering are also issues that actors must address. It's no fun to try to act and correct your speech all at the same time!

One actor I worked with knew he had a speech problem but hadn't gotten around to addressing it. It wasn't until he was shooting a movie and the star said, "You have a problem sibilant s'!" that the panicked actor finally went to a vocal coach. Don't let yourself get in a situation like this.

VOCAL WORK

As you develop in your acting training, you need to take a class or work with a coach on vocal work. No matter how good an actor you may be, if you can't drop into your voice properly and get your body resonating with sounds, you can't fully access your emotions. The placement of your voice is an invaluable tool. Knowing how to relax into your voice when you are highly emotional opens you up to feel more deeply. You're not blocked by shallow breaths and tension in your throat. It also makes your acting better, because you develop lovely subtle colors and velvety tones that enhance your acting. Frank Langella is a great example of an actor who worked very hard and developed his problem voice into one of his greatest acting assets.

Remember, the implements or techniques in your toolbox are there to help you do the acting "job". However, like all precision tools, they must be properly maintained if you want them to work for you.

9

SIMPLE BUT PROFOUND KEYS INTO THE WORK

Many of the core techniques handed down by my teachers and directors, developed out of questions and the need for answers. For years, these techniques have built the solid foundation that actors have relied on when performing.

Actors also develop techniques as they evolve in their craft. Some actors have shared their techniques in their quest to be better, clearer, and go deeper in their craft. An actor does something wonderful that works and everyone wants to know, "How did you do that!? How do you get that dimension? How do you get that style? How, how, how?" We want to know what makes it possible for an actor to achieve a wonderful performance.

Much is changing in the world of acting. Actors accustomed to working slowly in a classroom get left in the dust because the profession is moving so fast. Actors receive less attention from stressed and impatient directors. You can't depend on the director showing you the way. You have to know the way yourself.

8 EXERCISES TO GROW YOUR CRAFT

1. THE ACTING BARRÉ

Dancers begin working at the dance barré. They then move to the center of the floor to develop their technique. Similarly, the Acting Barré guides you through a structured progression of steps. Each step flows one into the other, building and deepening your process. Each exercise is designed to work out the muscles necessary for specific techniques that the actor requires. After doing these exercises over a period of time, you'll start to trust, relax, and let go into your emotional and creative center. The effects of this process will trickle down into all of your work.

My students do this series of exercises individually every week in front of the class. Practicing these exercises will add to your concentration and help you to lose your self-consciousness. The Acting Barré will make your work specific, creative, and fearless.

The Acting Barré consists of five exercises that have specific goals:

I'M SO PISSED! A technique to bring up the highest level of anger that is then fully released.

I WISH I COULD...! Switching the emotional gears from anger, to gleefully taking control and using your imagination "to physically do" a creative, yet specific action to the person who pissed you off.

RECREATE. Quickly, yet effectively re-creating and physically assuming the other character at the moment you were pissed.

CHARACTER BREAKDOWN INTERVIEW. Uncovering and revealing the specific structure of the other character on the spot.

RHYTHM & LIFT-OFF. Putting all the pieces together for artistic lift-off in the moment.

When I began teaching an acting class, I felt that it was taking too long to move the actors forward to their highest potential. I wanted to develop exercises that would move actors faster and deeper into the work without taking such long periods of time. That's when I found the "I'm So Pissed" piece of the Acting Barré. It just cracked actors open right away!

One of the most difficult challenges for actors is to effectively build the energy they need for strong emotions. Actors must know how to generate that hot steam and then be able to release that energy into the words. Anger is one of the hardest emotions for most actors to express authentically.

STEP 1—I'M SO PISSED!

The purpose of this exercise is to be able to create a bonfire of feeling from a few small sparks of emotion, and then to unload the anger fully and completely: To be in control of the uncontrollable, so that when you have to bring emotions to a character or script, you will know how to create tremendous real feelings without pushing.

To start, stand facing away from your audience. Think of someone or something that recently made you mad or angry. A fresh small incident often works better than something huge or traumatic. Recent incidents are still in your muscle memory. Choose a person, animal or object that made you mad. You want to learn how to open up your well of angry emotion to a "10"—the highest level. Then it will be no problem to pull it in and adjust that energy if a director asks you to be angry at a level "7" or "4."

Face the wall, to give yourself a private moment. Stand still. Don't move your feet or you'll diffuse the emotions you're trying to build. Imagine the recent "happening" on an imaginary movie screen in front of you. Hear the event on imaginary loudspeakers. Let it work on you and allow your feelings to come to a boil. Don't take too long, no more than about twenty seconds, or the "emotional steam" you are building will start to dissipate.

Just when you can't contain your feelings any longer, spin around, face the audience, and vent the anger in a huge explosive primal yell, phrase or a loud exclamation! Colorful language and expletives are encouraged. Don't think about what you're going to say, but allow yourself to be out of control of the anger you have just created. Don't explain the story or the circumstances. You want to unload and release the emotion completely. Be careful to explode that energy from your diaphragm, not from your throat. Only a few words are necessary. Some examples are "F**k you!" "I hate you!" "Stop it!" Let it rip.

Once you have emptied yourself completely, unloading the anger, immediately move to step 2—"I wish I could...!"

After the actors were able to access their anger consistently, some of them started festering in the angry feelings for too long, and I thought, "Wait a minute! You can't stay in that anger forever. Let's now go to something happy and empowering!"

STEP 2—I WISH I COULD...!

The purpose of this part of the exercise is to expand the actor's imagination in a creative and explicit way, so that ideas will come easily and creative impulses will be free. You are taking the angry energy that the "I'm so pissed" brought out and turning it into a positive energy. You are then empowered to use your imagination in a clear, precise manner in the moment, to do something physical to the other person. You want to make choices that are not just real, but interesting and stage worthy!

After you have turned around and fully vented your feelings in step 1, immediately say out loud, "I wish I could...!" Here's the fun part. Use your imagination to inspire you to create real action under imaginary circumstances. You are empowered to do anything you want to the person who made you angry! Don't sit indulgently in the anger but let go and enjoy being in control. Use that "steam" you've created to propel you to the opposite end of the emotional spectrum and imagine in your wildest dreams what you "wish" you could physically do to the person, animal, or object that ignited your anger.

Make the "I wish I could...!" fun for yourself! Conjure up what you would do to that person if you were in a cartoon. For instance, imagine spraying whipped cream all over them, or give yourself magic powers to be able to shrink them, squash them, and eat the little bit that's left. Or you could give them brain transplant surgery to open their eyes so they can see what they're doing to others. There are no limits! Be specific with your imagination. Improvise what you would physically "do" to that person. Show and describe out loud and in detail the action you would take to exact your revenge. Make it interesting! Go from anger to the joy of, "Oh goody! Now I get to do whatever I want to you!" This gets rid of internal barriers so you can access your fullest imaginative range quickly.

Add the conflict that the other person doesn't want you to do this action to them! If you are pushing your nasty boss out of your office window, he is fighting back. Of course, you win! When you add conflict, you become more physically and mentally involved with your creation. (and you don't worry about your audience) Pay attention to detail. If you're going to tie the person up, we need to see the size and weight of the person as you move them and sit them down. Work with the details to give you the exact width and texture of your imaginary rope. He's struggling, so you have the added challenge of the difficulty of tying him up.

You only have a minute or so to finish the "I wish I could...!" Don't stand there and think about it. The idea is to get out of the emotional rut of the anger right away, switch gears to empowerment, go right into your imagination, and be precise. It feels great to let your subconscious take over. Jump in and trust yourself. Just go!

Actors who are new to this exercise often hesitate because they don't want to "hurt" the person with whom they're angry. However, what will you do if you are cast in a role where you have to kill someone close to you? Are you going to hold back and not be able to go for it? This exercise allows you to explore what it would be like in a safe environment. Everyone has a "Walter Mitty" fantasy occasionally. One of the joys of acting is to be able to take bad things that have happened to you in real life and express them through a character. You're using these experiences in a positive way through your craft to fuel your acting work.

Now that you've been brave enough to use your anger against that person in a fun, empowered way, let's "Recreate," to show what happened.

STEP 3—RECREATE

The purpose of this exercise is to accustom you to transforming into people, or triggers in your life that can be used to develop characters. It also teaches you how to create clearly, quickly and effectively. You will learn how to move from anger to empowerment, and then switch gears to jump into the other person's shoes to illustrate what happened at the exact moment that angered you. If you've completely unloaded your anger in the first part of the Acting Barré, you can then shift over easily, and fully become the other person/thing/animal.

Return to center stage. Now, you will show us the moment that made you most angry from the perspective of the other person/character.

For example, if your boss said condescendingly, "Let me show you how to do that right," in front of customers. Jump into his skin and become your boss at the instant of the trigger. Repeat his words. Hone in on the exact moment that pissed you off. What did he look like? Sound like? What were his mannerisms and posture? Don't try to show the whole story of what happened, but recreate the "freeze frame" moment that got you angry. If you're recreating an animal or object, imagine what it would say and how it would speak.

You will stay as this person/character for the remainder of the Acting Barre. You do not become "yourself" again.

Now that you've jumped into the other person's skin, and have shown or "recreated" what happened, you are ready to be interviewed as the character.

STEP 4—CHARACTER BREAKDOWN INTERVIEW

The purpose of this fourth step is to make the actor aware and facile in breaking down and finding what people are made of on the spot. The faster you can center on the Core and driving aspects of your character, the more free and creative you will be in fast-paced professional environments. Also, because you are thinking from another person's point-of-view, you become aware of what makes other people tick.

The character interview is the next step in the process. Here's the catch: the character that you've just created is the character that's being interviewed. If you're recreating your boss, you are your boss answering the questions. You have his energy. You change your voice pattern to reflect his squeaky voice. Your mannerisms become all gangly and jumpy—you can't stand still, and are shifting constantly from one foot to the other as he does.

In class, I ask you the same questions that you would ask yourself when you break down a character for a scene:

Respond as your character. Now make these decisions as your boss—first, what is your boss':

Core?
Boss: Control.

Happiness?
Boss: "Cover of Time magazine as 'Man of the Year.'"

134

<u>Driving question?</u>
Boss: "How can I make this peon honor my way of doing things!?"

To help figure this out, I always say to the actor, "If this were a cartoon, what would you (as your boss) be doing physically to the other character (you) to get your driving question?")

<u>Inner Action?</u> (
Boss: "to cattle prod."

<u>Outer Tactic?</u>
Boss: "by monkeying" (since he reminds you of the animal)

Now you are ready for the final step. "Rhythm and Lift-Off!"

STEP 5—RHYTHM & LIFT-OFF

The purpose of this last step is to release the actor into spontaneous acting flight. By combining several specifics together that keep the actor involved in "doing" in-the-moment, everything comes together to create artistic lift-off!

This exercise teaches you not to get ahead of your energy and to stay out of your brain. Settle into your body and let the instincts of your subconscious take over. When you layer the outer tactic and inner action together, the actor starts to release, then the conflict is added, and finally, it's lift-off!

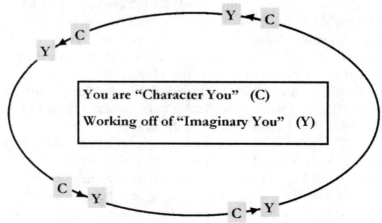

You are "Character You"   (C)

Working off of "Imaginary You"   (Y)

Stand center stage facing the audience. Repeat the key phrase you chose for the character (the boss in this case) three times in a row, simply and very relaxed. "Let me show you how to do that right." Don't move your feet. You want to feel the rhythm of the words without diffusing your energy. Don't "act" the phrase—just say it.

Now slowly begin to walk in a circle around the stage or room repeating the exact phrase over and over. Moving in a circle keeps you from focusing on the audience and allows the energy to build without coming to a standstill upstage or downstage. Again, don't think, don't force anything, and stay relaxed.

Let your instincts take over. As you feel ready, (as you keep circling) gradually allow the outer tactic, "monkeying," from your character interview to happen. Don't think about what you are going to do in advance. Leave your brain alone and let your subconscious take over. Continue to travel in a circle and say the phrase, "Oh here let me show you how to do that right!" Slowly evolve that same phrase and rhythm into embodying a monkey.

Once you're comfortable with the outer tactic (monkeying), explore and play with it in different ways. Let the phrase or sound become louder, softer, faster, or slower. Change the tone of your voice. As the movement gradually develops, add in different monkey elements to your physicality until it takes on a life of its own. Forget about what you look like or what people think. Go with your impulses.

Once you have the rhythm and are playing with different aspects of your outer tactic, it's time to add the boss's inner action, "to cattle prod" to the mix. Keep the "monkeying" going, as you layer in "cattle prodding." As you move around as your character, "boss you," start cattle prodding "imaginary you" in front of "boss you." Begin to combine the two and release into what's happening in the moment, (lift-off) while continuing to repeat your phrase. Let go into the momentum and allow your most creative impulses to take flight. This helps create the overall acting goal of the Acting Barré, where the creation becomes a force in itself and takes over from the brain.

The last element you add-in is the conflict. The conflict is what you did to the character during the "I wish I could..." section of the Acting Barré. You threw your boss's character out of the office window. Now imagine "boss you" struggling against being dragged over to and thrown out the window by "invisible, imaginary you," all of this while continuing to repeat your phrase using your outer tactic and inner action. Of course, doing all three at once starts to make the exercise difficult, almost impossible. That's the point. By actively trying "to do" all the specifics at once, spontaneous impulses start to happen. Acting gold! Then you get to finish off yourself as "boss you." Finish the scene. You can slow it down, end it quickly, or have a five-part "death," but give it a finish!

The Acting Barré keeps actors in shape while giving them a feeling of release, control, and empowerment. The Acting Barré also gets actors used to creating work in front of an audience without embarrassment or inhibition.

The key phrase and sound (of the character you're recreating) when repeated over and over becomes a rhythm that seeps into your body. When a writer writes a play or a screenplay, the work is infused with their energy. You want to be in tune with their rhythms and impulses, so you're not working against the energy and rhythm of the writing.

The Acting Barré stretches you consistently, in different ways. As you start to relax and drop into the different steps, the exercises become deep-rooted. The effect is profound.

One student said, "When I came into the master class, I saw people who had experience doing the Acting Barré, completely release into the momentum. That gave me courage to jump in, instead of worrying what I'd look like. It's like bungee jumping. You reach the point where you have to leap. Stepping into the other person's shoes, I have to see the whole situation from their point of view. I learned to switch gears, to turn around and become someone who has upset me. That's important to learn; especially when I'm creating people I'm close to."

If you've been consistently practicing the Acting Barré, it will serve you well. If you're on a set or in a rehearsal process, you will be able to open up your connection with the director quickly. This is because you will be receptive and flexible to taking the director's adjustments quickly, without fighting them or putting up defenses.

Great artists are always stretching and bringing tremendous range to their work. An artist working in different and imaginative ways finds diverse sides of themselves. How freeing to learn not to fight, but embrace what makes you uncomfortable, instead saying, "This is fabulous!" You can take direction and not only run with it, but know how to run with it.

HOW TO USE THE ACTING BARRÉ

There are different ways to work the Acting Barré. If you are rehearsing with another actor, one person can watch and lead while the other goes through the exercises. If you are a teacher, you can guide your individual students through performing the Acting Barré in class or in coaching sessions.

You can also work the Acting Barré by yourself. First, learn each section separately. Start by practicing the "I'm so pissed" technique, and then add in each subsequent exercise. Instead of asking the questions of the character interview, make statements out loud as your character, i.e., "My Core is power. My Happiness is to become the next heavyweight world champion," and so forth. Once you understand each exercise, weave them all together.

(To view a video of actors doing the Acting Barré go to http://pennytempletonstudio.com/acting-resources to download a video of this exercise)

2. THE PILLOW THROW

The purpose of this exercise is to physically feel the impulses of energy flowing back and forth between you and the other actor when you are in character. This exercise also builds your instincts to send energy over to the other actor on the most "effective" word with the most effective energy. For the following exercises, actors can use any scene or audition sides to work on.

Place two chairs facing each other, about three feet apart. Two actors sit in the chairs in an upright but relaxed position. Actor A, the first actor to speak (as their character), holds a small throw pillow. Speaking the first line(s) of material, they throw the pillow across at Actor B's solar plexus (diaphragm) on the word that should have the most impact in the material. For example, "Emily tells me you've decided to stay." Pillow thrown across on "stay."

The other actor, Actor B (who now has the pillow) throws the pillow back on the most impactful word in their section. For instance,

"That's very interesting. You've got some nerve!" Pillow thrown on "nerve."

The actors continue to throw the pillow back and forth through the scene. You should feel a focused, relaxed concentration of energy affecting each other, without tightening muscles you don't need. The goal is to physically impact or affect the other actor on the most important words. Aim the pillow at the solar plexus area, not anywhere near the face.

Throw the pillow with enough energy to wake up the other actor on the emphasized word. You can also hand over the pillow gently for a different energy.

Throw the pillow only once a sentence, unless that sentence is extremely long and loaded with two dynamite words. In this case, or if you have many sentences in a row, reach over to the other actor who has just received the pillow and take it back for the next throw.

Do not try to "act" the scene. Throw back and forth as efficiently as you can, without pauses, except for the rare exception of a needed pause.

You may also do this exercise on your own, by throwing a small pillow at a chair or similar setup, and retrieving it back before your next line(s).

This exercise can help you clarify what you want to say by throwing the pillow on different words. The emphasis and intention of a line will change depending on whether you throw the pillow on the word "Emily," "you've," or "stay." Especially on an important line, you can experiment by throwing the pillow on each word to discover the strongest impulse.

3. THE SWORD FIGHT

The purpose of this exercise is to develop the sense of "something at risk that must be won," while getting the actors to engage and respond in a back and forth use of energy on their feet. The choice and use of the sword develops the actor's imagination. The actor strikes physically, and must react visibly and audibly when struck.

Two actors stand about five feet apart holding imaginary swords. Actor A, the character with the first line, starts the fight. Actor A moves toward Actor B, as they thrust and parry with their swords on the most important words of their lines. If the line is, "I hate you and I wish you were dead!" "Hate," "you", or "dead" could be the operative word on which to try to strike Actor B.

If Actor A's sword lands an imaginary blow, Actor B reacts by making a reactionary sound or "Ow!" Actor B now takes their imaginary sword to Actor A. Actor A reacts with sound in the moment if and when they are "hit." The actors move back and forth, giving and taking, in a life and death battle for the stakes in the scene, striking and reacting. An important key to this exercise is allowing the scene to build subtly from a lower intensity level to the highest.

4. THE DANCE

The purpose of this exercise is to realize that every scene is a dance between characters. Like a dance, an actor needs to know when to lead, but also be open to following when the other actor/character is leading. It's important to feel the connection and give-and-take with the other actor in a scene, in the same way you feel the close physical contact of a dance.

The actor who has the first line (Actor A) takes hold of Actor B and starts to lead them in a "character dance." This is not a perfected ballroom dance. This is a character dance with all the passion, conflict, or silliness that is between the two characters as a couple.

If the couple is male-female, this does not mean that the male always leads or dominates. If the female takes the reins in the scene, she leads. She might even twirl or lean the man back in a dip. Who leads is determined by who is in charge of the scene at this moment. Don't always try to lead or dominate. Be open to the moment-to-moment give and take of the characters/actors.

Maintain physical contact. If the scene calls for your character to walk away, only then can the partner break contact. If the scene continues, the other partner could move and pull his partner back into the dance. The rhythms of the words, filled with the characters' emotions, should affect the dance. The actors should not go against the pacing and feel of the music of the words.

Characters that can't stand each other like Shakespeare's Katherine and Petruchio in *The Taming of the Shrew*, might engage in a rough, tango-like dance. Romeo and Juliet meeting for the first time might dance like two lovers at a prom, oblivious to the world. If it is the balcony scene, it might turn into an exciting waltz-like mating dance, full of sexual promise, joy, and discovery.

The dance can be between partners of any gender. Dancers can be male-female (Blanche and Stanley), female-female (Thelma and Louise), and male-male, (Cheech and Chong).

5. THE TAP DANCE

The purpose of the Tap Dance is to effortlessly release into the natural timing and rhythms of a scene. All pieces have rhythms, and tapping them out helps discover the heart of the beat.

Actor A and B stand side by side or facing each other and tap out the scene. Actor A as one character taps and then Actor B as the other character responds with their taps. Like "The Dance Exercise", this is not meant to be the tapping of a professional dancer. Make up the steps. The tapping should be relaxed and effortless, letting you fall into the rhythms of the scene. It is the tapping of your character. A Walt Disney scene might be light and fantastical, while a Mamet scene could be angry and relentless.

This exercise can be rehearsed individually. If rehearsing by yourself, you can just tap out the lines of your character. You can also tape the other character's words on an audio tape recorder, leaving space between the lines for your character's lines and responses. Work the scene as if the other character is there. You can also work out the rhythms of a monologue or soliloquy.

It is also possible to feel the rhythms of a piece through table tapping. Use your fingers on a hard surface to tap out the beats.

6. THE PAINTING

The purpose of this exercise is to explore and express the characters' emotions in a physical way, with different energies and rhythms through the precise brush stroke of an artist.

Actor A and Actor B face each other. Each actor imagines there is a large canvas directly in front of the other person. They can also imagine the other actor/character is the canvas. The first character to speak uses their imaginary brush as they verbalize. They paint on the large canvas, using the brush stroke to express their feelings and emotions through the words. Using the entire imaginary canvas, they can paint in bold, broad brushstrokes, or delicate, contained brush strokes. The other character paints on their canvas in response. Actor A and Actor B continue painting in the moment, back and forth in character, throughout the scene.

7. TEN TO ONE (OR HOW TO CRY IN 10 SECONDS)

The purpose of the 10 to 1 exercise is create a structure and technique that will allow you to bring up strong emotion under any circumstance.

For years I was on a journey to find an organic way to bring forth tears when needed for my work. Although I was able to access deep feelings, tears would not happen naturally in performance the way they would in rehearsal.

Finally, I discovered the key in an emotional scene in a production where the director wanted me to hold back the emotion. He did not want tears. The pressure of "showing the emotion" in performance was off. I started to relax. I would imagine seeing my "substitute person" as I worked off the other actor, which would trigger emotion. As I held back, tears would immediately spring to my eyes, but I wouldn't allow the tears to fall. It worked so well that it became a step-by-step structure that brought me to crying without forcing. Having my own technique gave me the control and joy of being able to access myself emotionally in a consistent, relaxed, and specific way.

A brilliant little actress, Katy, showed me the basic structural idea of this exercise when she was seven years old. *"Wanna see my acting game?"* she asked. Then she started happily counting down from the number 10, ending in tears at the number 1. I adapted this idea for my students, adding in specific elements to make it a structured technique for crying.

Let me be clear—we are not always going for the physical effect of tears rolling down the face. The goal is to bring up real emotion. At the very least, your relaxed face will show the depth of your sorrow. If your eyes just well up with tears, great. Sometimes, as they say, it's more effective for the audience to cry—not the actor.

First, begin by standing facing upstage, away from your audience. Think of something that makes you feel elated. The substitution that you use can be simple. Some examples: your best friend's coming to see you this weekend, chocolate chip mint ice cream, sex, a turquoise sea in Aruba—whatever works for you.

After you feel the joy sparking inside, jump up and down a couple of times to bonfire the emotion even more. You want the joy to radiate through your whole body. Then turn towards the "audience," and release the ecstatic energy in a relaxed, open way, saying "10!" The energy should be full, but with no tension. Don't push the feeling to make it more than it is. You want to build the emotion from the inside out. If you push the emotion, you will cut off real impulses, and your system will work in a false way.

Continue counting down by clearly saying "9." Don't rush. Don't go too slowly. Each number should be about one second in length. Do not go to the sad emotion yet. Don't "do" anything, but allow the happy energy to drift down on its own, like a parachute, as you count down from "8" to "7" to "6" while staying relaxed. Keep the breath flowing consistently, like a violin bow on the strings. When you reach "5," plug in the sad emotion. Turn that original happy substitution into something bad or sad! You can also internally bring in a new substitution that will help bring you to tears. Let it "hit you" and really feel it!

Then put the tension of the "emotional hit" on the inside, while holding back the emotion as you relax the outside. Keep the stream of breath flowing while relaxing the jaw, throat, and tongue. Do not swallow or cough; these are brakes your system puts on emotions.

Feel the wave of emotion like gravity. Let it pull your feelings down deeper and deeper as you go from "4" to "3." With each number, try harder and harder to hold back the sadness, while relaxing and softening the outside (the throat, the jaw, the mouth) more and more. As you reach "2" and "1," allow the breath to bring out the feeling, evolving into tears if it happens. Never force the emotion.

We rarely cry at the drop of a hat. Something causes us to feel an emotion and we generally try not to cry. When you look at your script, figure out where you want to first "plant the seed" of emotion that you want to bonfire. Put a star (*) a beat or two ahead of where that has to happen. This planting would be equivalent to your number "5." Again, try not to cry. Continue breathing and relaxing through the words to bring up your substitution to trigger the emotion.

10	Highest level of elation
9	Joyful
8	Cheery
7	Happy
6	Neutral
5	Hit with sad or bad substitution 💣
4	Sadness—gravity slowly pulling down
3	Hold back sadness—while relaxing the outside
2	Keep breathing and hold back more
1	Allow tears to come

10 TO 1 ROUND

An alternate version of The 10-1 is the "10-1 Round." The basis is the same as the "10-1 technique," except instead of just going from the high of "10" down to the low of "1", you continue back upward again from "1" to "10," plugging a happy substitution in at "5," and continue upward letting the happy emotion bubble you up to "6" and "7," more and more joyful to "8," to the surface at "9," and feeling the highest level of joy at "10," where you started in the first place. Then you repeat and continue downward again. I have the actors work on three rounds at a time. Ten to one going downward and back upward to ten, repeated three times.

The advantage of working the technique this way is that the actors lose self-consciousness, since the exercise keeps repeating. The actors start to relax and drop into the rhythm of their breath. Also you can feel the emotional push and pull of the muscles through the happy to sad to happy.

Practice this exercise as often as you can. For instance, you can work on this exercise by yourself, in the shower or on camera. The idea is to find something that will take you into the moment by starting as far away from the sad emotion as possible. Do not prepare the sad emotion ahead of time! You are not "playing" the emotion. Rather, you are releasing into it. Learn to trust your instincts and trust the technique.

THE 10-SECOND PREPARATION

This tool allows you to tap into the trigger of your character's heightened emotions quickly, before stepping onto your mark or on stage.

Perhaps your character is feeling a blend of feelings for this scene of: fear, apprehension, and anxiety. Ask yourself, "When did I recently feel these emotions?"

For example, last night your lover showed up forty-five minutes late for a dinner date. Now imagine the real person from the current event (your lover) is standing opposite you. Immediately begin improvising, by expressing out-loud to this person what you are feeling, to get your emotional steam boiling. Vent. Spew out your most primal feelings (I call them icebergs) at the other person. Starting at a low level may take too long to build the emotion. You may diffuse it. Don't say, "Oh, I don't know why you're not here." Yell, "What the hell is going on?" If "10" is the highest level, start around a level "8." Use strong words to light your personal fire of emotion. Fire yourself up right away. You don't have time to go through the whole process of slowly building the feelings. Usually the first words you say aren't quite charged or spontaneous enough so keep going. When you feel the emotion "hit" you on one phrase, that phrase is your spark.

Perhaps I start by saying, "What the hell is going on? How could you! I'm through!"– 'I'm through!" Those words scare me. I can feel that. We're going to bonfire that primal spark. Do not change a word, or you may diffuse the energy you're building.

We're now going to blow directly on that spark. "I'm through!" Say it fuller. "I'm through!!" Then fuller, still. "I'M THROUGH!!!" Out of that feeling, release a sound. "Ah!" Say it fuller "Ah!!" Fuller still "AAAAH!!!"

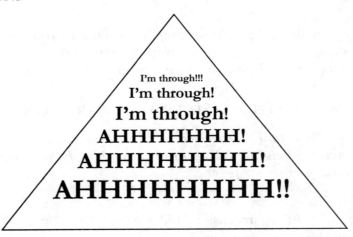

I'm through!!!
I'm through!
I'm through!
AHHHHHHH!
AHHHHHHHH!
AHHHHHHHH!!

At this point, the energy will be bon-fired. Then take that emotion and pull it into the level that is appropriate for your performance. For on camera, you might pull the energy all the way in. For theatre, perhaps you want to let much or all of it stay on the outside.

The sound is primal. It takes you right to your lower, dropped-in, primal place. As many actors are not used to working that deeply with sound, going to that unknown place is scary. That's where you really have to be brave.

With the ten-second preparation, you're coming from the primal, emotional, ready-to-react place of the character. Where most actors are "acting," you're feeling emotions. You're loaded with them! You're like a container that can be barely held. These feelings don't always have to be anger, but could be joyful, romantic etc. You can build whatever kind of emotional steam you need.

If you're auditioning for a casting director, work this technique at home. In your audition, as you walk to your mark or look over your lines, silently let the emotional phrase like "I'm through!" trigger your emotions.

IMPROVISATION

Improvisation is a quick way to cut to the real heart of "you." Many directors use improvisation techniques to find truth and spontaneity quickly.

When working on material, don't simply repeat the words over and over again. This kind of repetition can numb you to the words and make your performance flat. Instead, improvise the situation. Then release into the scripted words.

IMPROVISING REAL SITUATIONS

First, explore the emotions that your character is experiencing. Again, ask yourself what your most recent experience would be that would match most closely to your character's feelings. For instance, if your character just found out her husband cheated on her, she may be feeling vulnerable, betrayed and out of control. When did you feel these feelings most recently?

Yesterday you called your sister to connect with her. This was the third call and she never calls you back. You feel hurt, betrayed and out of control. Are you feeling the fullest emotions that your character whose husband cheated on her is? Probably not, but do you have some of the emotions on demand at hand? Yes. Now, let's stir it up.

In your private space, imagine your sister is there in front of you. Call her by name. Tell her how her unreturned calls make you feel! "Nora, what's your problem? You can't spare a few minutes away from your computer?" Imagine she's giving you a hard time. In other words, add conflict. She looks bored or angry or worse; imagine she's walking away from you. Create a tailor-made scene for yourself. Load it with conflict and let it explode. "Nora, Come back here!" Let yourself loose. The first goal is to get to the heart of your own feelings. You know you've reached it when you feel freed-up and released. You shouldn't be in your head, you should have "lift-off," the same way we have lift-off in our own lives when personal things affect us. Now that you've found your emotional energy, plug in the words from the script.

I teach this base improvisational technique in my classes. It releases your true feelings quickly and effectively. You can use this technique when working on your character or script privately, or you can use it when working with another acting partner. Always improv out loud. Expressing aloud allows you to access your primal emotions with ease.

Your goal is to marry the character's emotions directly to yourself. When you go to the scripted words, you will be filled with the same real, heightened emotions that your character is feeling.

When working with an acting partner, each actor should privately prepare with the improvisation technique just before rehearsing. After you are both fired up, come together and start improvising off of each other. Layer your substitution (your sister) into your acting partner and call your partner by your sister's name. In the reverse, the other actor imagines layering their substitute person into you. It doesn't matter that the two personal situations may be completely different. Allow yourself to react to the raw emotions that fly at you from your partner. Actors in the class are always amazed at the dramatic result of two people/actors going through real situations, pummeled back and forth by genuine emotions.

You can also improvise animals. If you're working on Stanley in *A Streetcar Named Desire*, improvising as an ape could be especially powerful. Finding the animal in you is an excellent way to embody primal energies.

In working with an actress on her one-woman show, we found an animal to represent each of her characters. Her uncle was a grizzly bear, her grandmother a vulture, her nanny a wounded alley cat, her mother a Russian wolf-hound and her personal character was a kangaroo.

As we improvised the animals suited to each character's primal quality, we found a solid base from which each role was formed. We would start with exploring the animal physically, evolving into the animal's primal sounds. Then, out of the animal's sounds, we would add lines from the play. Through the rehearsal process, the physical line of each animal through the character become clearer and stronger. When she performed, each role was full, clear, and well defined.

IMPROVISING AS THE CHARACTER

The next stage of improvising is as the character. Start by saying what the character would say in the script, but instead of using the writer's words, paraphrase the idea of the character's scripted words. Change them up. Say the words a little differently. What would you say if you were the character? Improv the words out loud and see if you can find more spontaneity and connection. If the character Hamlet says, "To be or not to be, that is the question?" you might improv, "Should I give up the ghost and kill myself?" Or in contemporary language, "Should I take a handful of Oxycontin and end my pain?"

WHY IMPROV AT ALL?

Improvisation frees up your feelings and takes you to the heart of emotions quickly. It also moves your body into a relaxed and responsive state. Improvising is a tool to personally connect you to the writer's different rhythms and words of the script. Improvisation allows you to marry your feelings to the character's feelings with comfort.

For actors, the purpose of learning improvisation should not just be just about being spontaneous or funny. I was in an acting class that included several professional comedians. I was blown away by how natural, responsive, and talented they were. However, once the actors were given a scene, the equation reversed. The comedians couldn't be spontaneous with someone else's words. Improv can free you up. Releasing yourself into material that someone else has written is a different matter. That's the challenge.

"Sometimes a scene is a very delicate thing where even though you can come up with something funny, it's like getting away from the intention of the scene and the rhythm of the other actor. You have to keep the reality going." —Ben Stiller

DEVELOPING
A CONSISTENT PROCESS

A tennis pro would never set foot on the court without having a game plan. They've mapped out how they're going to win "game, set, and match." Once on the court they don't have time to be thinking about their choices or their footwork. Their strategies must be ingrained. They must trust their impulses in order to play at the top of their game.

Actors also need a game plan. You work each of the beats with your choices to get them in your bones. You prepare the moment before you go into the scene, then trust and let go when you go into performance. You don't have to think about your choices in performance because, like a tennis player, you have worked your game plan until you have strong instincts.

"Working with Brando was fun. It was like a tennis match. We played unbelievably well together" —Uta Hagen

But in tennis and in acting, a player's strategy must be open to how that ball comes over the net. The energy that comes over the net from the other character may be entirely different from what you expected. You may end up adjusting the energy you impart to the choice to fit the moment. In some cases you may be need to come up with an alternative choice. You must react and change in the moment. That's okay. Some of your choices will work. Some may not. Don't try to make everything stick. If you did your homework and your choices didn't work, don't beat yourself up about it. Ask yourself, "Why did it happen?" Figure it out and learn from it. But if you didn't do your homework then you have only yourself to blame.

Fear comes from not knowing. You feel helpless because you're not in control. So what can you control in this business? Your "process." That's the ultimate. Love the process.

Learning new techniques may throw you off at first. Many actors think they have to know immediately what to do perfectly. Be patient. A tennis pro changing their backhand stroke expects a period of adjustment.

Devise a system to deepen your acting. View it like an exercise routine. Devote a set time to developing your craft outside of work or class. Even a half hour a day to practice your skills will enhance your technique. The effective habits you develop now will follow you throughout your career in whatever profession you pursue. Learn how to create a working structure for yourself. Often you won't have a director who has time to rehearse or direct you. This is especially true in film and television. Learn what methods work for you. Practice them consistently. Be ready to work.

10

BLOCKING & TECHNICAL ASPECTS

Contributed by Hank Schob

From an acting point of view, three primary components constitute the finished product of a play or film. There's the Written Word (the script), the Spoken Word (the actor's interpretation of the words), and the Visual (the total impact of the piece which includes the performances, the blocking, the set, costumes, and lighting). While it is part of the director's job to oversee the visual concept, understanding the concepts of blocking and how it contributes to the overall meaning of the production should be a part of every actor's craft.

In theatre, it is easy for the actor to have a sense of the picture the director is creating, because the audience is able to see the entire set and cast at once. In film and television, actors are often left in the dark. They may have no idea how the film will be edited, and which shots will be put together to create a completed scene.

For this reason, the actor must not be afraid to ask, "Where is my frame?" and, when possible, look through the camera to see the shot. That being said, the basic concepts of blocking are the same for both mediums. The differences are minimal and are a matter of adjustments in size and energy. With a solid grasp of the concepts of blocking, an actor can move easily from on-camera to theatre and vice versa.

WHAT IS BLOCKING?

The purpose of blocking is to:
- Focus the audience's attention
- Show the journey.
- Clarify the story.
- Deepen the levels

Blocking is anything visual that contributes to the scene. It is not only "cross up left" or "move camera right." Blocking is any physical move, no matter how small, that contributes to the picture the audience is seeing. The gestures a character makes—a turn of the head or roll of the eyes—should be thought of as blocking.

Make sure you know the basic vocabulary and the orientation of the stage before you ever get to a set or stage. You must know SR (stage right) from SL (stage left) and US (upstage) from DS (downstage) as well as DRC (down right center), XUL (cross up left), and XC (cross center).

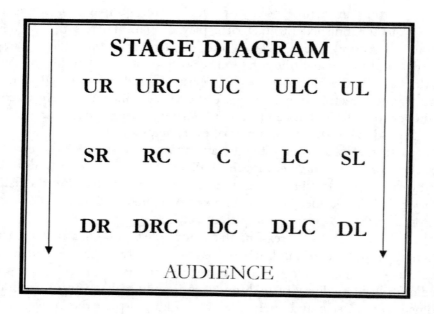

STAGE DIAGRAM

UR	URC	UC	ULC	UL
SR	RC	C	LC	SL
DR	DRC	DC	DLC	DL

AUDIENCE

Have these basics down. Nothing gives away a beginner faster than having to turn downstage and figure out where "stage right" is. This says "amateur" to the rest of the cast, no matter how talented an actor you are.

Along with these basic theatre terms, every actor should be aware of the film terms "camera right" and "camera left" meaning the cameraman's right or left. It is common for directors to use both theatre and film terms. Directors may use "stage right" when blocking indoor on a set and "camera left" when shooting outdoor on location. There's no technical reason for this. Usually a director will use the terminology they're most familiar with, based on their background.

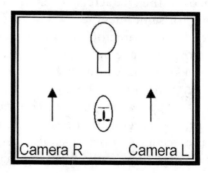

LEARN YOUR CRAFT

On a popular soap opera, there was a fairly simple scene set in a diner with several principals, extras, and an under-5 role of a waitress. When the notoriously mean director told the waitress to seat a couple at the table down left (DL), the actress had to turn to orient herself to figure out where down left was. The director was all over her yelling, "What! You don't even know where down left is? Just cross there!" The actress made the cross but then flubbed her line because she was now so nervous. This director then yelled at her for not knowing her line, causing the actress to cry.

The show was shooting on a fast block/dress/tape mode and had only about 20 minutes to get the scene on tape; there was no time to teach this poor actress. The director's response to her crying was a curt, "Where did they find you? You're fired!" He pointed to an extra and said, "You do her part." While the director was over-the-top with his initial yelling, he really didn't have much choice other than replacing the actress when she broke into tears. A whole taping schedule cannot be thrown out because an actor doesn't know their craft.

HOW ACTORS ARE BLOCKED

Directors can give blocking in several ways, so be prepared for anything. When time permits, some directors may let the actor play with a scene to see what basic blocking occurs organically. Then they will clean it up, setting the camera shots for film and adjusting the sight lines for theatre. Some directors will give the actors the opening and final positions in the scene, and then let them find their blocking based on the emotional needs of the characters. Then, once again, the director will adjust the blocking for sight lines.

There are also the directors who come in with every move pre-blocked. As an actor, you have little freedom in this situation, but if you have a specific idea that you can justify, you should never be afraid to ask if you could try something. The worst that can happen is that the director says no. This approach is most often used in television and film, where time is short; the director has preset every shot and knows exactly how they want the scene to look. It is also used in theatre when the rehearsal time is short, although the blocking might gradually change as rehearsals progress.

This happened with an Off-Broadway show with a four-week rehearsal schedule. Seeing as the fourth week would be all tech and dress rehearsals, there really was only three weeks of actual rehearsal. After two days of table reads, the director let the actors "find" their own blocking. By the end of day three, the cast wasn't even halfway through Act I. The next day the director gave out all the blocking. Today's reality is that there is no longer time for the actors to play and "discover." Do your homework, but remain flexible. You have to come to rehearsal or set knowing what you want to do but ready for anything.

PRE-BLOCKING

This more dictatorial form of blocking doesn't have to take away an actor's freedom and creativity. After doing your script analysis, begin working on each scene, breaking it down. Try to imagine where you are in relation to the other characters. Certain lines almost dictate strong eye contact with the other character or that you're avoiding them. Pre-block the scene for yourself. It won't match exactly with the director's blocking, but this homework will allow you to understand the director's choices better. If the director has you standing close to the other actor and you feel that you should be avoiding him, you can make a strong case for a blocking change, backed up with script analysis. You might get the change.

If it's film, the director might say no because of their visuals or the cost of another camera set-up. They may allow you to do a half-turn and look away, and in a tight shot, that could accomplish what you wanted in the first place. The more prepared you are going in, the more relaxed you can be on the set. When you pre-block a scene yourself, it helps to set up the scene organically for you. You don't suddenly find yourself with the camera rolling wondering, "What do I do with this fork in my hand?" When you go to the set, you are not learning "new" blocking, but making adjustments to "existing" blocking. This is always easier to do.

WRITE IT DOWN!

Listen very carefully to the director when they give the blocking. And always write it down, that's what the pros do. Many actors get into trouble because they rely on their memories and don't write their blocking down. When writing down blocking, don't try to act or figure out the "why" of the move. Just make sure you understand where you're supposed to go. If you're not sure about the move, ask about it immediately, not later. Always use a pencil when writing down blocking. Blocking will change and you must be able to revise your script.

Blocking for the camera is a bit more complicated and exact than blocking for the stage. Because of camera angles and shot setups, on-camera blocking is precise and involves a lot of cues, beats, and marks. The director's exact blocking is important, so listen carefully.

BLOCKING TECHNIQUES

Certain technical aspects of blocking can make an actor stronger on both stage and screen. First, try to be still when you are speaking. Move either before or after the line. If you have to move on a line, try to be still for a portion of the line. When you are still the audience can hear you better and what you say has more impact. Compare the performances of "Old Pros" to those of talented younger actors on stage and in film. You will be amazed at the economy of movement in the seasoned actors. They have learned not to move unnecessarily. When they move or make a gesture, it is for a reason and they will capture the audience's attention.

Another technique that can strengthen your work is to "take stage." In theatre, you do this by directing your important line downstage. In film, you direct the line squared to your camera. This does not mean upstaging other actors. It is important for an actor to know where the focus should be for every line in a scene. If it is on you, take stage. If it is on another actor, give him the stage.

Where you direct your attention and how you do it can go a long way in focusing the audience on the purpose of the scene. When focus is on your character in theatre, ideally you want to be upstage of the other actors so that as you are delivering your line, you are facing the audience. In film, you want to have your hips and shoulders squared to the camera and then turn your head slightly to the other actor. This is how you "take stage" in film. With your shoulders squared up, you fill the frame and look like a star.

COUNTER MOVES

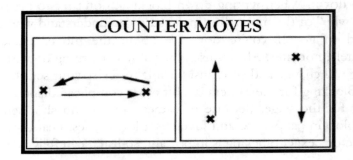

Another basic piece of blocking often given by directors in theatre, film, and television, is the counter move. The "counter" is a simultaneous move by a second actor to provide balance to the scene. It might be given as "John, cross left and Sally, counter up." This means that as John crosses left, Sally crosses right, passing upstage of John (counter up). Or Sally could be upstage left (UL) and be told by the director "cross downstage" while John is merely told to counter her. His move would be to cross straight upstage, thus keeping the set in balance. Counters are used to shift the energy in the scene or to create a new visual picture.

CUES AND CUE LIGHTS

Being cued for a move or an entrance is primarily for film and television, but it can happen in theatre. On a television set go to the Stage Manager or on a film set, the Key Second AD. Either they or one of their assistants will be giving you your cue. If there's more than one cue in the scene, make sure you ask which one is yours. There is nothing worse than standing on-set under bright lights and hearing "Cut!"

because you missed your cue. It can be hard to see someone in the shadows giving you a quick wave for your cue while you're involved in the scene. Know where the cue person is just in case.

Often you will be making an entrance from off the set or from the wings and no one will be available to give you a cue. Your cue may then come from a "cue light." When cue lights are used, a light will come on to give you a warning for your entrance. It will go off to "cue" your entrance.

TIMING/BEATS

Mostly in film and television but occasionally on stage, you will be told to hold for two or three "beats" (number of seconds). Beats are a part of blocking and are important. They are primarily for technical reasons, but can be used for adding emotional moments to a scene. Just as an actor puts pauses into his lines, the director will also put pauses into scenes.

TECHNICAL BLOCKING

Many blocking directions are for purely technical reasons. For example, I played a police officer on a television show. My character and a star playing a detective were arresting one of the other stars. I was told to step back over a hedge on a certain line and then "on cue," cross back onto my mark. I did my best to motivate my two moves, but it was really hard to look graceful climbing over a hedge. As we rehearsed, the crew was in stitches. Between giggles, the director told me I just had to duck down out of frame and move to the other side of the hedge, then on my cue, reverse the process. The camera was on a tight close-up of one star, so I wasn't seen at all. The whole purpose was to get me out from in between the two stars so they could get them in a two-shot without my being in the way. You don't motivate a blocking move like that. Just do it.

Another example was in a TV courtroom scene. The district attorney was aggressively questioning the star on the witness stand with rapid dialogue. At one point, the blocking called for him to hold for five beats (five seconds) for a cue to continue the scene. The actor had to "freeze" after the star's line and wait for a cue from the stage manager to continue, as if there was no pause at all. The purpose? To save money in the editing room. During the five beat pause, the director cut to reaction shots of three other stars watching the cross-examination. This "live" edit saved on production costs. Instead of motivating the five beat hold, the actor held onto his impulse for his next line so the pause would be completely unnoticeable to the audience. By the way, this is not exclusive to television. On stage, you may have to "freeze" while another actor has an "aside" to the audience, and then pick up the scene as if there was no interruption. The more you learn, the more you realize there are not many real differences in blocking between theatre and on camera.

GESTURES

Any movement an actor makes is a form of blocking. The director may tell you to move from position A to position B, but you get to block everything else yourself. This gives you great freedom, but at the same time, great responsibility. Everything in a scene should be there to help the audience understand the purpose of the scene. In real life, you may gesture madly to try to get your point across. You want to show the person what you mean because you're not quite sure you're getting your point across.

In theatre, when you are gesturing to show the audience what you mean, it's called "indicating." No actor ever wants to hear a director say, "You're indicating." If you study great speakers, preachers, or friends who capture everyone's attention, notice they make few gestures. Generally they stand very still when speaking. When a move or a gesture is used, it's strong and has impact. Get rid of random gestures—they diffuse your work. When you make a gesture or turn your head, do it for a specific reason.

SIZE OF THE GESTURE

Now, how should you gesture? The size of the gesture is influenced by the venue. In a small black box theatre or a film close-up, you may raise a finger slightly to point and everyone will see it. In contrast, in a 1500-seat Broadway theatre or a wide-angle master shot, you may need to point with your whole arm to get the same effect. One overriding rule of thumb is to keep your hands away from your face whenever possible. Acting is about allowing the audience to eavesdrop and see what you are thinking and feeling. The audience has to be able to see your eyes as much as possible for this to happen. Hands around the face are a major distraction. This is especially important in film. Hands flicking in and out of the frame in a tight close-up distract, and can make the shot unusable. Often scenes are shot with two or more cameras rolling simultaneously, each shooting from a different angle. One may be shooting a two-shot of the actors, while another camera is getting a close-up of one actor.

Recently an actress was shooting a film and, after the master shots were done, she was told they were going to shoot her close-up. She made sure her hands stayed out of the shot. The director stopped the scene and asked the actress why she cut out all of the gestures and animation that were in the master shot. She explained that she was controlling everything for the close-up. The director then told her there were two cameras rolling, one for her close-up, and one for a full body shot. He needed all her gestures for the second camera. One solution to this two-camera problem is to make your gestures in a horizontal fashion, keeping your hands below shoulder level and moving your arms and hands from side-to-side, as opposed to up-and-down. This way, when you have to match your movements for continuity purposes, you won't be in danger of getting your hands in front of your face.

CHARACTER GESTURES

When creating a character, it can be useful to create a specific gesture for the role. This is called a "character gesture." It is one specific action that is unique to your character and informs the audience of your character's emotional state or neurosis. This can be a one-time action or repeated. This type of gesture can be a powerful tool to help both you and the audience understand the character better. A great example is in the film *The Caine Mutiny*. To telegraph his character's neuroses, Humphrey Bogart chose to roll ball bearings in his hand to illustrate Captain Queeg's paranoid state of mind.

EATING AND DRINKING

Eating and drinking in a scene also require blocking. There is nothing worse than a fork waving around throughout the scene like a baton or a beer bottle coming up in front of an actor's face. A good rule is to keep eating movements to the absolute minimum. You are going to have to match your moves from at least two angles. First, never hold on to a glass or fork. Eat or drink, then put it down. Second, plan every sip or bite in advance. Rehearse the movements the night before with a video camera. Third, do not eat or drink on another actor's line. Always time your move to be immediately before or after your line, or in the middle of your line. Treat eating or drinking like any other gesture or blocking move. Every bite, sip, or picking up of a glass, should have a purpose. Taking a drink before a line can create suspense over what you are going to say next. Likewise, purposefully putting a glass down on the end of a line adds an exclamation point.

BLOCKING FOR CAMERA

While this section is about camera work, many of the overall concepts apply to stage as well. It is said that the camera doesn't take pictures of people's faces—it takes pictures of their brains. For the camera to take a picture of your brain, it must be able to gain entrance through your eyes. Two of the most important concepts of film acting are to keep your eyes up and find a way to "cheat" to the camera. These rules also apply to the theatre, which is why actors are taught early on to turn out to the audience. If you can make finding the lens a habit, you will be amazed how strong your acting will look.

The first skill to master is to always know where your camera is located. The camera is your audience. Let it see your complete performance. A good rule of thumb for keeping your eyes up even in the most depressing gut-wrenching scenes is to "Ask God." When we are sad or overwhelmed, the natural tendency is to look down. It would look odd if you didn't, but then bring your eyes up to the sky to "Ask God." Now the audience can see your performance and share in the scene with you.

Sometimes the director's blocking makes it seem impossible to share your work. There is always a way. An actor on a TV series came in to proudly show the rushes from his first episodes. In one scene, he was at the zoo in a penguin house, exchanging information with another character. The director blocked them side by side, looking at the penguins as they spoke. Both actors did exactly as the director asked. The result was mostly hidden, because you couldn't see their faces. It could have worked if, a few times during the scene, one of the actors watched a penguin swim in the direction of the camera. That actor could have taken his eyes toward the camera without looking at the other actor. When there is activity occurring off camera that only you can see, block in all of these imaginary creatures in a way that takes your eyes to your camera. If you see them and believe it, the audience will see them.

CAMERA SHOTS

BANANA IN

To do a "Banana In" merely means that as you cross to your mark, instead of walking in a straight line, you come to your mark on more of an arcing path (shaped like a banana). This puts you in the frame for several extra seconds. This method of crossing into a scene gives the audience a longer and better look at the character making the entrance. It also allows the audience to sense what is going on from the character's demeanor before the character starts speaking.

PIGGYBACK

The "piggyback" is one of the most important camera shots in film and television. In this shot, both actors are facing the camera, one behind the other. The unique advantage of this shot is that while neither character can see what the other is thinking or feeling, they each can have a private moment while the audience gets to see both characters at once. The key is to fill your character with interesting and "hot" thoughts. For the actor in the background, this shot is fairly easy. They merely need to focus their thoughts on the back of the other actor's head. For the actor in the foreground, getting used to this shot can be difficult. The biggest problem to overcome is the urge to turn your head to look at the actor behind you. This defeats the whole purpose of the shot. You must find a way to get comfortable talking to a spot, either over or just six inches to the right or left of the camera. The director or director of photography ("DP") can tell you which looks best. If not, ask. Maintain contact even though you're not looking at the other actor. In real life, you can be talking to someone who is behind you while you're doing something, like driving, and that is exactly what you need to do in this kind of shot.

The main things to remember in a piggyback are: keep your eyes front, don't put your hands on your hips (you could block the other actor), and keep absolutely still (don't sway). If you sway, you will either keep going in and out of frame, or you will block the shot of the actor behind you. If you are the actor in the back remember, if you can't see the camera, it can't see you. If the other actor blocks you missing their mark, often shifting slightly to one side or the other can clear you for the lens and save the shot. For theatre actors, the piggyback is also frequently used on stage. All of the same rules apply.

OVER THE SHOULDER

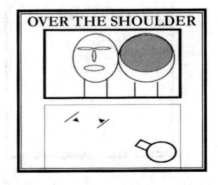

The "over the shoulder" shot is the exact opposite of the piggyback. In this case, the foreground actor is facing away from the camera, looking at the other actor or scene. This shot reveals to the audience what the character is seeing from the character's POV (point of view). This literally puts the audience in the character's shoes. Again, moving or swaying could ruin this shot. You can't cheat to the camera on this one.

TWO-SHOT

The other important camera shot is the "tight two-shot." This one takes some getting used to. If you are taking a snapshot of a group, you ask everyone to move in as tightly as possible. Why? You want to see everyone's face as closely as possible. This is what the director is creating in a two-shot. They need the actors close together. The hard part is getting close enough. Most of the time you need to be touching shoulders. This puts you so close that you may have trouble focusing on the other actor's eyes.

While that is a problem for you, the director loves it because the shot looks great. Very often, you will be so close that you feel are invading the other person's space. You would never stand this close in real life, but this is not real life. Get comfortable with this shot. The reality is that the camera adds distance and space.

Look at your family photos. Does everyone in a group shot look crowded together? No, and you won't look like you are standing too close to the other actor either. When you don't get in close enough you "spread" the shot. When you "spread" the shot a gap is created between you and the other actor, and you don't fill as much of the frame.

The director will often film these shots from two angles, giving each actor a good shot as the camera shoots across the other actor. If you don't get close enough in your shot, you can be sure the camera-savvy actor will and their shoulders will be squared to their camera. When the result is edited, their face will be much larger than yours will. This will make them more interesting and much of your great acting work may be left on the cutting room floor.

TECHNICAL ASPECTS OF BLOCKING

MARKS

"When I'm acting, I'm two beings. There's the one monitoring the distance between myself and the camera, making sure I hit my marks, and there is the one driven by this inner fire, this delicious fear." —Jeanne Moreau

Hitting a mark is an extremely important skill for the film actor, as discussed earlier. More shots are ruined because an actor missed their mark than for any other reason. If you are ever asked whether you want a mark, always answer "yes." If you are in doubt about needing a mark, ask. If you are being given a mark, freeze in the exact position of the shot until the marking is completed. If you even shift your weight, the entire shot may have to be reset.

Marks come in several forms. Often it is merely a small piece of tape placed between your feet. When a mark needs to be more exact, you may be given one for each toe or a "T" mark, which is a piece of tape across both toes with another piece of tape between your feet forming a letter "T." If the mark is really precise, you may have complete boxes taped around your feet. If the floor might be seen, you may get "spikes," tiny pieces of tape hidden by your toes. No matter what type of mark, your job is to hit it exactly and on cue.

Don't be afraid to occasionally look down. Everyone looks down naturally in life. Use that impulse. Just don't stare at your mark. With practice, you will learn to trust your peripheral vision. However, at times you must enter to a mark or cross to a mark while maintaining eye contact. In cases like this, you need to practice hitting the mark, either by counting your steps beforehand or by timing your steps to your dialogue. How many steps is the move? On what word do you need to be on your mark? Count back that many words and you'll hit your mark every time.

CARS & BARS

Scenes at bars or in cars have a similar set of blocking challenges. If you do your homework and take time to think about the commonality between them, you will find these scenes easy to do. The advantage is there are only so many places the director can put the camera if you are sitting next to someone at a bar or in a car.

BARS

At a bar, the camera can be behind the bar shooting head-on for a two-shot or off to each side, creating piggybacks when the foreground person looks away. It may also be set up behind the actors getting the reflection in the mirror (this would also create a two-shot).

CARS

In cars with two people seated in the front, the shot can be through the windshield or through one or both side windows. In all of these situations, there are times when you will be looking directly at the other character and times you may be avoiding them. You should be exact and block these head turns into your script. Practice with a video camera beforehand.

Next, adjust the moves based on the possible camera positions. If you do this homework, the scene will be no problem. Choose the options you planned for each camera position. For example, if the scene is being shot through the side windows, do not look through the windshield. There is no camera there. Look at the other actor or to the side of the other actor toward your camera. If the shot is through the windshield, look out the windshield instead of out your side window.

Cheat to the camera. No one will be able to tell exactly how far your head is turned so the shot will work and you will look great. If you're a backseat passenger in a taxi, the camera could be in the front seat looking back, through the side windows or shooting your reflection in the rearview mirror. Once you understand the types of shots for cars and bars, pre-blocking your moves becomes easier.

WORKING INSIDE THE FRAME

One of the worst misconceptions in acting is that your work must be smaller for film. This causes many actors to overcompensate and leave their performance at home. Instead, think of the camera frame (the space around you) as your theatre and adjust your energy according to the size of the frame. When shooting a master shot, you are working in the equivalent of a large theatre. Generally, as the scene progresses, the shots get closer and the framing tighter. In other words, your "theatre" gets smaller. Adjust your performance to the frame just as you would naturally do in a theatre. This is why it is always important to ask, "What is my frame?" or "How much room do I have?"

If you are shooting a close-up, how tight is the shot? If the shot is from the top of your shoulders to the top of your head with about a foot on either side, you can speak in a normal tone and turn your head to look at the other actor. If the shot is an extreme close-up and your face fills the entire frame, the scene suddenly becomes much more intimate. Your volume needs to come down and, instead of turning your head, you shift your eyes while keeping your head still. Your acting, your choices, and your emotions all stay the same.

If you're prepared, working on a set should be no problem. Blocking doesn't need to be hard. It does, however, take preparation. The director is only going to give you the bare bones of your blocking. Even if their blocking makes you feel constrained, remember you are going to do 90% of your own blocking with gestures, looks, and subtle moves. You have complete control over this 90%. Also, when you come in thoughtfully pre-blocked, the director tends to center the other actors' blocking around your clear choices.

11

CUTTING EDGE ACTING: USING A VIDEO CAMERA TO DEVELOP YOUR ARTISTRY

Along with the power techniques of Stanislavsky, The Method, and Meisner, every actor's acting toolbox should also have a video camera.

WHY A CAMERA?

When you use a video camera for rehearsal, it becomes your audience or "third eye." The camera allows you to work fully in the present moment, so you can then step back and review your work during playback. You can watch a video repeatedly, making adjustments to your performance along the way. In other words, you see what you really did, not what you think you did. Using the camera as an objective "eye" will help you uncover and work your own genius.

Unless you wish to professionally direct scenes or movies, the camera doesn't need to be high-tech or expensive. A camera with a rotating screen is best so you can frame yourself properly. Set your camera on a tripod and you are ready to work.

Use the camera regularly once you begin your acting "workouts." Don't be one of those actors with the bad habit of watching yourself in a mirror as you work. Seeing yourself as you are performing makes you too self-aware, and takes you out of the moment. It is too difficult to watch and critique yourself simultaneously.

WORKING ALONE WITH A CAMERA

You can work alone with a camera in many ways. The first that comes to mind is practicing sensory work.

I first used a camera for rehearsing sensory work when I coached an actress with a guest-starring role on the pilot episode of *Sex and the City*. Even though her character appeared throughout the episode, she was not speaking. She was shown in "story style," and the audience heard her in voice over. As it was important for the audience to "see" her feelings, we worked the scenes on camera until her face was filled with vibrant sensory detail for the screen. From then on I filmed sensory work of the actors in my classes. In watching their performances, the actors didn't have to look to me to describe their sense memory to them—they had the power to see for themselves. They could also compare their work with the other actors in a way that hadn't been available before.

HOW TO DO SENSORY EXERCISES ON YOUR OWN

One of my students, Bryan, created *The Sensory Bowl* exercise. Writing all the emotions that he can think of on slips of paper, he then folds the slips and puts them into a bowl. Pulling out three slips from the bowl, he works those emotions in depth on camera (anger, joy, fear, etc). Make your own list of different emotions and start working on them. Working every day is ideal. Practicing for long periods isn't necessary, but you must work long enough to get the feelings flowing easily and showing through your face.

Find a comfortable place. It could be an easy chair, a couch, or you can lie down. Have the camera zoomed in on your face in a fairly tight close-up. Start the process by consciously relaxing your face and body. Check for any feelings of tension. Tighten those muscles as hard as you can, then let go and allow the tension to dissolve. Imagine your face releasing like "melting wax."

When your entire body is relaxed, work on the breath. Become conscious of your inhaling and exhaling. Just notice the rhythm of your breath. Take a minute to feel the flow. Picture the image of waves gently flowing to and from the ocean's shore. Don't force or hold the breath. If you do, you will cut off access to your impulses and emotions.

Focus on one of the feelings you have chosen. If you've picked "fear" then steep in it. See what images or sensations bubble up for you. Allow yourself to be open—let your subconscious bring up whatever it will. If you train in this technique for a period, an issue that triggers the emotion will most likely surface. If this does not happen within a minute or two, ask yourself, "When did I recently feel this emotion?"

Hone in on this experience. Allow your feelings to come to the surface. Don't worry about how much emotion comes up, it doesn't matter, you can start with a spark. Marinate in the feelings and allow them to swell. Continue to inhale and exhale your breath, bringing the emotions to a head.

Once you feel this happening, start to say the alphabet slowly. I recommend using the alphabet because words will often cut off the emotions. See if you can allow the sensory impulses and the stirred feelings to come through the letters. Try this several times. See if the feelings increase. Now try to hold the emotion back. Attempting to hold back emotions often has the opposite effect and ignites the sensory. Often when we feel uncomfortable emotions, we try to stifle or restrain the emotion. We try to bury it.

Next, physically look up with your eyes into the camera. Bring your full sensory work into the open. This can be difficult. As stated before, in life when we experience strong feelings we frequently look down. You want to have control of the emotions and be able to bring your eyes up so that the audience can see your erupting feelings.

Director Martin Scorsese was interviewed about working with a young, shy, Harvey Keitel. Scorsese saw Keitel looking down while having these wonderful emotions. Scorsese said something like, "Now Harvey, that's terrific! Can you just share this toward the camera?" Bringing the eyes up while experiencing strong emotions, though mostly considered an on camera technique, is also important for theatre.

Another exercise is to practice crying and laughing on camera. See if you can make laughing and crying become organic responses, something easy and natural to do. Practice the breathing that comes with these emotions. Explore taping a scene and crying or laughing on a word or a line.

IMPROVISING

Improvising a situation can bring you to the emotion. For instance, imagine a minor incident. Maybe the clerk at Starbucks gave you "attitude" this morning with your mocha latte. Imagine the clerk being even ruder. React the way you would have liked to react, the way you were feeling on the inside when the situation actually happened. Let yourself rage. Film the improvisation. Now roll tape and see if you can go straight to the emotion without improvising the situation.

IMPROVISING WITH SUBSTITUTIONS

Experiment using the same emotion (like anger), but plug in different substitutions and see which substitutions affect you the most. Improvise what you'd like to have said when your boss made you work over the weekend, for example. The goal is to take techniques where you're working specifically with sensory awareness, like Stanislavsky or The Method, and bring those techniques to acting on camera. Then you can look at the playback and make adjustments on your own.

Ideally, you should rehearse scenes with a partner. However, there will be situations where you are shooting a scene without the other actor. In other words, you are performing to the air. See if you can plug in your substitutions and make them work without a partner. Using substitutions is also an excellent way to rehearse monologues. Create the scene as fully as possible. The more detailed and imaginative your substitutions are for your imaginary partner, the more interesting and specific your reactions will be.

Try filming one scene or monologue repeatedly, reacting to different people in your life to see how they affect you. Once your substitution is in place, be creative with your imaginary partner's responses, choosing those that affect you the most. Are they crying? Walking away from you? Interrupting you? Coming onto you? How do different "real" characters stir you up in your own life?

In his commentary, director, Peter Chelsom revealed that in the film *Serendipity,* John Cusack created a whole moment for himself without another actor present. In the movie, John's character is in love. He joyously kicks at a pile of snow, and then reacts as if, in his exuberance, he's hit another person. In reality, the "someone" was imaginary and not shown on camera. It was a great choice for the actor because it brought to life the purpose of the scene—that he is "head-over-heels in love."

How specific is your environment? Are you in a restaurant in a small town where you feel everyone in the place is trying to hear what you are saying? Are you in an open field? Busy office? Is it late? Early? Is it raining? With a camera, you can work deeply and take as much time as you need to get your environment in place. Using a video camera is a wonderful way to rehearse the Uta Hagen approach to creating a meticulous and specific environment (See Uta Hagen Chapter 3). Once you've created your environment in as much detail as possible, you can speed up your impulses and reactions to work with the timing of the scene or monologue.

Here's another idea—set up the camera to tape yourself when you are on the phone. Similar to Uta Hagen's phone exercise, but now with a camera and playback, you can actually observe yourself privately. You show your true reactions when the person you're talking to can't see you. After seeing how you really respond live on the phone call, now try to recreate that phone call and observe if you were as specific and real. In a scene, your character might cover their reactions. However, you want the audience to see and feel the character's private thoughts through a relaxed exterior. As one student exclaimed, "I get it! It's like seeing through a scrim!" (A sheer curtain).

Don't be embarrassed by your "private moments" when you're home alone. Get comfortable with your most vulnerable self. Lee Strasberg created the "private moment exercise" to help the actor bring private behavior to the performance. This will filter into all of your work, opening the door to true and powerful performances. This is one of the reasons I encourage actors to do on camera homework each week.

PREPARATION

Upset because she didn't get the lead role in a feature film, an actress coached with me to figure out and fix what held her back from being cast. As we worked, she became more relaxed and started releasing into her substitutions. As we filmed, she became uncomfortable because she felt her face held too much tension. I told her, "Don't worry about the tension—just improv the hell out of it, get the feelings out and trust it! Give yourself a really full preparation, but as you move to your mark, totally relax your face and do the scripted scene." All of a sudden, all of the work came together in a "Wow!" moment. The experience validated this process for me and made me appreciate this actress for being brave enough to figure it out.

Practice your preparations for camera work. Do a full preparation the same way you would prepare if you were on a movie set or before stepping on stage. I recommend the 10-second preparation discussed in Chapter 9. As the feelings start to build, jump up and down to bonfire them. Get the emotions alive in your body, fuller than you need them to be because they will dissipate somewhat. Keep the feelings going and relax your face as you walk to your mark, then begin your scene.

An actor rehearsed with his video camera the night before filming a short movie. He worked his camera angles, choices, sense memory, and walked onto the set owning his work. The DP and director were amazed. Even though originally the producer was looking to cast a "name" actor in the full-length version of the film, this actor won the role and was cast in the independent feature film.

The camera can help you to take responsibility for building your craft consistently. And that can pave the way for your career.

RELAXATION

It is essential to practice relaxation on camera. Relaxation makes it possible to be in the moment in a neutral and released state. Actors frequently think they look "boring" on screen in such a relaxed state. However, the next step is to add layers of emotional and physical life. The actor continues to build those feelings, until they can fully reveal the emotion through a relaxed face. Using the camera to record their process also reveals that the actor isn't boring anymore.

In Philip Seymour Hoffman's performance in *Capote*, his energy was pulled way in with a relaxed exterior. The audience was drawn toward him to see the depth of his feelings. Many actors work to reach out to the audience with their energy. Pulling the audience in is exciting work for the camera. How can you make the audience come to you like that?

Breath work is crucial in allowing you to reach a state of optimum relaxation on camera. Are there places where you are holding your breath? Are you able to inhale and exhale with consistency and ease? Focusing on your breathing relaxes the throat. It helps you drop into your center. It allows you open up to your emotional responses. There are actors who use tension to access emotion. Using tension to force emotion has the effect of distancing your audience instead of drawing them closer. The audience sees you working, and as a result they get tense. A relaxed actor who is in control permits the audience to sit back and relax too.

There may be times when you need to have physical tension and there are ways to use it in your work. Let the tension come to a head. Then take a breath, allowing a transition to happen while releasing the tension on the breath. Let your character have some "downtime" before the new waves of emotion ride in. Give yourself the freedom to explore all the crests and swells of your character's journey without unnecessary tension.

When you consistently practice relaxation with a video camera, you can reach a deeper understanding of the tension you habitually hold in your body and how to release that tension. By repetition and observation, you will come to the place where you don't have to actively concentrate on the relaxation techniques. You'll trust that you know how to relax. You've seen yourself do it. You can dive into the joy of your work, relaxed, confident, and in control.

EMOTIONALLY FILLING THE FRAME

- Instead of concentrating on physically fitting into the frame, how far out can you fill the frame with your feelings and sensory?
- How full can you make your emotions internally?
- How far can you go with your emotions and still stay physically relaxed?

Film yourself performing a scene or a monologue. Replay it with the sound turned down. If you are absolutely still, will the feelings and thoughts continue to show through? Are the story and the emotional journey all there?

TECHNICALLY FILLING THE FRAME

Here are some checkpoints to look for:

- Am I keeping my head still enough?
- Are my gestures clean and clear?
- Are my eyebrows at rest—not moving up and down?
- Are my eyes relaxed—not frozen or blinking?
- Is my jaw tense?
- Am I swaying?
- Am I mugging, or making exaggerated faces?
- Am I over-enunciating and biting down on my words?
- Am I vocally over projecting?

Don't worry about making all of these adjustments at once. It's a process. By observing yourself on screen, you can slowly eliminate what muddies and gets in the way of you.

BLOCKING

- Try coming on camera into the frame, then going off camera, leaving the frame.
- Practice doing a "lean in" towards the lens without going out of frame.
- Work on turning toward and away from the camera (turning on your own axis) correctly and effectively.
- Learn to sit down and stand up slowly enough to take the camera with you.
- Work on thinking your thoughts "up and around." The camera frame is like the stage for the screen actor. Your thoughts are like blocking.
- Practice eye synchronization. When is it most effective to look down or away from the other person? When is it most effective to look at the other person?
- Rehearse a scene using an extreme tight shot that only shows your eyes.

Develop your instincts until every movement on camera is clear, having a reason and a purpose!

BLINKING

It is distracting for the audience when an actor blinks too frequently on camera. This is especially true for film actors on a large screen. Excessive blinking often happens when the actor is nervous and isn't focused and concentrated to drop deeply enough into their character. Being tired or worrying about lines or blocking can also cause more rapid blinking.

"Blinking makes your character seem weak. Try it yourself. Say the same line twice, first blinking, and then not blinking. By not blinking, you will appear stronger on screen. Remember, on film that eye can be eight feet across." —Sir Michael Caine

Michael Caine practiced how long he could go without blinking (Don't overdo this, you could harm your eyes.). One of my working actors finds that choosing to focus on precise places when filming helps to keep him from blinking.

GESTURES

Very often actors who are over gesturing, and doing too much with their hands will say to me, "I'm an expressive person naturally." If the actor tries to remove or eliminate the extraneous movements, they can become stiff and uncomfortable. I tell actors, "Don't remove the gestures–use them in a different way: Imagine you have a football field on the inside. Take all that excess energy and release it on the inside. Yes, the outside needs to be clear, clean and simple, but you can do anything on the inside! Use all your gestures and more. Run around on that imaginary internal football field. Jump up and down. Do whatever you want! In other words, never confine or eliminate that wonderful energy; use it in a different, more useful way."

PRACTICING CHARISMA

The tension of having the camera on you can make you feel so anxious that you lose your personal magnetism. I was coaching an actress whose personality was alive, radiating feelings before filming. The moment she was in character on camera, she became anxious, and lost much of that spark. I replayed the tape and asked her to watch where she was casually talking as herself to me. She saw that in those relaxed moments she was vibrant, and full of life.

When actors get nervous, many just "dry act." That becomes their process. They don't know how to get the juices flowing and release into who they really are. This is why improvisation and substitutions are so important. You improv until you are released, and then marry it to the written material. You feel what the character is feeling. Like a symphony, great actors express different colors and levels of energy with a wide range of notes of emotions. The more feelings you have stirred up inside of you, the more you stir up the emotions of the audience.

CONNECTING WITH THE AUDIENCE

"I constantly play women who are damaged and out of touch, who are seeking without knowing, or knowing without the skills to transform their lives. Since I carry those same issues inside me, when I connect to that, it resonates in my work and I think women somehow feel the story is about them." —Olympia Dukakis

If you are really feeling the emotion, your audience will be stirred every time they watch your performance. When I play certain camera scenes over and over, the class laughs or tears up in the same places. Even though they've seen it before, the moment is real and a real moment touches people. There's nothing wrong with understanding how you affect other people. It's not that you're manipulating the audience. You have to go to the heart of yourself in order to reach the heart of the audience.

THINKING

Here's something to practice—thinking. Specifically, thinking on camera. One day I was coaching an actor when he stopped my filming to say, "Penny, I can't concentrate today. This weekend I was driving a hot blonde around in my sports car. I can't keep my mind on my acting!" I said, "Keep thinking about it because it looks great!" That was when I began exploring types of inner thoughts on the screen. I realized the importance of different kinds of thinking.

On the technical side, practice looking up with your eyes while keeping your chin slightly lowered. Relax to fully open up your eyes so the audience can see what you're thinking. Use your mind like a pinball machine. Make your thinking full enough that the audience sees it.

Imagine this scene: A man picks up a pregnant woman on a back road on a rainy night. He says to her, "Oh you're all wet—there's another coat in the back," but what he's really thinking is "Who are you? You're pregnant and you're hitching a ride on a dark road on this awful night? What's going on?" The thoughts you think can be different from the words you speak. That's what gives your performance dimension.

SEXUALITY

Experiment with adding sexuality into your work. A manager wanted me to work with an actor she felt was "boring." He was a great guy but he came across as a dull "Clark Kent type" when performing. He was appearing in a play, when I coached him to think of the most wild and dangerous sexual thoughts he could think as he acted. His performance was hot! I encouraged him to bring this element to everything he does. Sexuality is a form of primal energy. Some actors carry this hot current naturally. Some don't. Adding primal qualities into your work enhances your magic on the stage and screen.

Try this. Lie down in a comfortable place. Have the camera in a tight close-up. Now imagine a particular person in your life stroking you on the back of your neck. Take those sensual thoughts to other areas of the body. When the sexual energy comes through, say the alphabet or a nursery rhyme, and see if you can keep the sexuality going. Now try those hot thoughts on camera with a cold audition scene and see how you light up on screen.

WORKING ON CAMERA WITH A PARTNER

Do "acting workouts" and practice audition scenes with your partner as the reader.

- Take turns being in front of the camera with your partner as reader, and then play back the scenes to see if your sensory work is full enough.
- Are you compelling on camera? Do you have that twinkle in your eyes—that ball of fire sparked inside so full it can barely be contained?
- Are you reacting when listening to each other?
- Are you are looking down at your copy too much?
- Improv with your partner. Use your personal substitutions to ignite your emotions. Relax and release into the material. After improvising, do the scripted scene again, layering your substitute person into your partner.

Improvise the moment before the scene. If the scene is in the living room after a quarrel, improv the scene before the fight. From there, go right into the scripted material. Explore how you can add depth, dimension and a sense of release into the opening moments of the scene. If the scene begins in the middle of your conversation, you can improv the beginning of the conversation. When the camera starts rolling, you'll come in at the perfect pitch.

An actress I worked with played Al Pacino's wife in a movie. At four in the morning, the crew was setting up the cameras and lighting for a nightclub scene. Everyone was exhausted. Pacino pulled the actress from the table and started dancing with her. As they danced, he started improvising an intimate husband/wife conversation until the crew had the lights ready, when they just cruised right into the scene.

Investigate ways with your partner to fill the frame. Recently, two of my actors decided they would tape their scene using two cameras at the same time instead of filming each other individually. They were able to work their substitutions and capture both their performances simultaneously.

Artists exploring together can spark new and creative ideas and techniques.

USING THE CAMERA FOR THEATRE WORK

You can learn many things about theatre performance from on camera work. Many years ago when video cameras came out, I had an experience where my new video camera literally saved my performance. At the dress rehearsal for an important staged workshop performance, the director announced that he felt the casts' performances were too emotional. He told me I had to find another way to do my scene. The staged reading was the next day! I went home that night and set up the camera in an establishing, or long shot. I tried different approaches until I found one I thought would work. After the performance, the director was thrilled. He said, "How did you do it!?" I told him about working with my camera. As a result, I was cast to play that role in the full production.

When working with a camera for theatre work, set the camera back as if it's an establishing shot, as far back as the audience would be sitting if you were on stage. To see if your feelings are full and real, rehearse with a closer shot.

WHY THEATRE IS THE MOST IMPORTANT ON CAMERA CLASS YOU'LL EVER TAKE

Actors often say to me, "I know you also teach theatre classes, but I only want to be a film actor!" My philosophy is that to become a great film actor, you need theatre training.

What's it like if you don't have theatre training? It's like trying to swim a race without learning the basic strokes, and you don't even know how to float. It's like becoming a race car driver because you like to drive fast—or anything else that might look easy but requires mastery and skill. Just as ballet is the foundation for most types of dance, theatre is the foundation for all types of acting. Theatre is the hub. It's the base. If you have your foundation in theatre training, then you can easily make adjustments to the technical demands of other mediums such as film and television.

Film is like putting yourself under a magnifying glass. If you have no depth in your work, the camera sees that. The audience sees that. The place to train your deepest emotions is the theatre. When you pull your emotions inward for film work, the camera will see depth and complexity. In other words, there will be something interesting going on in there!

Theatre is physically fuller because it's done on a stage. It's live. Actors rehearse for longer periods and often do a run for at least a month or two. When you have to put yourself through the paces of theatre training, you go to the depths of your soul as an actor. Many of the great artists in film were theatre trained—Marlon Brando, Al Pacino, Philip Seymour Hoffman, Meryl Streep, Cate Blanchett, Liev Schreiber—the list is long.

What can you bring to film acting besides your limited personal experience? Shakespeare gives you a Grand Canyon experience. The Greeks take you through the wringer. When you're working on the great characters of theatre, you're working on creating a complex human being—a Hamlet, a Lady Macbeth, a Medea, or a Richard. Then when you go to film, that experience is inside of you. The characters become part of you and you've learned something from them. Actors will return to explore the great roles again and again. As you grow in age and experience and see life differently, you will see the characters differently. That's why these plays are timeless. That's why they still work. And that's why people are still performing them; they relate to the truth of the human soul.

"When you're a young man Macbeth is a character part. When you're older it's a straight part." —Laurence Olivier

To say, "Well, I'm not interested in Shakespeare," or "I don't need to be in a scene study class" is building an artistic foundation on sand rather than stone. There are professional film actors who regret not completing their training. They know they lack some of the great techniques that would make them feel more confident and at the top of their game. Theatre teaches you how to know what you're doing as an actor. If a casting director sees you performing on stage and doing great work, they'll know that you have an effective process. To have any kind of a career, you will need to have a process.

Theatre gives you depth. You're seeing a complex character through a person who has complexity. That's what artists have. It doesn't matter if they say one word or nothing at all. All they have to do is stand on that mark and you can't take your eyes off of them. When get on your mark and the camera sees your face, is it seeing a blank canvas or an oil painting?

"Brando wanted me to escape movies for a while – Take a year off. Go on. Study Shakespeare.' So it's one of the things that keep ricocheting around in my head. He told me that by the time he had got to the point where he felt he could do "Hamlet," it was too late. So he said, 'Do it now, (Hamlet) do it while you can.'"
—Johnny Depp

12

TRAINING

CHOOSING THE RIGHT PATH

SHOULD YOU GO TO COLLEGE FOR ACTING?

Whether you go to college for acting training has a lot to do with age. If you're under twenty, I would aim to get your four-year degree. If you plan to get your degree only in acting, make sure the school is one that will help you become a well-trained actor. Aim for an institution recognized as a leader in producing great actors.

In the cloistered environment of a university program, professors who don't have much professional or current experience may teach you. When you graduate, you are four years older in a youth-oriented field. It's not fair, but agents want to take on actors when they're young. In addition, you'd better be terrific because you'll be auditioning with actors who have had four more years of experience in the field. If you make the decision to go to school for four years, it's important to come out with a process and training you can use.

There is great value in a college education. College can help you grow as a person. Yes, it is more competitive when you graduate, but at least you're smarter. Some colleges are finding ways to bring the outside world to the students so they're not so insulated. That's wonderful because you have the best of both worlds. An agent shared that she likes to use certain college graduates because they are well-rounded and less likely to have a meltdown in professional situations. A good school will get many of the kinks out.

When interviewing for a particular college, ask what specific techniques they teach. You want to graduate with a solid foundation in at least one of the master techniques like Stanislavsky, Meisner, or The Method. Ask how many productions are mounted each semester and how often you will be able to get on stage. It's also important to ask the percentage of actors who get to perform. Some schools don't let their students do major roles on stage until their junior or senior year—and many of the favorites get the leads. It can be very political. On the other hand, one college production of *Hamlet* rotated eight different actors in the role of Hamlet. Hamlet was played by men and women, and it was a fair and interesting way to get everyone in the spotlight.

Colleges with better acting programs will require you to audition, often on their campus. You'll get a chance to see the energy and quality of the other individuals invited to audition. This is also a wonderful opportunity to observe how the program staff runs auditions. Remember, you're also there to audition them. Some colleges will run a program that takes you through your paces for several hours. For instance, they might have you do group exercises, such as a warm-up and improvisations.

Auditions always require performing at least one monologue, or sometimes two contrasting monologues. Be sure to get coaching on your monologues–you want to be prepared and confident for such a competitive event. Interestingly enough, a certain scenario happens when actors audition for different colleges. Going into the auditions, the actor has a favorite school that they want to be admitted to. After the auditions, that actor often changes their mind because of the environment or the energy of the staff at the audition. Reactions run from "They were such snobs." or "They were so disorganized." or "I didn't click with some of their theatre games" to "Wow! I felt like I met a lot of actors like me. I was inspired!"

Another suggestion is to talk to some recent graduates of the school. They may be more open than current students in relating about how well the program is put together and the quality of the professors and courses. Contact a college's alumni association and ask if graduates are willing to talk to prospective students. Beware if the only option is to talk to graduates whom the college handpicks. You may not get an accurate account of what that program is really like. There may also be blogs where you can get some frank opinions about the training and programs. Keep in mind that these are opinions, not necessarily facts.

Another warning—watch out for programs with no main acting curriculum, that divvy out the majority of training to outside individual acting studios. That college may not have a central foundation and clear structure to assure the result of a well-trained actor. Taking individual classes at an outside school or studio is likely to be much cheaper than college tuition. So what are you paying for? The college name?

Some actors go to college to pursue a major that will help support themselves when acting jobs are scarce. If you minor in theatre, you can still train in acting and have opportunities to perform at school to gain experience. With specific employment skills, you can avoid draining jobs such as waiting tables, catering, and temping once you're out of school. Also, you will have roots in a different career without having to start your education over again if an acting career doesn't work out.

WHAT ABOUT GRAD SCHOOL?

An agent came in to critique the actors in a MFA final class before they graduated. He said, "I am going to be honest with you. Most of you are not going to work in this business. So what are you going to do if you don't?" The students were shocked and hurt at the brutality of this declaration, but the agent was right.

Generally, you shouldn't study longer than four years to get a degree. If you want to teach or direct, go for an MFA program. But if you want to make your living in the business of acting, many in the business may feel you're too old to start an acting career by the time you finish grad school. It will be a struggle, especially if you're female. Additionally, you'll be carrying the debt of many years of student loans. I pass this hard truth on to you with a heavy heart.

One problem with actors in a college or graduate school is that they have all been together in a "fishbowl" environment for two or three years and often get stuck with labels, good and bad. When I taught a grad class on camera technique, the limitations of this fishbowl environment were reinforced for me. Some of the "leading" theatre actors found it hard to grasp the differences between stage and screen. Others in the group took to the screen and "shone." The leaders were angry and frustrated that certain actors they'd labeled as "not great" were breaking through on screen, while they were struggling.

Some programs are so focused on "the classics" that their graduates are not trained for the material they'll encounter in the real world. They might feel, "I don't want to do this pilot, I've played Antigone!" It is unlikely that a working actor is going to make a full time living performing Shakespeare or Greek tragedy.

There is also the issue of entitlement. Some graduate-trained actors believe that roles will be handed to them on a silver platter and that being a few pounds overweight will not work against them because they are "great" actors. Almost every actor in the professional world goes to the gym, some work with a trainer. So these recent graduates may be in for a rude awakening when doors quickly slam on them because they are not in shape, physically and professionally.

TWO-YEAR ACTING PROGRAMS

The theory of acting programs that claim you will become a "ready-to-work artist" in two years is questionable. There can be inflexibility of programs that insist on a rigid order of learning technique, which does not always work for individual actors. If you're way ahead of everyone in the class, you're held back and stuck. These programs are usually not taught by the artists who created them, so you may not have a great teacher instructing you. Worse yet, you may be stuck with a "clone" whose individual teaching style never evolves.

Some of these programs frown on actors getting any type of professional work during the length of the program. They may try to make you sign a contract that prohibits you from working professionally or from dropping out of the program. Some make you sign a contract with financial obligations. This obviously benefits the school because it then has the surety of your tuition for two years. If the teacher or the technique is working for you, why would you need to sign a contract? Why wouldn't you just stay?

IF YOU START LATE OR "THE OLDER ACTOR"

Don't start a college degree or a two-year program for acting if you're twenty-five or older. When you're an older actor, you don't have time to waste. You can't afford baby steps. Train with a master teacher and make sure you get to study with that teacher.

If you're a beginner, how do you get into a master class? Some acting schools will make you go through a long process before you get to work with the master teacher—that's if you ever do get to study with them. If you're really talented, there are always exceptions. Get a recommendation from other actors who are in a great master class. Ask to audition.

There are smart ways to learn and prepare for a master teacher. One is with a coach who can work with you one-on-one. You want someone to quickly guide you to where you need to be so you're not wasting your time. Even if you're just starting out and at an intuitive level with the work, some teachers will train you, especially if you're passionate about acting.

Whether you're starting out or have just graduated, go to a major acting center—New York or Los Angeles, Vancouver, Toronto, Chicago, Boston, Philadelphia, Miami, Dallas, Seattle, Minneapolis, San Francisco, Phoenix, and North Carolina. You must go to a cultural center, to one of the acting "Meccas." When you come to that center, find the right ongoing class immediately. When actors build their process correctly, they build careers. It has nothing to do with age. It has everything to do with being a complete, exciting artist.

When actors dabble in short-term courses that promise instant results, they're not building a great foundation. Beware of schools that advertise they get you work—"We have agents come in!" It's like a gold rush. Actors can end up spending all their money and energy on something that turns out to be a lie. A friend (and working actor) was hired to teach for an acting school that spends a fortune on advertising. He taught there for six months but soon realized he was hired just to make money for the school, so he left. He said diplomatically, "It's not my thing."

CHOOSING A CLASS

Look for a class that has a structure with a progression of steps that leads to deeper emotional levels and greater range in your work. If it's a class that seems like "Acting 101" kindergarten, get out quick.

The old masters—Stanislavsky, Meisner, and The Method—are great techniques. I call them the "big guns" in the actor's toolbox, and it's important to work on them for a period to make sure they're ingrained. But after working on a technique for a time, jump off your base and "move." There isn't time to work on one technique exclusively for years. If your goal is to continually study in a class to learn detailed exercises and hone your craft, that's fine. Not all actors are able to or want to work professionally.

FINDING A TEACHER

One of the best ways to find a great teacher is to ask actors whose work you admire, "Who do you study with?" Set up appointments to meet those teachers. Do your research. Just as each actor is unique, so is each teacher.

"Auditing," or observing a class, is another way to research a teacher. However, many good teachers do not allow potential students to audit for good reasons. Having an auditor can distract the teacher as they may be wondering if the person auditing understands what they're teaching. Students in class may feel vulnerable and judged by a stranger sitting in class for the first time. Auditors can take focus away from the group dynamics of the class. To allow potential students to experience their teaching style hands-on, some teachers have "open" or "free" trial classes.

If you are considering taking a class with a long-term commitment, be sure to interview the teacher. Most courses have a minimum number of classes in a session, but there should also be an "out." If the class is wrong for you, you don't want to waste your money. This is especially important with a one- or two-year commitment to an acting program.

Ask yourself these important questions when deciding if a teacher is right for you:

- Do I like this teacher as a person?
- Does this teacher have an inspiring energy?
- Has this person taken the time to get a sense of what I'm like?
- Does this teacher love what they do? Or is it just a job?
- Is teaching the craft the priority? Or is the priority making money?
- Do we click together?
- Does this teacher have training and experience in the field?
- Do they have a progressive structure based in a well-known master technique such as Stanislavsky, the Method, or Meisner?
- Does this teacher have a reputation for building great actors?
- Is this teacher or school making promises I know in my heart are not realistic?
- Do I think this teacher can take me to a higher level in my acting?

WHAT IS A MASTER TEACHER?

A master teacher is one who has studied the craft thoroughly, and then has refined and created their own unique and successful approach.

The role of a master teacher is to be your guide, honing qualities in you that lead you to fulfill your artistic potential. A master teacher helps you assimilate the imparted knowledge. They also assist you in understanding how to use the acting technique independently of the teacher.

Like playing catch, the teacher throws the ball of their knowledge to teach the student. Then, as the student evolves, they toss the ball back to the teacher. In this exchange, the student teaches the teacher something new that the teacher can pass on to other actors. This interchange of energy allows both actor and teacher to develop and grow as artists.

Some actors don't get work because of their personal energy. The actor may be a person who projects themselves as scary, immature, angry, afraid, or difficult. So a teacher's job is not just working with actors on their craft, but with the actor as a whole person.

SIGNS OF A GREAT TEACHER:

A teacher who:

- Is passionate about the craft.
- Cares about the actors.
- Keeps the class moving forward.
- Critiques in a truthful and constructive way.
- Has a class structure.
- Creates a professional class environment.
- Treats everyone equally.
- Appreciates each individual.
- Makes sure everyone performs at least once a class.

ELEMENTS TO LOOK FOR WHEN CONSIDERING A CLASS

BASIC BEGINNER CLASS

- The warm up exercises have a purpose—to open up the actors and make them comfortable with being in the space.

- A foundation in at least one of the recognized master techniques should be central. Working on basic skills such as sense memory or the Meisner word repetition. The foundation should be broken down and explained.

- Scene study from plays that are well within the range of the actors, which provide a foundation for putting techniques into practice.

- Scene structure and analysis and a clear teaching of terms, such as: super objective, scene objective, actions, and beats.

INTERMEDIATE CLASS

- The actors should be working on more advanced scenes that challenge and stretch their range.

- Structure and technique are developed into a more consistent process.

- Script analysis is key—digging for all the clues an information in scenes.

- A focus on improvisation and physicalized exercises to free up the actors and release their imagination.

MASTER CLASS

- The actors should be at an advanced level of talent and experience.

- The bar should be raised to a high level and challenge the actors; this is a thoroughbred class.

- Actors should have prior training and must be able to work on their own outside of class.

- The environment is professional and the purpose of the class is to develop artistry, leading to work.

- Many of the actors in the class are working professionally.

- The teacher should not take up class time continually explaining basic technique.

- The teacher's role is to critique and guide the actors' work. The actors take those critiques outside of class to work on their own and bring their work back for further critique and guidance. Actors develop their personal acting process.

- The actors are intelligent and "gutsy" in taking risks.

WHAT TO LOOK FOR IN A MASTER CLASS

A master class should train you to be a professional—to be on time, organized, and ready to go to auditions, rehearsals, and performing on-set or stage.

The classroom should be a safe and creative space where you are not afraid to fail. You should feel that you could try anything in class. There should be a positive environment while you're being guided, moved, and stretched. The teacher should assign the work. When actors choose their own scenes, they tend to pick unbalanced scenes with one character dominating. Or they choose "safe" scenes and characters they already know how to play instead of choosing material that will challenge them. If the scenes you are working on aren't stretching and strengthening your craft, you're wasting your time.

"WHAT IF MY TEACHER..."

Because actors can be open and vulnerable, they may not be aware they are studying with a teacher that is hindering and not helping them. Here are some situations that may make it easier for you figure out whether you are with the right teacher.

DISCERNING THE DIFFERENCE BETWEEN CRITIQUE AND CRITICIZING

Actors are encouraged to bare their emotions and put themselves in the teacher's hands. There is a difference, however, between the teacher who is actively helping you work through frustrating points and a teacher who constantly shuts down your process with verdicts like, "You're all wrong!" Being harshly judged can make you feel bad about yourself, instead of feeling inspired. It can become abusive when teachers yell at students, or angrily walk out of class. A teacher is responsible for their behavior at all times. That includes effectively communicating to the students. A good teacher can challenge an actor without slamming them down.

Some actors believe that working with a negative teacher proves "they can take it" and that this makes them stronger actors. Others in the same situation think, "This must be what I deserve because I'm a bad actor." Ask yourself, "Is this teacher helping me become the best actor I can be, or are they just abusive?"

Constant negative criticism can make you emotionally weaker, feeling fragile and full of doubt. If you find yourself feeling bad about yourself without growth in your process, it's time to search for a new teacher.

There's a fine line between teachers who help you figure out how the psychology of a character relates to you personally, and a teacher who messes around with you as a human being. It's scary when a teacher uses actors as lab experiments. For example, there was a famous teacher who was good at "opening up" actors. A woman in his class was extremely self-conscious about her age. He grabbed her purse, took her license out of her wallet, and read the year that she was born to the class. She freaked out. It's crossing the line when a teacher starts getting into people's personal, private business, and making that public in class.

SEXUAL BOUNDARIES

If you're in a class where a teacher wants to see you on the weekend or locks the door when you're alone with them, get out of there fast. There is a difference between a teacher having a cup of coffee with a student to discuss their process, and overstepping the teacher/student boundary by sleeping with that student. Teachers shouldn't date students. It's taking unfair advantage of the actor's vulnerability. There is a difference of power between a teacher perceived as an "expert" in the field, and a student who longs to partake of that knowledge. Sexual relationships with teachers twist the teacher/student relationship.

AUTHORITARIANS

Acting is not some ethereal, spiritual art. Acting takes a lot of sweat, hard work and knowledge to do it right. It is natural for actors to want to know "why?" And, at times, actors may even challenge the teacher. Some teachers don't want any questions at all. It's as if the teacher is saying, "I'm going to tell you what you need to know. I don't want to hear questions. I'm in charge." They expect that the actor should just know and understand everything they do. Even worse, they like it when the actors are in the dark. That is the teacher's ego getting in the way. Actors deserve the respect of the teacher and should be treated like adults, not children.

WHEN CLASS IS ALL ABOUT THE TEACHER

Class should be about the craft and the actors. A teacher talking about their experiences when they were acting should be like salt—a little for seasoning. The best acting stories are like parables, providing a metaphor for actors to understand the lesson. It's not a good sign when a teacher talks too much about themselves.

An actor recalls, "A former teacher would talk about himself and demonstrate sensory exercises while we had to sit there and watch him. I was in this acting class because I wanted to do the process. I didn't want to watch him do the process. The whole class was all about him." Generally speaking, the more the teacher has to demonstrate techniques, the less effective their communication skills.

"WATCHING" CLASSES

Actors have to do. James Kiberd, the first actor I worked with, used to say, "If you're not up working, it becomes a 'watching class.'" Find an environment where every person gets up to work scenes and techniques at least once a class. There are many scene study classes where you go in, sign up and you see maybe two scenes out of five. You sit and watch for hours. You observe other actors. If class is only once a week, watching is a waste of time. You have to get up in each class or you will be afraid to take risks with your work. You want to understand how to do the techniques on your own, not simply observe them being done. Not working in every class paralyzes actors. That's what class is for. Actors have to act!

WHEN TO MOVE ON TO A NEW TEACHER

There are times when an actor may have to leave a class. Some reasons are:

- You are at a different acting level from the other actors.
- You have learned the technique the teacher has taught and need to explore a different technique.
- The class has no structure and is too loosely run.
- You're bored and not inspired.
- You're not learning in the class; your technique is not moving.
- You have a weak link in your technique and need to go somewhere else to address it.
- You and the teacher don't mesh.
- You don't get up and work every class.

MAXIMIZING YOUR ACTING CLASS

Develop the work ethic you will take with you for the rest of your life. You have to learn before you can be good—that's what acting class is for. You don't want to be a rank beginner in rehearsal or on a set. Acting class is a great place to explore and try things without worry. Shoot for that confidence of "I've done everything in class. I've stood on my head. I've been horrible, but now I know what works for me." You either head into the storm and learn from it or you don't. How else can you hone and streamline your process?

BE WILLING TO FAIL IN A SAFE ENVIRONMENT

A wonderful actor surprised me by performing a monologue in class that was ungrounded and way over the top. Afterwards, he explained he wanted to do the monologue without a structure and choices, and just see what happened. He had never done that before. Though his risk didn't work, bravo to him for trying! It is essential to take risks like this in the safety of a classroom so you can see what works and what doesn't.

COMMANDMENTS OF THE CRAFT:

- <u>Be prepared.</u> Always do homework on your own. Don't wait until the last minute to breakdown and memorize your material.

- <u>Always know your lines.</u> (Professionals have to or they're fired!)

- <u>No excuses.</u>

- <u>Always be early for class</u>. Being on time is considered late by pros.

- <u>Consider rehearsing with a partner as a professional job.</u> Never direct another actor (a well-known rule in the pro world).

- <u>Take risks.</u> Embrace your fears. Learn what works and what doesn't in the safe environment of the classroom.

- <u>Raise the bar for yourself.</u> Practice keeps you prepared. Keep finding and enhancing your techniques. Keep stretching.

- <u>Consistently work on your craft</u>, not just in class. Develop a personal workout program

For example:
  o Put yourself on camera
  o Work on sensory
  o 10-1
  o Improvisation
  o Relaxation
  o Substitutions
  o Read new scripts
  o Practice reading cold copy
  o Rehearse monologues

Your training says a lot about who you are and how serious you are about your craft. It is the foundation that supports you. When I worked for an agent, the first thing she looked at was the actor's training on their resume. The actor's choices about what they choose to study, and who they study with say much about them and how committed they are. It also shows how much of a stake they put in their own future.

PART III
THE BUSINESS
OF ARTISTRY

13

YOUR BUSINESS TOOLS

Most actors don't want to deal with business. "It's dry, it's boring, and it's not creative." Understanding the business of being an actor, however, is essential to becoming a working actor. Your attitude toward your career will shape your future. This may be a business where other people have a lot of control over when and where you work, but they don't have control over what they see to make those decisions. You do.

After all the training and effort you've undergone to discover who you are, and learning to be the best actor you can be, you now have an incredible opportunity to present your best to the "buyers" in this business. You will spend a great deal of time auditioning, doing mailings, taking meetings, and networking. Auditioning and meeting with directors, agents, and casting directors is akin to a fashion designer getting to show at Bryant Park or a painter having an exhibit at an exclusive gallery. Taking hold of your career is an adventure!

BUSINESS TOOLS OF AN ACTOR

When you are ready to begin auditioning and searching for representation, you need to acquire the basic business essentials of an actor—professional headshots, a clear and concise resume, a brief, yet compelling, cover letter, and audition-ready monologues. Later you can add business cards and postcards to announce upcoming projects, and to follow-up with agents and casting directors. Lastly, when you're ready to step up your exposure after building credits and training, you can consider creating a reel and a website, which can be excellent tools for marketing yourself. Creating your business tools can be fun and exciting if you approach it as a creative process. The role of you!

HEADSHOTS

In the eighteenth century, miniature portraits were used to preview possible marriage matches for royalty. Today, headshots are previews of possible matches for agents and casting directors. Your headshot puts a "frame" around who you are and shows the professional acting world how you want to be seen. A great headshot makes a definite statement about you. It tells us not only who you are, but what you have to offer as an actor. Headshots are previews of possible matches for agents and casting directors.

Your headshot should mirror your energy and your "type." If it doesn't, it can cause great disappointment and hard feelings, just as it would have in the past if the proposed mate did not look like their miniature. After all, a professional has made the decision to meet with you after looking at your picture. If you don't look like your headshot, you've wasted their time.

PHOTOGRAPHERS

Price shouldn't be the main consideration when you look for a photographer. I have seen wonderful work at modest prices, and some awful headshots that cost a fortune. The following are some guidelines when searching for the right photographer:

- Choose a photographer that specializes in actor headshots, and who resides near where you work. Color digital photography is the standard. As color is so unforgiving, it is essential to choose a photographer who is trained and skilled in color photography.

- When looking at a photographer's book or work online, notice how they shoot your type, gender, age group, and skin tone.

- Never use a "model" photographer. A good headshot photographer has developed their particular craft over time. Agents and casting people expect a specific and distinct professional product. "Glam" shots or typical model poses do not make good headshots. Casting directors and agents want to see actors who are natural and "themselves."

- A good way to find a photographer is to go to reproduction labs in your city and look at their headshot books. Some of these reproduction labs have headshot portfolios available to view online, and photographers have websites.

- Ask working actors if they will share resources about whose headshots have been working for them. You can also check acting blogs, but be cautious, not everyone is an expert.

You want to choose a photographer who will give you exactly what you want. Take your short list and make appointments to go see each of them. Meet with at least three photographers before making a decision. Then you go through the photographer's book or computer screen of headshots, see if:

- The actors look comfortable and relaxed, not posed.
- Each picture shows off the unique qualities of the actor.
- The eyes are expressive, alive and vibrant, not glazed over.
- The lighting or the style of the photographer accents the actor. It shouldn't upstage the actor.
- You feel comfortable around this person's energy. If you don't, you'll probably feel uncomfortable during your headshot session.

THE PHOTO SHOOT

CLOTHING

Color photography adds a whole new dimension to consider when planning your headshot session. Be careful choosing your wardrobe. Look for hues that make your eyes pop and flatter your skin tone. Find silhouettes of clothing that fit your body type well. You don't want to have too much detail, layers of fabric, or prints. A caution for women regarding clothing: don't wear ultra-revealing tank tops. If you are going for a sexy look, you don't have to show everything. You don't want to find yourself typecast for mainly prostitute roles.

MAKEUP AND HAIR

Makeup should accent you, not change your everyday look. For example, if the makeup artist uses a lip liner and redefines your lip shape, you will look completely different in your headshots than you do in real life. You want to look as you would on your very best day. Actresses should generally never do their own makeup and hair. Always hire a makeup artist who specializes in color headshot photography who also styles hair. Make sure the hair and makeup artist is present for the entire shoot. You will be changing your clothing several times during the session and you will need someone to keep an eye on stray hairs and to freshen up makeup. Minor issues can be retouched. Men rarely need makeup.

Remember, you must be able to recreate the same look for every interview and audition, so you look like your headshot when you walk through the door.

THE SESSION

Before getting headshots, you should know exactly what you want to bring to the photos, and communicate that to the photographer. Your headshot should say clearly "This is exactly who I am." Look directly into the camera. Your eyes will express it all. Keep your eyes relaxed and open, not fixed or spacey in energy. Keep your hands away from your face. You don't want to have a disembodied arm or hand take focus away from you in your headshot.

Because of the pressure to get the perfect headshot, many actors feel stiff and nervous. To offset this, move while you shoot. When a photographer shoots a model, the model is in motion much of the time. Move, and then hold for a moment while the photographer shoots the picture.

I always tell actors to think of interesting things that are real to them in their session. Have substitutions in your life for whatever makes you shine—cool breezes in Jamaica, a sexy guy or girl, or winning an Oscar. Some actors find it easier to relax with music. Another technique is to imagine yourself performing fabulous roles. Whatever works to keep you loose and alive in the moment. A great photo is all about the eyes and the energy you are conveying, so think hot thoughts!

REPRODUCTIONS

When deciding on which lab to go to for prints, ask the photographer for a recommendation and actually visit the lab to look at their work. There are differences between "photographic" reproductions and "lithographs." Photographic reproductions are more expensive, but they are also sharper and richer in color. Some lithograph labs in LA produce excellent color reproductions, so in LA, you have a choice between the two kinds of prints. In NYC, labs mainly produce photographic reproductions. There are mail order labs for lithographs, but often the quality is too poor to use for headshots. In either case, get a test print done to approve color saturation, sharpness, and tone.

Actors often worry over the number of headshots they should have printed. Base your decision on the average of how often you audition each week and if you are planning to do headshot mailings to agents. Without large mailings, a hundred prints should last an actor awhile. There are electronic submissions so you will only need a hard copy of your headshot when you audition, not for every submission.

Never print your headshot on regular printer paper. Your headshot is your calling card. Nothing says "unprofessional" like a headshot printed on flimsy printer paper. If you have an excellent color printer, you can choose to print headshots at home, but make sure you use high quality 8x10" photographic paper.

BUSINESS CARDS AND POSTCARDS

FOLLOW-UP

Send thank you cards with a business card or your postcard after each audition or agent meeting to keep your face fresh in their minds. Don't beg for a role or representation. Later, when you're more established and known, send thank you postcards after important auditions or meetings. When you have career news, send a postcard updating casting directors and agents to keep them apprised of your work. With casting directors you would like to audition for or agents you would like to meet, the first mailing should be a headshot and resume, and then follow-up with postcards. Keep your messages short and simple. Once your face passes by their desk enough times, recognition will set in and they will remember you

BUSINESS CARDS

Business cards should be your headshot in miniature with your name, contact information and union affiliations. The photograph should be your main headshot. Business cards are easy to carry with you at all times.

POSTCARDS

Postcards are used for follow-up and promotion. They also should be your main headshot. If you use different headshots for different kinds of submissions, print separate postcards of each headshot. Don't put more than one headshot on postcards. Agents and casting directors meet thousands of actors each year. If you start sending many different looks, they will not remember you. Postcards are a cost-effective way to follow-up with casting directors and agents. Have something to write about, like your latest shoot, job or callback.

RESUMES

The following is detailed and specific left brain information. It may make your eyes cross, if this is "not your thing." However, this information is imperative. If you have one misspelling or list an incorrect billing category, you will immediately be pegged as a "novice." If you've never created a resume, it may be worthwhile to hire a business coach to help you.

A resume should clearly and cleanly list your experience and illustrate the type of roles in which you get cast. A resume should never be longer than one page.

Training is an important part of a resume that beginners sometimes overlook. The quality of teachers you work with and the consistency of your training show an agent or a casting director how serious you are about your craft.

What you leave off is just as important as what you choose to include. You don't have to list every production you've done. Often the agent or casting director only has a moment to glance at and take in your resume, so unless you're a brand new actor, list only important roles. They don't have to be in chronological order. Put the most prestigious credits first.

A resume is broken down into sections—basic information at the top, experience in various areas (such as theatre, film and television), training, and special skills. If you have done commercials and industrials, these are usually noted as being available by request on a separate list and not included on an acting resume.

YOUR NAME

	Phone number	
Height		Hair Color
Weight	*(Never put your home phone number*	Eye Color
	or Address on a resume!)	Vocal Range
	Email address	*(Only if you sing)*
	Website	

(List your work in each category in order of importance. In the third column you may have to choose between Theatre, Director, Playwright or Star, on any given project.)

THEATRE

Three Days of Death	*Bill Jones*	Broadway
Camelot	*Lancelot*	Nat'l Tour
Pericles	*Thaisa*	Off Broadway
Hamlet	*Laertes*	Stratford Festival

FILM

The Clown	*Jimmy*	Feature Film
Tangents & Transitions	*Bill Johns*	Independent Feature
Death at Home	*Brother*	Short Film
Help Me	*Robert*	NYU Student Film

TELEVISION

Guiding Light	*Inmate (u/5)*	CBS Day Time
Law & Order	*Officer Pike*	NBC Prime Time
The Runaway	*(Guest Star)*	Syndicated series TBS

COMMERCIALS : List on request or conflicts on request. (*Listing old commercials poses potential conflicts that could cost you work.*)

TRAINING

NORTHWESTERN UNIVERSITY - BFA
    Studies include: Acting, Voice/ Speech, Singing, Stage Combat,
PENNY TEMPLETON   Advanced On Camera Technique
                               Master Class (Acting Technique)

SAM CHWAT: Dialects
(TRAINING is one of the first things Casting Directors, Directors, and Agents, etc. look for.)

THEATRE COMPANIES
    SIGNATURE THEATRE COMPANY
    LA MAMA

SPECIAL SKILLS
Driver's License, Improvisation, Juggling, Tumbling, Ice Skating, Fencing, Typing, Running, Baseball, Tennis, Auto Mechanic, Water Skiing,
(You must be proficient in every item you list.)

BASIC INFO

First, in large, bold, clear letters is your name. Other immediate information follows such as: union affiliation, contact number or agent information, hair and eye color, height, weight and website and e-mail addresses. Some actors now print a color thumbnail of an alternate headshot on their resumes to show another look. If you have a reel available, you can indicate that it can be obtained by request or that it is available on your website.

EXPERIENCE

List your categories of experience according to your focus. If you are interested in a film and television career, that information should come first. The same principle applies to theatre. You should have a subheading of "Film," "Television" or "Theatre" and then list your experience under each in three columns—the name of the project on the left and the type (Film/TV or Theatre) and name of the role in the center. In the far right column, list the production company and director for film and television, or for theatre productions, the name of the theatre company and the director, if well-known.

BILLING

Each category lists billing a bit differently and it's important that you get this right. This information comes courtesy of LA casting director, Bonnie Gillespie:

For film, the categories of billing are; "Lead," "Supporting" or "Principal," and "Featured." Don't list yourself as "Starring" unless you are the lead star of the film. Because of the co-opting of the term "Featured" to describe background work, many actors no longer use it to describe small speaking roles. Instead, they will indicate featured roles as "Featured Principal" to distinguish that they had a legitimate speaking role. Make sure you spell "Principal" correctly!

For television, the categories are different depending on the type of television program. For television series and mini-series, the categories are "Series Regular," "Recurring," "Guest Star," and "Co-Star."

For soap operas, they are "Contract," "Principal" or "Recurring," "Day Player," and "Under 5" (or U5).

Television movies are a little different. Film billing is used for a television movie. After the name of the television movie, many actors put "MOW" in parentheses to indicate it is a "movie-of-the-week," not a series.

How do you tell what category to bill yourself? If it's a union production, look at your contract or your paycheck stub. Your correct billing is listed right on it. If it's a non-union production, ask or make an educated guess. Five lines on a non-union television pilot? That's a "Co-Star." A lead in a non-union film? You guessed it, it's "Lead" or "Starring" if you are the main character.

For theatre, list the name of the character instead of the category of billing. You can also subdivide the "Theatre" category into "Broadway," "Off-Broadway," "Regional," "Tours," and "Musical Theatre," if you have a lot of different types of theatre experience.

Do not list background/extra work unless you are just starting out. Limit your extra work so you will not be considered a background performer. Once you start to accumulate legitimate credits, delete the extra work from your resume. If you want to indicate that you have the experience of working on a big budget film but you did not have a speaking role, list "feature film on-set experience" in your Special Skills section.

EDUCATION AND TRAINING

List your most impressive and recent training first. You don't have to list every class you've ever taken. Show diversity in your training and name any well-known teachers with whom you have studied. Agents often look at your headshot and if they're interested, review your training before your experience.

SPECIAL SKILLS

Whatever special skills you list, make sure you're an expert at them. If you say you can speak with an Italian accent, you better be able to do it perfectly on the spot if asked. List unusual skills, such as being double-jointed, riding a unicycle, and sign language; and talents such as dancing, horseback riding, fencing, stage combat, accents, and dialects.

LYING ON YOUR RESUME

Don't do it. You will get caught! So before you beef up your extra role to "Principal" or "Featured," remember that it only takes a minute for casting directors to check IMDb and IBDb to verify your roles.

MULTIPLE RESUMES

Some actors create multiple resumes that highlight different areas of their career. If an actor is strong in musical theatre but wants to break into film, he might prepare a resume that plays down his musical theater credits. Many experienced actors will have a second resume focusing on all of their musical credits and acting training. There is nothing wrong with having two specialized resumes that draw attention to what you want to highlight.

PUTTING HEADSHOTS AND RESUMES TOGETHER

Actors worry a lot about how to do this, but there are only a couple of rules to remember:

- Your resume must be 8x10 to fit your headshots. Never attach an 8½x11 resume to an 8x10 picture. (If you do, trim the resume to fit the headshot).
- Staple the four corners or use a glue stick to secure your resume to your headshot.
- Another option is to print your resume directly onto the back of your headshot.

COVER LETTERS

When you do an initial mailing to agents or managers, you must have a cover letter to introduce yourself. Cover letters need to be simple and short. First, research the agent or manager on the Internet. Not just the agency—the individual. Agents and managers do not want to see some generic computer-generated letter with their names plugged in. They want to read a letter that shows the sender has taken the time to find out about them personally.

THE "HOOK"

Make a list of unique, interesting things about yourself. Include experiences and places you've lived, unusual people you know, things you've done, your interests and hobbies. Pick out one to use in your letter as your "hook" to catch that person's attention. Make sure that what you have chosen is appropriate for that specific business letter. Choose the strength you want to play up that makes you stand out. Not everyone has backpacked through India or knows how to fly an airplane or has recently moved from Iowa. Use these things to create interest so you can talk about them further in your agent interview.

PROFESSIONAL FIRST

Your letter should always have your name, address, and contact information at the top of the page. No cutesy paper or gimmicky fonts. Be creative, but be professional. Don't put things like glitter or confetti in envelopes. Agents and casting people don't want to have to clean up a mess off their desks.

ADDRESSING THE LETTER

Address the agent as "Mr." or "Ms." Don't call an agent by his or her first name unless you are already on a first-name basis. Letters should be addressed to one person at a time, so if there are multiple agents or managers at a single office, you should send individual letters with headshots and resumes to each. Never address a letter generically to the agency name or to the dreaded "To Whom It May Concern." Your letter, headshot, and resume will end up in the "circular file" (wastebasket) for certain.

WHAT SHOULD THE LETTER SAY?

The letter should be only one page. At most, your cover letter should be three or four short paragraphs. Generally, the first paragraph should include information such as a referral, if you have one. Include that sentence or two (hook) to create interest in yourself.

As far as the order of the remaining paragraphs, one should go into why you chose this agent or manager to send your materials to. This is where to include your research information. For example, if you saw that an agent has many successful sitcom actors on their roster and you feel you would be a good fit, write something such as, "I saw that you represent many respected comedic television actors on IMDbPro. With my extensive experience in improvisation and comedy, I think I would be an exciting fit with your agency." Another paragraph can highlight recent news about your career. If you've just filmed a role in an indie film or you're currently in rehearsal for a play or you've just gotten positive reviews in a major paper (send a copy), let them know. Talk yourself up without sounding pompous or egotistical.

Your closing paragraph should be warm and friendly without being desperate. Thank the person for their time. Tell them you're looking forward to talking with them or meeting with them soon. Don't beg for an audition or an interview. Be positive.

There was a great posting on an acting message board on the Internet about an older actor who just wrote one sentence for his cover letter—"I am too old to wait for success, so I am going ahead without it!" He received several calls from agents from this letter and is now signed with one of them. This actor made his letter his own.

MISSTEPS

There are a couple of things that you shouldn't do in cover letters:

Don't state the obvious. Of course you are looking for representation. Write something along the lines of being a good fit for the agent and wanting to explore a mutually beneficial relationship.

Don't overload the letter. Your experience is on your resume. Leave some mystery so you have additional things to talk about when you meet with the agent.

REELS

Your reel should showcase your outstanding professional material. Many actors make the mistake of including too much material on their reel. Your reel shouldn't be more than two to three minutes total. It should be like a movie trailer for "you." Cut out poorly produced scenes. Edit the clips so that the emphasis is on you. It's better to show a few seconds where your acting is fabulous than to show five minutes of film where you're not that great.

Many actors wonder if they should film monologues or class scenes to include on a reel when they don't have much material. Only do this if an agent or casting director is interested in seeing you and the quality of your work on camera when you don't have a reel.

WWW.

WEBSITES

Websites are the new calling card for actors. Having a website is becoming important to host your reel, to "brand" yourself or to create "buzz" about your upcoming projects.

Accessing a website is a fast and easy way for agents, managers, and casting directors to view your headshots, resume, and performance footage all in one place.

The best way to decide on a layout of your website is to view as many actor websites as you can and find ones that you like. Note what features you want, page layouts, and color schemes. What will highlight you the best to show your personality and who you are?

In addition to having your pictures and resume you should have a page that shows your best work, whether it is a scene from class or a monologue you recorded. Leave out any work that is not a high standard of quality. One of my students booked leads in two independent feature films from directors who saw her work on her website.

WEB DOMAINS

One thing you absolutely want is a Web domain that is specifically yours. You don't want to host at a site where your name is preceded by the site name, such as *www.actorsrus.com/yourname*. Domain names are inexpensive and are worth purchasing. For the best results, use your stage name as your website name.

DESIGNING YOUR WEBSITE

Either hire a website designer to create your site or learn how to build your own. You can also use a "template," a pre-existing website shell that you plug your information into. The option you use depends on how much you want to spend and how much time you have.

SOCIAL NETWORKING SITES

Internet sites, such as Facebook, Twitter, and MySpace have become a tool for showcasing actors' work.

A NEW WAY TO NETWORK

These sites are excellent ways to get your work into circulation. One student has been writing, producing, and shooting their own

207

webisode series that is posted on YouTube. The actor created a profile for the webisode series on Facebook and sends out announcements and reminders to create buzz about upcoming episodes. This created a "presence" for the actor, whose work has reached many more people than just by posting on YouTube alone. Now in its second season, the show has garnered over 2 million hits, and building.

WARNING!

It's a good idea to either keep your personal and professional postings on separate profiles, or be very selective about the personal information (including photographs) you post. Be careful about using social networking sites.

CASTING RESOURCES

Many Internet casting sites allow an actor to post a profile, including headshots, resume, and performance footage, for varying fees which can be monthly, yearly or per submission. These sites allow you to electronically submit directly to casting directors, attaching the headshot and footage you choose. A list of casting sites is listed in Resources.

Besides having an online site, Backstage and Backstage West are also published weekly in print versions which are available at newsstands or bookstores, and available online. Make sure you buy it or download it the day it comes out!

SURVIVAL JOBS

Figure out what you're going to do to support your acting. You can avoid poor paying jobs by getting education and training. There are popular side jobs such as waiting tables, bartending, and catering that can be lucrative and flexible. But, be careful, a job that has you working until 4am can play havoc with your career plans. Don't get stuck in impossible situations, such as trying to be energized and positive for a morning audition when you've just worked a graveyard shift.

TEMPORARY VS. PERMANENT JOBS

Many good temporary employment agencies cater to actors both in New York and Los Angeles. If you're skilled with computers or word processing, you may be able to work on days that fit your auditioning schedule. Sometimes you can land a permanent job with flexible or evening hours if you have specialized skills like legal word processing or computer programming.

START YOUR OWN BUSINESS

Another option is creating your own business. One of my students owns her own boutique with an excellent staff, leaving her the freedom to audition when she needs to. Another former student, a Broadway actress, is a life coach who has written several books and teaches about the "business of acting." If you're very physically fit, you can be a personal trainer or a yoga or fitness instructor. If you're talented with graphic design, be a website designer or offer services to create resumes, business cards and other promotional material for actors. Producing actor reels or other video services is another option. There are limitless opportunities springing up as fast as technology changes.

OR, GO FOR IT

Sometimes the opposite can be true. There is also the viewpoint that if you have a day job you'll never be hungry enough to really use everything you've got to get the acting job.

Morgan Freeman on not getting a survival job:

Upon getting work as an off-Broadway actor in 1967: I made $70 a week as an actor and I'd been making $60 in LA. Making more than that as an actor was just unbelievable to me. I never went back to typing but had some real lean times in-between. But I didn't have to go to work for anybody else. I didn't have to wash dishes, I didn't have to wait tables, I didn't have to drive a cab or wash cars. I deliberately left myself nothing to fall back on. If you've got a cushion, where you land, you stay. You can't climb a mountain with a net. If you've got the net, you'll let go. —

AVOIDING SCAMS

There are some rules of thumb:

- Never pay for promises.

- If it sounds too good to be true, it probably is.

- Become familiar with cons and rip-offs before you become tempted by any. Use the Internet to Google key words.

- Check out actor blogs and messages boards. If it's not legit, actors will be venting and warning others on the Internet. Read many of the forums describing the various tactics used including paying upfront for "jobs" or "opportunities" or "shortcuts."

- Run the name of the agency or person through the Better Business Bureau website search (*www.bbb.com*) or the Consumer Protection Agency for your state (this can be found through the Attorney General's office website for your state).

- *www.easybackgroundcheck.com* targets scam "modeling and acting" agencies.

- *www.ripoffreport.com*, *www.scambusters.com*, *www.consumeraffairs.com* are resources to search out consumer complaints against scams.

- If you know someone who has been a working actor or professional in the business for more than a couple of years, ask that person.

- And last, but not least, always get the offer in writing, including verbal promises. If you're not sure, have a lawyer look at it.

As an actor you are the president and CEO of your own company. Once you have your craft, it is your understanding and follow through of the business of acting that bring you to your goal of being a working actor. Your professionalism, attitude, marketing skills and the quality of your tools have a lot to do with direction your career takes.

14

How To Get Work

Know who you are

"You get to a point where you've become that person for that day, and you dilute your personality to the point where it's actually non-existent. You walk into a room, and you don't know who you are or who you should be, and they can't connect with you because it's not a truth."—Naomi Watts

Actress Naomi Watts recalled she would often lose roles in her 20's because she was told, "Not beautiful enough, not sexy enough, and not quirky enough." In responding to this pressure, she tried to be the pretty girl, the funny girl, the sexy girl, be whatever it was they wanted. Her friend, Nicole Kidman, kept encouraging Ms. Watts to be herself—and that it just took getting one job, and "she was right in the end."

You have no control over the casting process. Even if you give the exact performance "they" are looking for, you might not get the job because the star is 5'6" and you are 6'3", or you remind the director of the person his wife ran off with. There are a million different reasons why you might not get the role, even when you are the best person for the job. You have no control over any of them. The only thing you have control over is your performance. You have a chance to show them who you are as a human being and what you have to offer as an actor. An audition is an opportunity to act. If you go in trying to please "them," you water yourself down. When you go in confident with strong choices, even if you don't get the job, you will leave a lasting impression. Someday the phone will ring because "they" need what you brought to that audition.

It's crucial to be the best at your craft <u>before</u> you put yourself in front of casting directors. You can't just be competent. You have to be brilliant. Why would you place yourself in the position to be remembered in a negative light by people who have incredibly long memories?

SHOWING WHO YOU ARE

For many actors that first impression is made at a "general" non-specific audition that has been set up for the purpose of screening unseen talent. Contrary to popular belief Agents and Casting Directors are constantly looking for new, exciting, talented and well trained actors. Their careers depend on it. Many of them regularly hold general auditions in their hunt for the next undiscovered star. The usual format is a combination interview/audition. The audition portion most often consist of one or two short contrasting monologues. Every actor should have several really good monologues that showcase both their talent and who they are. As a person and an actor you are complex and have many different sides. You want to have a variety of monologues in your repertoire that reflect that complexity and the many varied facets of your personality. This requires finding great material that allows you to tell the world who you are.

FINDING GOOD MATERIAL

Many resources for scenes are available on the Internet. Just search "scripts" and you will find many sites with free scripts to download. See References for a starter list of online references.

MONOLOGUES

If you are planning to audition for theatre, especially in NYC, you should have at least two contemporary monologues ready to perform, one dramatic and one comedic, and one classical monologue. Choose Shakespeare for your classical monologue, either dramatic or comedic, because it will generally fit all categories of "classical." Build your repertoire to get more and more specific in showcasing the different sides of yourself.

You should also have at least one contemporary monologue from a film or play that would be appropriate for on camera, where it is slowed down to show sense memory, reactions and moments. An on-camera monologue can be a good choice to use for auditioning in an agent's office, where you are usually in a tight space and want to convey more intimacy with your listener.

Keep your monologues performance ready. Work with a coach who specializes in monologues. You are being compared with every actor who has performed a monologue at that casting or agent office.

Since casting is primarily film and television in Los Angeles, cold readings are most often used for auditioning. However, this doesn't mean that you'll never do a monologue in LA–some agents still request them.

FINDING MONOLOGUES

Often there are many actors all doing the same monologues from the latest hit plays. To avoid this go back at least a few years when looking for material. Go to libraries or bookstores and read plays. Film monologues can work when they are well-written, if you have a sense of how to use them in different spaces. Just be careful—unless you can perform it better than the star who is generally remembered, stay away from well-known monologues.

There are scripts available from most films and television shows that are available online. My general feeling is that material from plays work best. The characters have been fully developed, and the material has already been tried and tested in front of audiences. Research the plays and films of actors who are your type. Read material such as Studs Terkel's *Working* and *Coming of Age*, which are interviews that can be shortened to monologues. One-Act plays can also be good sources for monologues.

If it's the right monologue, you should feel that it was written for you, that it's you speaking. You should be so passionate about your monologues that you would love to perform them every day. Keep searching until you find them, and then keep perfecting them!

WRITING YOUR OWN MONOLOGUE

I don't recommend writing your own material, unless you are a brilliant writer. If you do write your own monologue, don't tell them you wrote it, use a pen name. You want them paying attention to your acting not your writing skills. Generally, try to stick with monologues that are taken from scripts—theatre, film or television. The director wants to see your acting skills, which include your ability to interpret a character and bring it to life.

HOW LONG SHOULD A MONOLOGUE BE?

A good length for a monologue is around one-and-one-half minutes. Generally, it shouldn't be longer than two minutes total. If you are asked to do two contrasting monologues, you will usually have a total of three minutes to perform both. Occasionally, classical theatre companies require a monologue of greater length, and the audition notice will tell you so.

A recent trend is requesting monologues that are one minute, or two contrasting monologues that total no more than two minutes. Don't try to get too many colors into a one-minute monologue. Make one or two strong choices and save showing a range and journey for longer monologues. One-minute monologues are harder to find. Sometimes you can cut a longer monologue down to one minute, but run it by someone you trust to make sure that your editing makes sense and shows you in a strong way.

AUDITIONS VS. MEETINGS

Auditions

Auditions consist of readings of sides (scenes or portions of scenes) from a script or a monologue performed for a casting director.

Meetings

Meetings usually occur with directors and/or producers, and can involve discussing the director's vision for the role and how the actor feels they can embody that. If you're a big enough star, you may skip through auditioning and immediately meet with a director or producer or sign a contract. Don't fall into the trap of refusing to audition once you have a few legit credits. Unless you are a "household name," count on having to go through the audition process.

AUDITIONING IN GENERAL

When your acting is fantastic, the excitement of it creates action. People recommend you. Work comes to you. The mistake some actors make is to audition with limited training and auditioning skills. Many actors think, "I went to college, I went to grad school, I took a scene study class, so I'm ready." You might not be ready.

Auditioning requires different acting tools from those of performing. You may rely on techniques such as script analysis and substitutions, but with auditioning, these are done in a rapid process.

After you have the role, you can fill in the details and the richness of layers, but for auditioning, focus on the important details that will help you get the role. You must become proficient at cold reading, bringing up sense memory, and substitutions on the spot. You might only have minutes to prepare. Having these skills ready to go makes you stand out.

HAVE AN AUDITIONING PROCESS

Unless you're a star, much of your time acting will be auditioning. Take the time to create a process for auditioning, just as you do when you work on a role. If you are afraid or consider auditioning a chore, that energy will permeate your audition. Make each audition an exciting, adventurous experience. Conquer the elements of the audition process.

- Auditions are a chance for you to perform.
- To show your talents and meet new people who are excited about this business and discovering talent.
- Auditions lead to work—your goal!

A casting director shared that out of approximately 25 actors he auditions for a role, he might call back 5 who gave great auditions. He shared with me that what these particular actors do is show him what the scene is about, perhaps in ways he never considered before.

An agent revealed there are three questions she asks herself when she auditions or interviews actors:
- Are their emotions accessible?
- Are they vocally clean?
- Are they released physically?

She looks for a complete performance with no encumbrances.

THE END OF "GENERALS"

Casting directors used to have what was known as "generals," individual meetings with actors to look for new talent. Generals rarely happen today as casting director seminars have become a venue for getting yourself in front of casting directors.

215

EPAs

For theatre, the general auditions for the members of Actor's Equity Association (AEA) are called Equity Principal Auditions, or "EPAs," and are usually union-mandated auditions. EPAs are conducted different ways in different cities. If you live in New York, be prepared to stand in a long line early in the morning. EPA time-slots are assigned on a first-come first-serve basis. In other cities around the country, EPAs are "appointment-only" auditions, where the Equity actor calls in or signs up at the Equity office on a specific day at specific times to schedule an upcoming audition. Both types of EPAs have "alternate" lists, whereby Equity actors without appointment times can sign up on the day of the audition. If an actor with an appointment time does not show up, the next alternate gets the time slot. All actors, whether members of Equity or not, can get the current Breakdowns of all Equity shows being cast from coast to coast at the Equity union website: http://www.actorsequity.org/CastingCall/castingcallhome

In most cases, with the exception of some EPA's, there is no requirement that the actor be a member of a performer's union.

WHAT TO EXPECT WHEN YOU AUDITION

NON-UNION ACTORS

Non-union actors have a seemingly insurmountable task—to audition for prominent casting directors they need to have union-level experience. In order to get these legitimate credits they need to be acting in union projects. That being said, there is absolutely nothing stopping a non-union actor from submitting for union projects.

If the casting director wants to see you, then you will be seen.

GETTING SEEN IN NYC

One of the best ways for non-union actors to be seen in New York is through theatre. Join a respected theatre company and perform in plays. Work with other actors in a creative theatre environment. Casting directors and agents in New York will go to plays by reputable theatre companies to look at new talent.

GETTING SEEN IN LA

There's a saying about LA—"Don't go to LA until they ask you to come." I've seen actors go to LA too soon and never hear from them again. Just think of how many aspiring actors flood LA every year! There are more auditions, but three times the competition. A move to LA is not only expensive, but also can wear on your spirit. Make sure you have a realistic and solid plan for housing and employment in place before you make the move.

Actors who are prepared for the business of LA can do well. If you're a fabulous actor with a strong resume, great recommendations, and a terrific reel, you're ahead of the game.

Theatre in Los Angeles doesn't have as large an audience, so one of the best ways for non-union actors to be seen is through respected showcase performances and independent films.

EPAS FOR EMCS AND NON-UNION

You may be an Equity Membership Candidate ("EMC"), an actor who has earned "points" toward your Equity card, but you are still considered a non-union actor at EPAs. After you stand in line, you sign up on the "EMC" list in chronological order. EMCs are seen ahead of other non-union actors, who sign up on the "Future Members" list. That being said, the reality is an EMC or non-union actor may not necessarily be seen. The casting director or director always has a say as to whether they will be seeing non-union talent and/or EMCs. If non-union is not being seen, you will usually be invited to leave your headshot. After waiting for hours hoping to get an audition time, this can be frustrating.

If the casting director is seeing non-union actors and EMCs at an EPA, you will have to wait your turn for all Equity members to be seen first. This includes the list of Equity alternates. It is difficult to get seen at EPAs, but it's not impossible. In fact, I have coached non-Equity actors who were cast in Equity productions through EPAs. Remember every Equity actor was once non-Equity. They made it.

GETTING BREAKDOWNS ILLEGALLY

The breakdowns are provided by subscription from Breakdown Services. I do not condone getting the official breakdowns illegally, although I don't understand why the breakdowns are kept such a big secret. Breakdowns are copyrighted material and if you receive them without subscribing, this is a crime. Therefore, getting the breakdowns illegally can have serious repercussions. The breakdowns offer agents and managers the opportunity to subscribe to the daily casting notices posted by casting directors. The public version of the breakdown listing is available daily via the Internet on Actors Access, but a casting director has the choice of whether to post their breakdowns publicly or only on the subscribed service.

You may be thinking, "Well, I want to audition for *Law & Order: SVU* and they only list breakdowns through Breakdown Services, not Actors Access, so I need to find a way to get the breakdowns..." There are other options:

- You could send in your headshot and resume to the casting teams at *SVU,* following up with postcards.
- You could attend casting director workshops and seminars with these casting directors.
- You could do physical drop-offs of your headshot and resume at their offices.

If you're a smart actor and do your homework about who is casting which projects, you can have the same level of success as someone using illegal breakdowns. Investing in *IMDbPro* and getting the *Call Sheet* put out by *Backstage* every couple of months is a great way to stay on top of what projects are in development, pre-production, and filming, along with the names of the producers and casting directors.

There's no rule that says you can't submit directly to a production company or director.

THE "ROLES" OF CASTING DIRECTORS & AGENTS

Casting directors are "buyers." Agents are "sellers." Many actors think they must have an agent before auditioning. Agents are not going to be interested in you until you can get roles that bring them a commission. The advantage to having an agent is that casting directors are limited to the breakdowns they are currently casting. Agents have access to all the up-to-date breakdowns being cast. Actors are more appealing to agents if they already have established relationships with casting directors. Unlike agents, casting directors have no limit as to the number of actors they see. They are always looking for fresh faces and new talent.

The golden rule is:

Make sure you can consistently deliver outstanding work in auditions. It is expected of you, because you are competing with professionals.

Casting Director & Agent Seminars

Generally, casting director/agent seminars or workshops are one-shot meetings. In the workshops actors pay to have a short question and answer session with a casting director then perform scenes, cold copy, or monologues. Actors should ask questions that will benefit everyone in the room. The questions should not have a limited focus such as, "Which headshot do you like best?" One of the biggest mistakes actors make is asking questions that, if they thought about it, would come up with the answer on their own.

The auditions are often with the casting director, sometimes with a reader, or sometimes paired with other actors attending the seminar. On occasion, you will audition in front of the entire group of actors. These seminars can also be brief (5-10 minutes), timed (yes, on a timer) interviews, with the casting director/agent or panel of casting directors, sometimes followed by the actor reading cold copy or performing a monologue. Short-term classes (also called "workshops" in NYC) are offered by casting directors with particular specialties, such as: cold reading skills, on camera skills, etc. They usually last four to six sessions and meet weekly.

Some casting directors will not offer seminars or workshops. They don't believe that actors should have to "pay-to-play" (pay to audition). But the reality is that seminars and workshops are taking the place of mailings for many casting directors. Rather than just a headshot, there is a distinct advantage for the actor to being seen live and in action. There is also the question of ethics of actors paying casting directors (whose job is to find actors) to be seen.

The bottom line is that you, as an actor, have opportunities to audition through seminars. Years ago you didn't have a choice, except to mail in headshots and resumes. You have to decide whether it's worth the money.

HOW TO CHOOSE

Just like choosing what breakdowns to submit to, you need to be selective as to which seminars you attend. Who is actually present at these seminars? Three levels of casting directors give seminars: casting directors, assistants, and associates.

If a casting director is giving a seminar, it is because this is a time-expedient way for them to see fresh faces. Be prepared and take these seminars as seriously as you would an audition. It could pay off. For example, an actor in LA attended a seminar with the lead casting director for a major series on a Saturday, was called in by the casting director the following Monday, read for a guest star role on Tuesday and was cast on Wednesday. This proactive actor attends high-profile casting director seminars frequently and sees them as opportunities to build relationships. However, he is very experienced, has an agent and a body of work, and treats these seminars seriously.

Doing seminars with major casting directors can be a good way for you and your work to be seen. However, the downside is, that long term classes with a casting director tend to dim their initial excitement over your work. While you may shine in a single class, over a series of 4-5 classes you will also reveal your weaknesses as an actor—something you don't want them to know. Another thing to consider is that casting directors are specialists in casting. They may or may not be good teachers, and they may or may not have acting training and acting experience. Some casting directors have a great eye and can give sound advice; others will say things in order to look like they're an expert, and those things may not always be accurate.

RESEARCH

Research the company providing the seminars. Some require actors to audition first before attending. These companies can even charge a fee to audition in addition to the fees for the actual seminars. On the plus side, auditioning can weed out a lot of beginner actors with little or no training, so there are fewer discrepancies between the actors at the seminar. There are large companies that offer a wider variety of seminars and workshops with a bigger pool of casting directors. The downside is that many of these seminars may be with assistants and associates rather than casting directors. Do your homework. Talk to actors who have attended seminars and workshops at different facilities.

Try a few out. Don't allow yourself to be pressured into buying large packages of seminars. These are businesses that need to make money first and foremost, so be smart and keep your own goals in mind.

FREE SEMINARS

Lastly, investigate free seminars. These do happen! Casting directors may give talks on various topics at the performing unions: SAG, AEA (Equity) or AFTRA. Check colleges and universities for seminars offered through continuing education programs. Some of the seminar companies offer free seminars each month on different topics such as the business of acting, developing a one-person show, or taking care of your health and well-being. Take advantage of these. You have nothing to lose and knowledge to gain.

Just as casting directors and agents have diverse personalities, auditions have differences, but all share certain core components. Let's break down this process in detail.

SUBMISSIONS

- Type casting is the Rule!
- Type casting is your best friend. How else will the casting director remember you?

There was an audition for a Broadway show where the producer had posted the following note:

"I know you are all talented actors with lots of range, but if I need a 6'5 actor with a club foot, one eye, flaming red hair and no teeth, I don't need you to get out your make up kits. There are 80,000 actors in NY. He exists!"

A lot of actors were very offended. They didn't get it. We are all a type. If petite 5'3" actresses crowd into a call that specifies "Actresses must have red hair and be at least 5'8"," those petite actresses take up time and space, thus keeping the director from auditioning actresses that would have had a real chance at the role.

Be smart. The selfish attitude, "Well I got the casting director to see my work," usually backfires. It also makes you look green if you have no sense of the roles that are right for you. It wastes their time, which annoys them, so they remember you in a negative way. You may also keep a fellow actor from getting the job that was perfect for them.

When you are starting out, it is important that you submit for your primary type. Once you've established yourself with casting directors, then you can stretch your range.

ELECTRONIC SUBMISSIONS

The biggest innovation is the electronic submission. All casting breakdown sites have means to submit electronically, or a breakdown may have an email address to send your headshot and resume. Many sites offer the option of attaching video reel clips along with your headshot, allowing casting directors and directors to have access to your work immediately.

DVD AND ONLINE SUBMISSIONS

Another alternative to live auditions is casting directly from DVD or online submissions. You download sides, tape your scene, burn it to a DVD and mail it in or send the file electronically. Although this means you don't get any adjustments, which may take you out of contention for the role, you still have control in these situations because you can perfect the final product that is submitted.

SUBMISSION ETIQUETTE

Don't call the casting director after submitting your headshot and resume. If they want to see you, they will contact you. If you persist in calling them to see if they received your submission or to pitch yourself, you will make them angry. If you have an agent or a manager, it is that person's job to pitch you for a role, not yours. If you don't get that particular audition, it's not the end of the world! There will always be more.

SCHEDULING

If the casting director of a project wants to see you, you will be scheduled for an audition. When making appointments, be sure to take the time to schedule an audition time that doesn't conflict with other commitments, get the address of the audition, and ask if there is anything special you should be aware of for the audition. A casting director shared that it is frustrating to put the time and effort into scheduling perhaps tens of actors to be seen on a project, and then have actors wanting to reschedule because of conflicts.

AUDITIONS AND CALLBACKS

Every project has its own unique requirements, which means there are no hard and fast rules when it comes to the audition process, but there are some general concepts that may help you to understand the audition process.

TYPES OF AUDITIONS

- Sometimes, a casting director brings in a number of unknown actors who are submitted by agents, producers, directors or writers or who self-submitted. This step is called pre-reads or pre-screens.
- This group gets whittled down to a small number who join the known actors for the rest of the audition process.
- Sometimes actors are cast without callbacks, straight from the audition.
- Now it is possible to audition online. Skype, and other various online services let an actor perform live over the Web. You can be working on a film in another country and have a live online audition for a role in Los Angeles or elsewhere.
- For network television shows or other big name productions, producers have their say and you may be called in again to audition for them. Sometimes this is a live audition with executives; other times they review the video from callbacks.
- In theatre, selected actors are called back for one or more live auditions until the role is cast. Occasionally an actor who is working on another job or out of town will be asked to submit an audition electronically.
- In the theatre callback process, you sometimes read with other actors being considered for other roles, and you may be paired with various actors to see what chemistry works. The director is usually present at callbacks. There may be a second callback.

SCREEN TESTS

Screen tests used to be a standard part of the casting process but have fallen by the wayside in recent years. You are rarely asked to screen test. However, screen tests do happen.

British actor Linus Roache, who joined the cast of *Law & Order*, said in an interview, *"Dick (Wolf) had me audition in a courtroom full of extras and cross-examine a witness."* So you never know what you might be asked to do.

Screen tests are now often done by actors at their agent's office, with their coach, or by even themselves at home. They are then uploaded and sent to the producers. I shoot several of these "screen tests" every month.

PREPARING FOR THE AUDITION

PREPARING COPY

You generally have anywhere from a few days, to the day before, to day of, to prepare for an audition. This is where you use your process to be consistently effective:

- Read the material through slowly to get as much information from the script as you can. Never skim.
- Then make your choices—the purpose of the scene, your job as an actor, your Core, happiness, driving question, actions, tactics and feelings.
- Choose the most important substitutions and plug them in.
- Make the most significant lines resonate by selecting strong substitutions and dynamic actions and tactics for those few lines.
- If you only get the copy when you arrive, choose two or three shifts of intent to drive your audition, creating a journey. For example, you decide your character will come in strong, lose control, and then get inspired. You may not have time to completely break down your script in this situation but do as much as you can.
- Then run through the scripted lines once more. If you have additional time, you can then improvise the scene with your substitutions, quietly to yourself in the hallway. By the time you

have done this work and allowed yourself to marinate in the feelings, it will be time for you to go.

The number one complaint of casting directors is poorly prepared actors. Just doing these simple things gives you a big edge over the herd of other actors doing the minimal amount of preparation.

DO YOUR HOMEWORK

You will often be told that memorization is not necessary for the audition. Not true. First, break the scene down, then, learn the scene, then, memorize your sides. This is a professional actor's job. It is what we do. It makes a difference. Make choices that will make the meaning of the scene clear, support your take on the character and build on your strengths. For instance, if you have a great sense of humor, find a place to show that humor, even if you are auditioning for a drama.

"You may not be right for what we're casting today, but you may be perfect for what we're casting tomorrow. How will I know who you are if you don't show me?" —Joan D'Incecco, Casting Director

RESEARCH

- Research how to pronounce names, places, and things. Google anything you don't understand, such as medical and technical terms.
- Know what's going on with the other characters.
- Understand the complete arc of the storyline.
- Use the Internet and *IMDbPro* to look up information on the director, the production, and other projects this director has worked on. Know who the producers are and what they have produced in the past.

By doing all this you can knowledgably discuss the role and the project with the director and casting director. They will know you are a smart actor who did your homework.

HAVE A POINT OF VIEW

Audition with a strong point of view that's truthful and specific. An actor was auditioning for a "bad-guy" role in a feature film. He thought, "I know other actors are going to come in playing the 'bad ass'.

How do I want to do it?" When he read the script, he discovered that in another scene the character's girlfriend felt betrayed by him. She had completely trusted this character before he tried to kill her. This supported the actor's choice to give the character a loving side. When people closed in on him, he would kill those he loved. The director loved his interpretation, and he got the role.

PREPARE BEFORE THE AUDITION

You can prime yourself at home before you leave, in your car, or out on the street if you want. Don't work yourself and your material so hard that you leave yourself emotionally or physically drained for your audition. As far as doing a full-out preparation in the audition room, I'll discuss that in a bit when I talk about taking the "temperature of the room" and preparation.

DRESS FOR SUCCESS

If you are told by the casting director or your agent to dress a certain way, do it. You don't want to obviously wear a costume (unless you've been told to do so). What you want to do is suggest the character. If you're playing a business person, wear a suit. If you're playing a Victorian woman, wear a longer skirt and a covering blouse. If you wear your usual jeans and flip flops, you will not make a good first impression as you walk in the door—unless it's how your character would dress.

Also, it's important to look distinctive. You don't need to spend a lot of money but you need outfits that convey the center of you, no matter if you are told to be nerdy or sloppy or stunning. You can suggest the character while showing your unique style. How would Sean Penn dress as opposed to George Clooney? Kate Hudson as opposed to Angelina Jolie?

HOW NOT TO DRESS

An agent told an actress, who was auditioning for the part of a nerdy roommate, to dress sloppily. She didn't do that. She came in looking nice and professional. As she walked into the room, the casting director looked at her, and said, "Didn't your agent tell you how to dress?" This actress felt like an idiot. The casting director said, "I'll have you read since you're here, but you don't look right for the part." The actress was really upset with herself and walked out muttering, "What was I thinking?!" only to see another girl out in the hallway rehearsing sides dressed in an old baggy sweatshirt and a pair of ripped up jeans. By not dressing appropriately for the role, this actress hurt her audition.

BRING YOUR HEADSHOT AND RESUME

Many casting directors complain about the number of actors who come to auditions without hard copies of their headshot and resume. Casting directors use the hard copy to make notes on during your audition. They use those hard copies to sort actors to call back and to file for future projects. So have headshots and resumes on you. Make sure that your resume is current and immaculate, with no handwritten entries. Be sure to have the headshots and resumes already assembled with staples or glue. It's unprofessional to bug the monitor or receptionist at the office for a stapler or scissors.

THE WAITING ROOM

If possible, try to get to the audition 30 minutes early. If you don't have the sides, see if you can get them without signing in. Find a quiet place to work on your audition and stay out of sight. Many an actor has blown an audition because they were rushed into the audition early by the casting person without being fully prepared. Return 10 minutes before your assigned time to sign in with the monitor. You may be required to show your union card. If audition sides are being handed out, you may receive them at this time or, as in the case of EPAs, the sides are posted on the wall and you will receive a hard copy 20 minutes before your scheduled audition time.

Instead of looking at your lines over and over while you're waiting, use that time to think "in character." Be cordial, but don't get casual and start talking to other actors. To prepare herself, one of my working actresses goes out in the hall to be in the thoughts of her character. She discovered that it's like a perfect wading pool until you're ready to jump into your audition.

WAITING BEYOND YOUR AUDITION TIME

If you are forced to wait more than 30 minutes past your appointment time, have a plan in place to keep your energy up and your focus on your audition. Bring water and a snack with you just in case. If you decide to step outside for some fresh air or use the bathroom, tell the monitor where you are going and for exactly how long. It's horrible for you to be called for your audition when you've stepped away for a minute and the monitor thinks you've left. At EPAs, if you fail to show up 10 minutes before your scheduled time, an alternate will take your place. This applies even if you're in the bathroom and forgot to tell the monitor. Always let the monitor know.

If you've been waiting for an hour or more and are suddenly called in, ask for a few minutes to regroup if you need it. If you're not allowed, use your current feelings to fuel the triggers you need to jump into the role.

One of my actresses was forced to wait over two hours before auditioning for an important role. She knew she did not give as good an audition, because she was exhausted from waiting so long. She called the casting director and asked for another audition, and was immediately included in the callbacks. The casting director knew the wait had been unfair and affected the actress's audition.

If you are a union member who is forced to wait beyond your scheduled audition time on a union project, you are eligible to be paid for your audition time after a certain point. The same thing applies if you are called in for multiple callbacks beyond union rules. Check your union's guidelines on how to claim payment for these auditions. If you are non-union, you have to decide whether waiting is worth it. Since many non-union calls are open calls, waiting is just part of the process.

WALKING INTO THE AUDITION

"There are no second chances for first impressions"
—Unknown genius

COMMAND THE ROOM

The first moment when you step into the audition room, you want the casting director to think, "Wow! This actor's got it—the complete package!" Excite the casting director. Make them want to hire you. This doesn't mean you have to be extroverted. It means that you step into that room with complete confidence knowing exactly who you are and what you're doing. Command the room in a positive way. Casting directors may not have an outward response when you come into an audition and take the room, but inwardly they will sit up and notice you.

USING THE ENERGY OF THE CHARACTER

Come in with enough energy of the character, so they think you're perfect for the role. That doesn't mean be rude if you're auditioning for an edgy character. But if you come in really nice and all of a sudden you start reading for a role with dark energy, the casting director might think, "Yeah, he's right for the role, but…he's so nice."

One of my actresses was shocked that a casting director told her manager that even though she gave the best audition, she lost a role because she was "too nice." This actress learned to measure which casting directors wanted an edge when she walked into the room. She said, "It's not that I'm rude or have an ego, but I just enter with a different, more professional energy."

DESPERATION

Entering through the casting door desperate puts you at your weakest. Professionals pick up on that immediately. "If I don't book work, my agents are not going to work with me!" One actor was so hysterical about getting work that he was absolutely not going to be hired. When an actor tells me that he must be hired now, what he's telling me is that he's not ready to work at all. He's not even at peace with himself. You are enough. Don't try to make yourself into someone you're not or what you think someone else wants you to be.

At a talk back with my actors, Kevin Spacey said that after living under terrible conditions and struggling for a long time in the acting industry, he had to make a decision whether or not to continue in the business. When he decided he would, he first chose to work diligently on his craft and be the best actor he could possibly be. The second, and equally important decision, was that he would be an actor for himself. He acted because it fulfilled and empowered him. Auditions weren't about trying to get a role; auditions were opportunities for him to act. His two concepts turned his career around.

THE INTERVIEW

TAKING THE TEMPERATURE OF THE ROOM

When you walk in, judge the feel of the room. Never try to shake hands, unless the casting director offers first. If the casting director wants to interview you, they'll make eye contact and talk. If not, say hello, introduce yourself and go. They have a lot of actors to see, especially if it's the first round of auditions, so just start and don't try to chit-chat. On the other hand, if a casting director has extra time, don't be thrown if they want to talk with you for a few minutes before your audition.

SHOW WHO YOU ARE

If the casting director hasn't met you before and starts a conversation, be prepared. The most common question is "Tell me something about yourself?" It's a great question. That opens the door to anything "you" want. Figure it out ahead of time. Always have a couple of interesting stories to tell. If something is currently happening in your career, talk about that to get the casting director excited. It should be true and give the casting director a sense of who you are. Don't ramble. Don't push your energy or push being nice. You want to give the casting director an impression of you being the head of your own corporation— an artist and business person who is moving forward with your career. Bottom line, "know who you are."

THE AUDITION

THE READER

In most situations where you have copy and will not be performing a monologue, you will have a reader who will be reading the other character's lines for your audition. This could be anyone from a casting director or assistant to a hired actor. Always acknowledge and say hello to your reader when you come into the room. Always work off of the reader because generally it's the reader and the director or the casting director in the space. When you leave the room, the reader has a lot of power. If you haven't connected with the reader and they're asked for their opinion, they will give it.

Readers sometimes read flat because the casting director wants to see how everyone will make it work, but other casting directors will bring in an actor as the reader to see what kind of chemistry you can generate with them in the audition. Have an effective substitution from your life for the other character and layer that substitute person into the reader, so that you can react under any circumstance.

Sometimes the reader will skip or fly through their character's monologues or pauses and jump to your cue line. This can throw an actor, who is prepared to listen to the reader recite the entire section of the script. Even when the reader skips sections of the script, you can take your time with your reactions because you're not relying just on the reader to give you what you need for those reactions. That's why it's important to have a solid substitution for the reader's character. It's great when the reader takes time and gives you something to work off, but don't expect it and you won't be thrown.

Working with the position of the camera and the reader

Most casting directors know that they need to have the reader next to the camera, but you never know what directors are going to do. Sometimes they'll have the camera in the corner of the room, far from the reader. You can ask to move the reader, and the director might say, "Don't worry. Don't think about the camera." Here's what you can do:

- Square yourself to the camera.
- Work off of the reader, but
- Think your thoughts and reactions toward the camera.

Turn a disadvantage into a huge advantage. Don't tell the director you're squaring yourself to the camera. Just do it. Many actors like to verbalize that they know what they're doing in terms of blocking and framing. It is never appropriate to do this, either in an audition or on-set.

Memorization—Listening and reacting

Have your script memorized but always hold your copy; it's not a final performance. If you go up on a line, they will not throw it to you.

Remember the camera is only recording *your* performance in an audition. You want your eyes up because you don't want the casting director staring at the top of your head. When the reader is speaking, do not look down at your script for your line. You must listen. If the camera is only on you, it will show that you are not paying attention and connecting to the reader/character. If you're not listening, your impulses are cut off. Don't stare blankly at the reader. Breathe and take the moments to feel and connect. Think and react.

If you need to look down for a line, stay in character. So many actors become flustered when they need to find a line and completely drop their energy and their character.

- Wait until the reader stops speaking...
- Have a reaction as the character to what the reader said, and then:
- With that reaction go down to pick up your line or lines in character.
- Look up at the reader and then deliver your next line. It's better to look down as your character, read the beginning of your line that's on the page and then come up to make contact with the reader for the end of your line. Most actors do the opposite, when in fact the connection/meaning/response often comes at the end of the line.

Remember that you want to create chemistry with the reader. You also want the casting director (and camera, if there is one) to see your face, sensory impulses and reactions as much as possible.

WHEN YOU ARE GIVEN OPTIONS

If you are given an option, such as sitting or standing or being allowed to choose what scene to do, don't ask the casting director what they want. Make a choice. If there is more than one scene, be prepared and make a decision ahead of time. If you mess up, and you're not too far into your material, start again. Diplomatically say, "I'd like to start again." Let them know you have it under control, but don't make a habit of stopping in the middle of your auditions to start over.

Don't over-apologize, whether it's not reading the script, messing up a line, or having to start over. Just do your work as a professional. No one expects you to be perfect, but they do want you to be in control of your audition. They may see what they want in one moment or reaction. Trying to make it perfect is scholarly and not the process of an artist. After all, you haven't had the material for long. Casting directors and directors want to see a great actor, not a perfect one.

SLATING

Slating for on camera auditions usually consists of stating your name and contact information directly to the camera, prior to beginning your audition or immediately after. Sometimes you will be given a sign to hold for your slate. You should slate with somewhat the energy of your character. Don't let the slate take away from what you need to do in the scene. If you're auditioning for the role of a murderer don't slate with a sunny energy of the "girl next door." In some auditions, you are asked to turn and give profiles after stating your name. In a theatre audition, state your name and what monologue or role you will be doing. Know the play and playwright in case you're asked.

BLOCKING.

Adding simple blocking like a cross, a turn or a lean in makes it interesting, active and clear. It also shows that you know what to do with the space. Keep it simple though, because too much blocking at an audition is distracting and looks "gimmicky."

KNOW YOUR FRAME

If it's an on-camera audition, always ask, "What is my frame?" If the camera is in a tight close-up, your blocking is more limited—maybe a slight head turn. If they're shooting you chest up, then you might choose to do a turn or take a step or a lean in. You have a little more freedom. Again, keep it simple.

"FRIENDLY AGGRESSION"

One casting director said he likes to see "friendly aggression." He said, "We may be as cold as ice on the outside, but on the inside, we're excited and anticipating seeing what you will do next."

"Friendly aggression" means you have confidence that you have a good grasp of the role. You say to the reader, "I'm going to lean in at this point" or "I'm going to come in on camera" or, in the case of a theatre audition, "I'm going to place this chair here." It lets the casting director know you're setting the scene.

For on-camera auditions, always tell the casting director and the reader exactly when and what you're going to do. You must inform them, for instance, if you're going to go in and out of frame or you're adding a pause or reaction at a certain moment. Do this quickly and efficiently. Only add movement if it's important to the scene and make sure that if you choose to enter the frame, you hit your mark. Be extremely clear. If you confuse the casting director or the reader with sudden movements or pauses, your whole audition could be lost.

USE THE SPACE LIKE A PRO

- Find your light: Look for the best place in the space to be seen so the casting director can see all of your work.
- The strongest place to stand for a theatre audition is not necessarily center stage. You don't want your face in shadow. Not finding your light can make you look like a novice.
- The further away or more upstage you are from the casting director, the more you look like a star. The closer you are makes you appear more human and fallible.
- LA casting director Mark Sikes says actors shouldn't "break the bubble" by getting closer than three feet to the casting director. If actors break the bubble, they can distract the casting director and take away from their audition.
- Another professional rule is: never touch the reader during the audition. It's considered violating the reader's personal space, and makes many casting directors very upset.

PROPS

Actors always ask whether or not they should use props in an audition. Less is more. The casting director wants to see you, not your props. What you would normally carry on your person can be appropriate to use in an audition but only if it is necessary for the scene. If the character is on the phone, then use a cell phone. Don't go crazy with props. If the character's smoking is not necessary for a scene, eliminate it. If it's important, use an unlit cigarette. If your character is smoking marijuana, you can twist a small piece of paper to simulate a joint. Keep in mind actors relying on multiple props are a real pet peeve of many casting directors. One important thing is to never use even a fake gun. It scares the hell out of everyone!

Preparation

If you've had a conversation with the casting director for a few minutes and lost some of your energy and concentration, don't be afraid to take a quick preparation. If you feel the casting director is uncomfortable with you taking a preparation, bring up the emotional triggers you prepared at home as you walk on stage or set to your mark. You can also stir up the feelings while pretending to quickly look the scene over. There's no point in being there if you can't do your best work. Casting directors don't want to see an actor go through a long series of acting exercises. However, if you have to go to the corner for a moment, go ahead. If your audition is effective, they'll get over it.

There's an actor that I train who purposefully does a brief fierce preparation for his auditions. He view is, "They don't know what they need. I know what they need. I like to get them excited. I want to give them what no one else does." It's right for him. It may not be right for you. Do what you're comfortable with.

Redirection

Many actors internally freak out when the casting director or director redirects them after their first reading of the material. Don't get discouraged. If they're taking the time to give you adjustments, it's not because you did something wrong—it's because you showed them something they liked, even if they disagreed with the choices you made. Or, they may have loved you, and are going to the next step of seeing if you can take direction. If you pick up on the director's adjustments and make the scene work, they're going to seriously consider you.

Redirection is not personal. Directors direct. That's what directors do. You've shown them something in your work that got them excited and now they want to add something to your work. It is the process.

Create chemistry with the director by working with them, not against them. You should think, "Aha, they're directing me! They must be interested." This is your goal.

LISTEN CAREFULLY TO DIRECTION

Focus and listen carefully to what the casting director or director says. When you are given a note, just do "the note." Don't discuss it or embellish it. Just do it. They want to see if you can make the adjustment. One casting director got angry when an actor, out of nervousness, ignored the redirection.

The casting director said, "You just wasted the time that I took out of my busy day to give you an adjustment, and you didn't even have the consideration to apply it. How do you think that makes me feel?" This was a real wake-up call for this actor. Actors will think, "Oh, you're redirecting me, you didn't like it," but the truth is they did like it and that's why you're being redirected. Otherwise they wouldn't bother. Actors who zone out when redirected often lose out because they're not paying attention.

COLD COPY—BE PREPARED FOR THE UNEXPECTED

What do you do when you walk into an audition for a role and the casting director says, "You know what? I want you to read for another character instead." Don't panic. It means "You're not right for this role, but I like your acting and you're more right for this other role." Again, it's a matter of being prepared for the unexpected. Don't be afraid to ask for time to go out in the hallway and prepare for a few minutes. What if the casting director tells you that's not possible? Don't try to look ahead, or understand what the scene is about—stay in the moment. Other actors may have had the sides for this role for a week and yes, you will be judged against these other actors. It's a shame, but the big advantage you do have is being in the moment. If you try to read ahead and figure out what the scene is about, you're not being present. In the moment, you may be able to bring a unique reaction that the director has never seen before. You can react truthfully because you're listening and reacting spontaneously.

When one of my actresses flew to LA, her agent had an audition waiting for her. She learned the sides in the car on the way from the airport to the audition. After she auditioned, the casting director said, "That's fantastic! You had it memorized and did a beautiful job, but you're more right for this other character. I'm so sorry." She handed the actress different sides. The actress had 15 minutes to work the scene. She came in, had it memorized and nailed it. The casting director then asked her to go to the screen test that day. At the screen test, the actress was told she was now going to be shooting a different scene. She took a few minutes with the new sides, came back in and aced the screen test. They offered her the role. She knew how to take charge of her process because she learned how to prepare, make choices and memorize quickly. She was a lead in a critically-acclaimed series for years, and recently was signed for the lead in a new series. When you can do work with cold copy with confidence, it makes you very castable.

FINISH YOUR AUDITION

After you complete your audition, give a genuine "thank you" and leave promptly. Don't hang around hoping to have a chat. Be organized, have your things where you can get them quickly and exit. Know that you are special and always leave them wanting more.

AFTER THE AUDITION

After the audition, the best thing you can do is forget about it. Move on to the next one. Tormenting yourself endlessly over auditions, what you did, or think you should have done, can destroy you. There are many factors as to why you are cast or not cast and some have absolutely nothing to do with the audition you gave. You may not be physically right for the role. The producer or director may want to go with a blonde and you're a brunette. You're too tall or too short. Or the role may already be cast, but they're just going through the required auditions. The list goes on and on and on. As one of my LA students says, "I leave it in the parking lot."

You never know how you are being perceived in an audition. Never assume you're not right for the role. I auditioned for a play where I was totally the wrong age for the role—everyone else there was ten years older than I was. The director wound up rewriting the part younger. I could have blown it if I didn't take being called in seriously.

"WHAT DOES THE DIRECTOR WANT?"

Don't worry about what the director wants. Show the director what you have to offer. When I conducted a seminar at the Screen Actors Guild for over 200 actors, I kept getting the same question over and over again—"How can I know what the director wants?" If you start by asking the director, "What do you want me to do?" First off, they have probably given the same direction to every other actor auditioning for your role. Make a choice, but make it for a reason. Base it on the scene's purpose, what it needs, and what you can bring to it. Don't be afraid to tactfully ask, "Can I show you what I worked on?" You may have come up with something they didn't think of, and they may change their idea to what you've done. Choose.

An actor I work with auditioned for an HBO movie for the role of a drug addict. The other characters were undercover FBI agents, and his character was trying to sell his daughter to them for sex, in order to get money for drugs. When we worked on the sides before his audition, we deduced that the daughter, who was 11, knew what he was doing. He added conflict to his character that this was the first time he was going to sell her for drugs. Because he loved her he was battling with his conscience, as she was fighting and struggling with him.

The casting director was impressed, but didn't expect that choice. The actor was redirected that his character was hardened and didn't care. He took the adjustment and did what was asked. Later, the casting director called the actor back and said "That choice that you made? We couldn't forget it." He got hired because it was a more explicit choice, a real choice and it made the scene more powerful. That choice also heightened the scene for the actors playing the FBI agents. It intensified everything. If you've made a choice for a reason, be brave enough to use it.

NUDITY AND EXPLICIT SEXUALITY

THE PRESSURE TO ADD NUDITY

Pressure for nudity and explicit sexuality happens to both male and female actors. Never do anything physical that you're uncomfortable with. An actress who came in to coach on an audition said, "I don't know what to do with this scene!" It was badly written and gratuitously sexual. She was so upset about the upcoming audition, she was crying as we were making choices. I finally said to her, "You can't do this. If you get this role, you're going to have a nervous breakdown." She finally called her agent who said, "Oh, yeah, you and 100 other people turned it down." One of the reasons she got the audition was her agent thought she might do it as a last resort. Don't do anything as a last resort!

PROTECT YOURSELF

Be aware of directors or casting directors who try to sneak nudity or explicit sex into an audition, especially where nudity is not in the breakdown. You are not required to be nude at an audition, even when the breakdown specifies nudity. According to union regulations, "body checks" (showing your body at an audition to the casting director and director) are only allowed in the final stages of callbacks. If it is a non-union project, choose what you will do or not do, but you choose. Sometimes at an audition, a director will say, "I really want you to do the part but we may have to add a love scene." (Red flag!) If you are uncomfortable with nudity, don't allow someone to pressure you to do it.

If you do agree to do any kind of nudity, have the type of nudity spelled out in detail in your contract. Make sure your agent protects you. If you don't have an agent, be smart and go to a lawyer. If you're going to do any form of nudity, you should always have an attorney look at your contract.

ALWAYS GET IT IN WRITING

You really don't know what is being shot. The director may say to you, "Oh, we're just going to show a suggestion of your breasts," but they're really shooting you from the waist up. You won't know that until the film comes out. Get the details in writing of what will be shot and what will be shown and for how many seconds, i.e. from the top of breasts upward, 3-second side view. Make sure your contract is clear, because if they shoot something else, the director will have the right to use that footage.

One actress was in an action adventure feature film. After editing, the only thing left of the actress's role was a love scene and a scene with her semi-naked and dead. The footage is now on the Internet and is promoted that you can see so-and-so naked. Be very cautious.

ACTING LIONS

Footage that has been shot could also end up on the Internet, even if the footage doesn't appear in the final cut of the film. And, remember, everyone on-set has a cell phone with a camera!

UNEASY? TRUST YOUR INSTINCTS

There are many organizations that are upfront and professional, but there are also individuals and groups that try to take advantage and exploit actors. If you feel uneasy about the motivation behind a casting or the ethics of a project, trust your instincts and do your homework. Some warning signs:

- When the breakdown description doesn't match the reality of the audition—when you get there and you're being asked to audition for an entirely different kind of project.
- When it's an organization that wants you to join and/or sign a document for them before your audition.
- When you arrive and the project has been canceled or put on hold, but you are asked to join their group.
- When the copy contains repetitive words that seem strange or out of place that you think could be a sign of some kind of mind-manipulation.

Make sure you use professional casting sites that screen projects before they put up the breakdowns. It takes little time to search the web to check the legitimacy of the job and the people involved. Do your homework, and if you arrive at an audition and feel suspicious about their motives, leave. Don't wait to find out your instincts were right.

15

FINDING AN AGENT OR MANAGER

FINDING REPRESENTATION

Agents. Managers. Casting Directors. Producers. Directors. What do they all have in common? All are vital components of the industry of "Show Business." Too often these relationships can become adversarial, especially if we don't fully appreciate the job everyone has.

The common denominator is that casting directors, agents, and managers need a client list of exceptional, well-trained, professional actors. If you want to work or have good representation, you want to become that exceptional, well-trained, professional that they all need.

Every year, thousands of new actors flock to NYC or LA hoping to get their big break. It can seem daunting, if not impossible, to break into the business. Remember every one of those successful actors taking those jobs was once a beginner, was once non-union, and was once as intimidated as you. They all made it. You can too. Look at the casting directors and agents. What do they need? They need the best you that you can be.

FINDING AN AGENT

Remember:
A casting director looks to cast actors in projects. An agent looks for actors who can have careers.

While I talk about agents in this chapter, much about what I say about agents applies to managers and the process of signing with an agent or manager can be very similar. The best way to figure out what an agent/manager wants from an actor is to step into their shoes and ask, "Who would I want to work with? What would I want to see?" Agents

241

want actors who are well-trained, know who they are, how they would be cast, and are ready to go work to make that agent money.

Agents do look at training, especially for actors with less experience. If you're a new actor or coming back to the business, training shows that you are serious about your craft and focused on having the staying power for a career.

Before looking for an agent, you should have enough film and theatre experience, so that you won't be thrown if the agent sends you out for auditions. If an agent sends out actors who melt down or flub in high-profile auditions, the agency develops a bad reputation with casting directors. If you're just starting out, you can get away with having less experience if you're young and beautiful. Even so, if you don't quickly prove you can get callbacks or cast, an agent will probably lose interest in you. At this point, the agent may insist that you get more training before continuing a working relationship.

RESEARCH FIRST

When you feel you are ready for an agent, how do you start? There are many ways to research agents:

- Talk to represented actors and see if their agents might be a fit for you. One of the best ways is to ask for a referral to their agent (to be explored later in this chapter). Recommendations from an actor, director, or casting director are the best way to meet an agent. You can also attend agent seminars.

- Google search the agencies. Look on websites like IMDbPro to find what types of actors are represented by an agent or agency, what level of work the agency's actors are cast in and how many actors an agent has on their roster. It is important to get a snapshot of the specialty of actors an agent and agency handle. For example, if you are just starting out, it is unlikely that an agent at ICM or CAA would work with you given the caliber of A-list actors these agencies represent.

- Many agents specialize in certain types of talent. There are agents who mainly represent "mob" types. They hope the casting director will call them directly for the next gangster movie before the breakdowns go out. There are agents whose specialty is musical performers or beautiful people. Agents also cultivate relationships with the casting directors, hoping to gain an edge.

- Look at the agent seminar listings online. Some of these companies allow actors to browse their listings for free, and often the description for the seminar will tell you exactly what type of actor the agent is looking for, such as musical theatre actors, actors in a certain age range and look, etc.

- Other tools are informative publications such as *Call Sheet* (formerly *Ross Reports*) and *Breakdown Services Agency Guide*, and various services that market mailing labels and the latest information on agents and casting directors. These are helpful with contact information and keeping track of who is at what agency. Agents move from one agency to another, so don't assume that if you read something one month that agent will be at the same office the next. *Call Sheet* is available online for a monthly subscription and is published every two months. *Breakdown Sources Agency Guide* is published twice a year. When doing a mailing, if you're not sure of the gender of an agent, Google them to find the answer. You can also politely call and ask the agency whether to address a submission to a Mr. or Ms.

- Research the SAG, Equity, and AFTRA's websites to find out whether or not an agent you're interested in is franchised. You don't have to go with a franchised agency, but agencies that follow the various union franchise guidelines have been reviewed and certified by that particular union. For instance, franchised agents only take a 10% commission and all agencies in major markets agree not to charge upfront fees to actors to be included on the agency's website. Many agencies follow SAG's guidelines.

- Find the agencies that you want to target and mail out to 10 or 20 agents at a time. Write a short, personalized cover letter expressing why you want to work with each agent. When mailing to large agencies, make sure you send separate headshots and resumes to each agent because they're all different. While one may toss out your headshot or represents a client who looks like you, another may be looking for exactly your type, even within the same agency.

- Agents do not want phone calls or drop-ins, generally not even from clients. Don't expect agents to respond to your letter for a couple of months, unless you are a type they currently have a need for. Many agents wait for lulls in the audition seasons to review mailings. Some agents just throw out unsolicited submissions. Others might be interested in you, but won't call you in until they see your headshot and resume cross their desk a couple of times.

NEVER PAY AN AGENT UPFRONT!

If an agent or manager wants money upfront for anything, you are in the wrong place. Run. Agents are only paid commissions when you book work. If an agent or manager wants money up front for pictures and expenses—that is a real warning sign. However, many times an agent will give you a list of recommended teachers and photographers at your interview— but these lists should always be suggestions and not requirements. When an agent insists you must go to a certain class or certain photographer, it can be because they're very passionate about that resource, but be aware that there are some who may be getting a kickback.

AGENT INTERVIEWS

PLAYING THE "ROLE" OF YOU

Just as when you interview with a casting director, you are playing a role when you interview with an agent—the role of yourself. You need to have that role well-prepared and polished. Typical questions agents ask are "Tell me something about yourself," "What's the last project you did?" or "Where are you from?" You want to give the agent a sense of how intelligent you are and what your energy is like. Work your answers to these questions using your video camera to practice getting comfortable with playing the role of yourself. Have a friend or acting partner interview you. Play it back. Refine it.

PRESENT YOURSELF AT YOUR BEST

Just as in an audition, how you come through the door is almost as important as your interview. When you walk into an agent's office, present yourself as a well-trained, clear, focused, professional actor, who knows exactly who they are. Walk in looking like a star. You must look exactly like your picture—your makeup and hair must be the same as your headshot. Dress your best, no matter what your type, and go in with complete confidence that you are unique. If you look sharp, your acting is terrific, and you've got the right training, agents will respond to you.

Know what you want from this interview. Convey to the agent that you're already getting your career going, but you would like the agent to help you get even more work. You are looking for someone to collaborate and build a career with. Agents no longer have time to develop actors. This has changed a great deal in the last 10 years or so. Many actors still hold that myth in their minds—"I'll get an agent and they'll make my career!" No, they won't. Only you can do that.

Always take 10 headshots and resumes, and copies of your reel when you meet with an agent. It is possible that if you and the agent click, the agent will want hard copies of your material immediately to send out to casting directors. Be prepared.

VARIOUS MARKETS AND SETTINGS

Agent interviews vary in different markets. In Los Angeles, agents will have you read copy, if they have you read anything at all. They may just want to look at your reel. In Chicago, you might just interview. In New York, you should always have two contemporary contrasting monologues ready to go. When you perform your monologues, adjust the performance level to the size of the space. If you are in a cubby hole, make your performance more intimate. If you are in a large open space, fill the room. However, the worst thing you can do is over-act within a space.

Unless directed to do so, general protocol is that you never look the agent in the eye when you are performing. It's hard for them to judge you and make notes if you're looking at them. Imagine the other character from your monologue is in the audience or a few feet away from you in the space. Place that character close enough to the agent so they can see your choices and what you're doing.

When an agent takes the time to review your reel, listen. Don't be defensive. A frank professional opinion is a valuable gift. It's better to have no reel than poor quality material or a shoddy reel that shows your flaws.

In some situations, you have to audition or interview in front of a group of other agents who are there to be intimidating on purpose. Just know that it is a possibility. Imagine they are all really on your side, just testing you. Think about and prepare ahead how you will gracefully handle this kind of situation.

Occasionally, agents will invite actors they are interested in to a single performance evening. They may ask you to perform monologues, songs, cold copy, or scenes. They may even hire an accompanist for musical theatre actors. Prepare for an "agent night" as you would for any audition or performance.

ASKING QUESTIONS

It's okay to ask the agent questions during your interview, as long as you're respectful. Ask the questions as if the agent is the expert. Approach it something like, "I know you know everything about being an agent, so how do you go about representing your people?" Combine that energy with indicating, "I'm already getting work, but I need a pro because then I'll get more work." If you have researched the agent, you can ask whether there are other actors of your type being represented. See how the agent sees you being cast, and if the agent "gets" you.

Take note of the agent's environment and their effectiveness within it. How many actors does the agency represent? Out of those, how many clients does each agent handle? If an agency has a lot of agents, their client list may be much bigger, but each agent may, individually, only handle 20 to 25 people.

You should also ask the agent how often you can call or meet with them. Some represented actors won't hear from their agent and don't know what to do. Ask if you could call, how frequently you could call, or should you stay in touch by email? Actors need to follow-up in some way, but agents need the time to do their job.

FREELANCING AND "HIP-POCKETING"

In New York, some agents won't sign you immediately but will offer to freelance. The agent will send you out on auditions to see how you do and how your relationship is working. Signing may come from freelancing, but many actors freelance with multiple agents for years and are happy with this arrangement.

In Los Angeles, this practice of trying out an actor is called "hip-pocketing" and works similarly to freelancing, but it is exclusive. That is, you only have a hip-pocket arrangement with one agent at a time, whereas in New York, you can freelance with multiple agents simultaneously. Keep in mind though that freelancing means they're not going to be as committed to you as they are to their signed clients.

You must be diligent if you freelance with more than one agent. Make sure that each agency calls and clears you before submitting you, or you may find that you are submitted by multiple agents for the same role. If you are cast, there may be problems sorting out who gets the agent commission. Usually, the first agent who submits you is the one who gets the credit for the actor, but it can be word-against-word to determine this. You don't want to get involved in a lawsuit over a commission and have two agents mad at you!

"Engagement" before "marriage"

If an agent wants to represent you and you're not sure they are right for you, ask for an engagement period. The old saying "any agent is better than no agent" is not true. Don't sign with anyone you don't feel confident about. Many actors feel desperate to work with an agent. If you're feeling something funny or uncomfortable about the agent's energy, your intuition is probably right. You don't have to have the first agent who wants you. It's like a marriage. Don't marry the wrong agent! Even if they're franchised with the unions, you should have an entertainment lawyer look at your contract before you sign. This step will save you a lot of time and headaches in the long run.

Once you have representation

You finally sign or are freelancing with an agent and you think, "Whew! Now I can start having the career I want!" But—now that you have representation you have to stay on top of your game for the opportunities that may arise.

Be proactive

Continue to dig for work on your own. Find out what's going on in the world of casting and production, even if you have an agent. Some agents say you are "the president of your own corporation," so act like one. Don't expect your agent to get you all of your work. Be organized, follow through, and find auditions in addition to those your agent lines up for you. Don't wait for the agent. There are a lot of ways to get into doors. Be aware that even if you find your own work, generally you still have to give your agent their commission.

Many resources exist that tell you what's in production—*Variety, The Hollywood Reporter, IMDbPro,* and *Backstage,* among others. Work in tandem with your agent on the kind of career you want and the types of roles that would be right for you. You want your agent to let you turn down projects that are not going to help build you as a professional.

Some agents play it too safe and are reluctant to send actors out on projects that are on the next level. Now that you've done a few day player or supporting roles, you may be ready to audition for guest star or secondary lead roles, and you have to convince your agent to submit you. Your agent may hesitate. But if you are ready and have the confidence, you can prove that you can get cast in these kinds of roles. It may take some persuading. Just be sure that you are right.

TOO MANY AUDITIONS

Don't allow your agent or manager to overbook you with auditions. If you are self-submitting, be selective. Submit only for projects you are right for. If you have an agent or manager, discuss with them exactly what kinds of roles to be submitted for and the maximum number of auditions per week you should do. It's better to go to fewer auditions fully prepared than a slew, just winging them with a hope and a prayer. The main point of this chapter is that you must be at the top of your game when you audition. Auditioning takes stamina, focus, and commitment.

COMMUNICATION IS ESSENTIAL

Communication issues often derail agent/actor relationships. If your relationship with your agent isn't working, diplomatically address that directly. If you have legitimate concerns, such as not being submitted for appropriate roles, take your agent out to lunch and tell them how you feel. Don't be angry or aggressive, but clearly state what the problem is and how you propose to solve it together. You may be able to work things out beneficially for both of you.

LEAVING AN AGENT

An agent can always release you from your contract. If neither of you is happy, it's time for another agent. When you leave an agent, don't burn bridges by getting nasty or aggressive. Be professional and courteous.

Think about what is best for you and your career. Try to look for another agent while still signed with your original agent. The fact that you are already represented is appealing to other agents looking at you. But never criticize an agent to another agent. If a new agent asks why you left your former agent, have a diplomatic answer prepared.

THE 90-DAY RULE

If the agent doesn't want to release you from your contract, take advantage of the 90-day rule. According to SAG guidelines, if your agent doesn't secure you at least 10 days work in a 90-day period, you can terminate the contract. For agents who offer their clients a "General Service Agreement" (which offers actors less protection than a SAG-franchised agreement), an actor can terminate the contract if he has not been offered one day's worth of employment within a period in excess of four months. Equity and AFTRA have similar guidelines for their franchised agents, so read the information available on their websites or call and ask. Bottom line, if an agent isn't helping you do your job—leave.

MANAGERS

An actor might need a manager if the actor is older, or is a particular type and needs to have contacts made with casting directors and agents. Usually you should only have a manager if you have a career to manage. A good manager can get you in to see agents and casting directors, and pitch you for projects. Managers also have smaller clientele and can help develop and promote an actor as a complete package. Legally in the states of New York and California, managers are not supposed to get you auditions without working with a licensed agent, but this still happens. If you are cast, a contract must be signed through an agent.

A good manager can help, but they're rare. An actor I work with who is starting to work in studio projects consistently researches all of the movies in pre-production and the roles he's interested in. He has his manager contact the director and say, "This wonderful actor wants to meet with you and is interested in this role." You have to look down the road before everyone else and working with a manager who is invested in your career can help open doors.

MANAGER COMMISSIONS

Managers will be paid commission above and beyond what you are paying an agent. Commission is paid 10% to the agent who got you the audition and 15-20% or more to the manager. That's 25-30% right off the top of your salary. Then you have taxes. So think about whether or not it's essential have a manager.

USE A LAWYER FOR ALL CONTRACTS!

It's imperative to have an entertainment attorney review a contract with a manager. Managers' contracts usually run three to five years, and can be difficult to get out of. Getting work often extends the contract longer. It is not uncommon for contracts to have a clause, stating the actor must give written notice of his intent not to renew 90 days prior to the expiration date of the contract. Since you probably won't remember that "minor" clause you initialed 5 years before, you are automatically now signed for 5 more years.

To understand all the terms and conditions set out in the contract, I recommend that you hire a good entertainment lawyer to go over it. A good contract for the actor will have reasonable "out" clauses. It will also have limitations on commissions after your relationship with the manager has ended. If the manager refuses to make reasonable changes to the contract, you should strongly consider walking away. You will be sorry if you sign a contract that binds you to an unfair relationship with that person. More than one actor has been sued by their manager and had to pay thousands of dollars to get out of a bad contract.

Remember, Choosing the right agent or manager makes the difference between having the career you want, or the career you wish you had. Don't be so anxious for representation, that you sign with an agent or manager just because they will represent you. Value yourself enough to actually choose who will be worthy of you.

16

YOU'RE HIRED! NOW WHAT?
HOW TO PREPARE & DO THE JOB

"I like to act with people that know what they're doing." —Ed Harris

GETTING THE MOST OUT OF YOUR REHEARSALS

TABLE READS

The first step in the rehearsal process is usually a table read. The director assembles the actors around a table or in a circle of chairs to read the script. Often it's the first time all the actors have read together. The director tells the cast, "Just read the words. Don't act. You've all been hired, so don't worry." Like a proud parent waiting with excitement, anticipation, and nerves, they are watching and filtering many thoughts and emotions. But what is the director really thinking?

THE DIRECTOR'S FIRST IMPRESSIONS

When a group of actors comes together for a first table read, certain things become apparent. Some actors will listen and respond to the other actors and allow real emotions to surface. The director might think "Great!" Then the director notices an actor who is not listening and appears uninvolved with the other actors, and thinks, "Hold it!" In fact, the director can have thoughts such as:

- That actress seems scared and unsure. I can't hear her.
- The romantic leads don't have any chemistry together, and the movie depends on it.
- She seems to be privately mocking him. Can I deal with her?
- That actor's style is different from everyone else's. Will this work?
- Alternatively, the director may be thinking, "This cast is terrific!"

251

During the table read, the director makes mental notes of any challenges that are immediately arising as well as what's working.

The director notes any weak links in the cast. Will it be worth their time to work with that actor? Some directors will consider immediately replacing the weak link. Once actors are further along in the rehearsal and have bonded, it becomes harder to replace a cast member. It can be bad for morale and disheartening, causing the other actors to wonder if they'll be next. So before the rehearsal process gets further along, the director may decide to quickly make a change.

BE PREPARED

Now that you have the job, and you want to keep it, it's important to understand what to bring to a table read. What can the actor do to be prepared for a table read that's supposedly an "exploration," when the director is calling for "no acting?"

"No acting" doesn't mean reading the words flat and lifeless. It doesn't mean reading in your zone, unaware, and unresponsive to other actors' impulses. You want to bring your best self to a table reading.

First, understand you were hired because you're you. You brought certain elements, choices and your own unique energy to your audition. Don't throw those choices away. This is your opportunity to work those choices in the moment with the other actors, in the intimate environment of a table reading.

After the table read for a feature film, one of my actors was the only one left standing from the original cast. Why? Because he took that read seriously, did his homework and was prepared, just as he would be for an audition or the actual shoot. Remember that the table read is like a call-back. Think of it as such and you'll be ready.

Do your homework before the read. Read the script as many times as you can. Explore the material very slowly at least once. Take the time to feel out the words and, as opposed to skimming, drop in and allow your sensory impulses to start resonating. Use your script analysis technique to take your understanding of the material to a deeper level. Research the play or screenplay. Layer your substitutions into the individual actors as their characters, but be open to receiving and responding to their impulses in the moment. Allow yourself to react. Don't hold back, but don't push past the fine line of what you are actually feeling as the character.

AFTER THE FIRST READ

After the table read, the director may share their concept of the piece with the cast and go over important points of the text. Some directors will have the cast read the script again. They then begin an initial script analysis, by exploring the beats and asking questions. There are some directors who will encourage an open discussion and exploration of the material. Other directors tell you what they are looking for without discussion. Either way, this initial session will give you a sense of how the director will lead. This lets you formulate a way of working with this individual. If you have done your homework, you will come to the table with a higher level of understanding of the material, especially if it's an open forum format and the director is receptive to your input. You're all searching together as a team, looking for pieces that will help the puzzle come together in the right way.

REHEARSING FOR THEATRE

BLOCKING

Blocking rehearsals can be a daunting step for actors. There are different techniques for blocking, so it's easy for an actor to become insecure. The director also has a lot at stake in transitioning rehearsals from the table read, to getting the script up on its feet. With the director as the captain of the ship, the liner is leaving port and going out on the open sea. The director must be competent and fully in charge, so the actors relax, trust, and let the director lead.

I believe the blocking rehearsal works in a deeper way when actors go through a longer process at the table. This doesn't mean just reading the material over and over, but having a progression of steps that lead the actor to a greater understanding of the material and their character. The director can work acting moments between characters, exploring and working scenes until the actors can't bear it and feel they must get up and move! They now have an understanding of what they are doing with the words, where they have to go, and why.

Come to the blocking rehearsal prepared. Look at the scenes that are to be blocked beforehand. As discussed previously, some blocking will be obvious and some will be chosen. Have a point of view. Ask yourself questions like, "Where do I need to be in relation to the other characters at the beginning of this scene?" If you diplomatically present your reason, the director may allow it. After all, if it is a better choice, it will make the director look better. The director may also want to start with your ideas and what you feel would work best for your character. Or they may give you certain places where you have to be and allow you to fill in other areas. Some director's work with improvisational techniques and interesting blocking can also be found this way.

As one director shared, "Never come in empty. You may have to change everything, but you're changing it off of something." If you're included in discussions about blocking, have ideas. Just remember, the director has the final decision.

CONTINUING REHEARSALS

After blocking, you will have scheduled rehearsals with other actors for particular scenes. At some point, the director will start to put the scenes together and have run-throughs of scenes or acts. Some directors have a run-through at the end of each week, while others every couple of days. It varies. You should be making new discoveries and find new moments with each rehearsal and run-through. Some directors get out of the way and let you run with the ball, if they see that your process is effective and moments are coming together.

When you first get off book, even though you know the material perfectly, don't be surprised if you have to call for lines. This is normal. The first time you do anything new, your nerves will throw you off a little. For instance, while trying something, such as layering in a style or a dialect, you may lose focus on some of the other character aspects you've been working on. That doesn't mean you've lost them. You can't do it all at once. Layer in one element at a time. Two steps forward, one step back. Don't get upset, that's what the rehearsal process is all about.

A director might take scenes apart and move away from the "normal" process to explore. This can be scary, especially if the director seems to be losing track of time. Actors have horror stories about the wonderful rehearsal process for the first act, that then turned into panic as time ran out and the second act was thrown together. It is what it is. You can't anticipate this and you rarely know what it will be. Your job is to remain flexible and make it work.

Rehearse at home or with a trusted coach to fill in the blanks. Don't try to take over or direct the director. Do not talk with the cast behind the director's back. Aside from hurting the director, it also compromises your integrity and can get you in real trouble.

A Broadway director I worked with invited me to see a run-through of his show. I was surprised that an actor in the show, whom I knew, seemed lost and unsure. When I mentioned this to the director, he shared with me that this actor had tried to direct the show. The actor told this director what the actor's wife thought the show needed. The director was so angry he said the actor could "sink or swim," and he never gave him another direction! I'm sure he didn't hide his feelings about this actor to other professionals in the NYC acting world. The show got great reviews, except for this particular actor who was never even mentioned. Bottom line: do your own job; never tell a director how to do their job!

"That was a strange production. There were moments of extreme tension on the set. Between the producers and actors, between the director and actors, between everybody. Just this personality stuff between different groups. Very strange. Let's stop talking about that one" —Morgan Freeman—on working on The Shawshank Redemption (1994)

Every job will have a challenge you aren't prepared for. This often happens because actors are thrown into a new environment that's fast-paced, loaded with high-stakes and fear. Every job is a war of some kind. Expect mayhem and make it work!

THINGS THAT MAY THROW YOU:

- The script's not ready, or worse, there's no script.

- The weather isn't cooperating. (When *Jaws* was filmed they dealt with terrible weather.)

- The director is new, or it's their first comedy, or they don't know how to communicate with actors.

- The actors don't get along, and people in the production are taking sides.

- The star of the movie gets injured, and you have to start filming your scenes right away!

- An actor or director or writer is unexpectedly fired.

  Jeff Bridges on his experience on the *Iron Man* set:

They had no script, man. They had an outline. We would show up for big scenes every day and we wouldn't know what we were going to say.

Bridges and Robert Downey Jr. would improvise their own roles, and then each other's, to find the dialogue.

You would think with a $200 million movie you'd have the shit together, but it was just the opposite...that was very irritating, and then I just made this adjustment. It happens in movies a lot where something's rubbing against your fur and it's not feeling right, but it's just the way it is. You can spend a lot of energy bitching about that or you can figure out how you're going to...play this hand you've been dealt...Oh, what we're doing here, we're making a $200 million student film. We're all just fuckin' around! We're playin'. Oh, great!' That took all the pressure off. 'Oh, just jam, man, just play.' And it turned out great!

Be prepared. It's going to happen. You don't want to look back on the project and see yourself on stage, or the big screen, with all the stress and turmoil clouding your performance.

Take a step back and breathe. Know that this situation has probably happened many times before in different productions. Don't jump into the crazy energy that might be going on. Be the consummate professional and calmly access what's taking place. Is there anything you can do, realistically, without muddying or making things worse?

I went to see an actress I worked with perform in an off Broadway play. The production was wonderful, and the cast terrific. When I went backstage to congratulate the actress and the rest of the ensemble of actors, they had an amazing story. The director quit and walked off the first week of production! Rather than let the show fold, they decided to team together and direct it themselves. They helped and inspired each other, got through it and even received wonderful reviews. By the way, the original director who quit was credited for directing the show. The actors didn't care; they had created artistic gold together.

REHEARSING WITH OTHER ACTORS

You learn to work with different types of performers and various acting styles through rehearsing with other actors. Usually you will rehearse under the guidance of a director. Certain boundaries need to be established in rehearsing with other actors. Here are some guidelines:

PROFESSIONAL BEHAVIOR IN REHEARSALS

Be on time. Rehearsal time is your call time. One of the marks of professionalism is being on time, ready to go. You need to be centered, relaxed, and focused, so being on time actually means arrive early. Do your homework. No excuses. Make time to do it. This is your profession. Be off book when you need to be. If you leave your homework to the last minute, something will always come up and get in the way.

Don't direct the other actor. It's unprofessional and "not cool." You may have more experience or know more than the other performer, but when you're working, keep your opinions to yourself. Respect the other actor's personality, feelings, and differences. Never tell an actor to do their work in a certain way so you can react off them. Don't give line readings. Your job is to do your job. That includes minding your own business.

Personalities can clash. This often happens when actors are scared, unsure, and working with heightened emotions. Don't take things said in the heat of rehearsal personally. If something upsets you, use those feelings to fuel your work. It will make your acting better.

Except for theatre, rehearsals are generally a luxury. Rehearsals are the only time you have to work in-depth with the other actors. That's why it's important to do your homework. When you are relaxed and prepared for rehearsal, you are more open and aware to what the other actors are bringing to the scene. This in-the-present approach allows you to discover special moments with the other actors. Then you can make adjustments and fine tune your script. You can adjust and change what's not working and layer in your new discoveries. Learn to love rehearsals!

REHEARSAL TOOLS

Every actress should have boots and a long skirt for working on period pieces. Every actor should have traditional shirts, ties and bow ties, a couple of hats and different jackets. You need just enough to give a feeling of the period.

Actors should own some props to rehearse with. Scout around for rehearsal costumes and props at garage sales, flea markets, thrift shops, Craigslist, eBay, and in "Great Aunt Mildred's" attic.

Research different periods of style. There are paper doll books of different eras to look at hairstyles clothes, shoes, and accessories. If you Google "1920's images," pictures will come up from that decade. Search YouTube and other video sites for film clips. Wearing a couple of costume pieces or a sassy wave in your hair can be just enough to help you find a connection to your character.

TECH REHEARSALS

"Tech rehearsals" are the part of the rehearsal process where all of the technical and visual aspects finally come together. Another name for this phase is "Hell Week." This is the time where the lighting, sound, set pieces, and transitions are worked and refined. Costumes and wigs are tried on and final choices made. For actors chomping at the bit to perform, it can be a challenge to wait while these technical issues are ironed out. However, your job is to let the technical people who have been waiting in the wings to finally have their turn on stage, to ensure that every element of the production is the best it can be.

COSTUMES

A good, hardworking costumer wants the actors to be happy, and they will often burn the midnight oil to accomplish that goal. Tech can be a very stressful time for the costumer because there are always last minute problems and adjustments. If you have a problem with the fit or need a minor alteration to one of your costumes, mention it privately at your fitting. Be diplomatic. If there is a larger problem, for instance, the costume doesn't look like what you feel the character should be wearing, discreetly speak with the director. The director should work it out for you.

Choose your battles. If you are bothering the costumer and hair and makeup for unimportant issues, the air will turn cold and nasty quickly. When wearing a costume during tech rehearsal, make sure you go through all your character's physical moves. This is the time to discover any problems and take care of them. You'll also want to work with all the necessary costume pieces you'll be handling, including gloves and hats. One of the purposes of a full tech with costumes is to make sure all the costume changes can be accomplished in the allotted time.

At a tech rehearsal for instance, you might find you need backstage assistance with props or a costume change to make an entrance for a scene in time.

HAIR AND MAKEUP

On a professional set, you will usually have a hair and makeup artist. For theatre, you may have the design created for you during tech week. If you will be doing your own makeup during the run of the show, be sure to recreate the design with the professional makeup artist, or hair and wig person, so you will have no difficulties when they're not around.

If you are working on a production without hair and makeup artists, research the styles appropriate for your character. Once you have the hairstyle you need, work with a professional stylist to create the look and learn how to do it yourself. The same applies for makeup. Use the staff at department store counters and beauty product stores to help you create your look. Established theatre companies can be a good resource for finding professionals to create specific looks for hair and makeup. Use your video camera to record the hair and makeup session. Replay it as you reconstruct your look.

LIGHTING

A lighting tech will often be run "cue-to-cue," which means moving from one lighting cue to the next lighting cue. You may be right in the middle of your monologue and acting your heart out when the director says, "Okay let's stop here and go on to where the blue lights come up on the last line of your monologue." Don't resist. Just stop and move on. They'll be grateful for your full cooperation.

Cue-to-cue is frustrating to actors who just want to rehearse their scenes to be ready for previews. One of the worst things you can do is to try to perform during tech week. You will exhaust yourself. Rehearsals can run 10 to 12 hours. You will need to conserve every bit of energy you can. If you have to act, find moments to go over your work with your fellow actors in the dressing room on your "down time." Be patient and present even if it's 2am. Don't just stand around—anticipate what the technical crew might need. They will appreciate it! Tech rehearsals are where you need tolerance, endurance, and especially, humor. Tech rehearsals separate the divas from the professionals.

DRESS REHEARSAL

A dress rehearsal is a full performance of the show, with costumes, props, lighting and sets. There may or may not be an audience. If there is an audience, the attendees are invited, non-paying, and often supportive. The dress rehearsal is the actor's chance to give a full-out performance in costume and to get comfortable running the entire show on the set, with props, hair and makeup, etc.

PREVIEWS, NOTES, AND PICKING UP CUES

Previews are essentially dress rehearsals with an invited or paid audience. The show is a work in progress, and changes can still be made. From an acting point of view, the purpose of previews is to hit your stride and get the performance into your bones. Previews help you work off the audience, figure out your timing, and pinpoint where laughs will occur. For the writer and director, previews are also the time to make last minute changes, based on the audience response to given scenes. This can mean cuts, rewrites, new scenes, or all of the above. Be ready for anything!

It's a difficult situation when a scene is completely rewritten. It may take several days to learn the new lines. In this case, you may be performing one version of the scene at night while rehearsing the new version during the day. Just keep your eye on the ball, do your best and get through it. You can do it!

PERFORMANCES

The only way to endure the rigors of a run of a play is to make sure that you are in top physical, mental, and spiritual shape. You could be performing six days a week with multiple performances a day.
The obvious:
- Be sure to go to the gym often
- Eat healthy
- Meditate
- Get enough sleep
- Don't overdo the partying

KEEPING IT FRESH

Be open to the subtle changes in the moment that occur with the other actors in each performance.

- Embrace understudies, whose fresh and new energy can to shake up things and open you to finding new discoveries.
- Be aware of that the energy of each performance and the interchange with the live audience that varies every night.
- Occasionally re-read your script to continue finding new discoveries.

REHEARSING FOR FILM

There are a series of steps that occur with regularity in filmmaking: the table read, blocking, lighting, dress rehearsal, adjustments, shooting. How individual directors handle these steps varies.

REHEARSALS PRIOR TO THE SHOOT

Some directors like Clint Eastwood or the late Sidney Lumet would have rehearsals before filming. A director uses this process so they can explore the script in chronological order. Since the movie will probably be shot out of sequence, the rehearsals give the director and the actors a greater sense of the whole storyline of the script. In rehearsing the screenplay, the actors can feel the arc of the film. They can also understand the emotions the characters are feeling in a deeper way, so that when they are on-set, they have that base of understanding to call upon.

This is particularly important in movies dealing with strong emotions or centering on relationships between the major characters, such as *Saving Private Ryan*, *The Big Chill*, and *Crash*. Connections between the various characters need to be detailed, in the moment, and honest. Think about five of your closest friends. How different are you in your interactions in each of those relationships? In film, the audience must be able to notice those subtle differences immediately. The relationships must come from the heart and gut.

ON-SET REHEARSING

If there are no pre-shoot rehearsals, some directors will rehearse the leads the night before shooting the scene. Even more likely, they will rehearse right before the setup of the shot. As scenes are shot out of order:

- You must know exactly where you are in your character's emotional arc.
- You need to be aware of what your character knows and doesn't know at this point in the script.
- Where did your character emotionally end in the scene immediately preceding the current scene?
- What note will you end the current scene on, that will carry you into the following scene?

(Review the character roadmap chart to track your emotional arc in Chapter 6 for precise guidelines on how to do this.)

PREPARATION IS KEY

The more preparation you do on your own, the more productive your limited on-set rehearsal will be. The night prior, set some preliminary blocking. The director might even ask you on-set if you have blocking ideas in mind. Rehearse how you are going to handle your props and what your timing will be within the structure of the script. If time allows, work this out with your own video camera as discussed previously.

NO REHEARSALS

Many movies have no rehearsal at all—even for major roles. If you're coming in as a Day Player or for one or two days on the shoot, be prepared to have no rehearsal time. Do your homework.

REVISING DIALOGUE WITH IMPROVISATION

On some projects, improvisation is done on-set in rehearsal. Some directors will have the actors improvise to find real spontaneous moments, especially if a scene isn't working. As the actors improvise the scenes, the writers are present and make changes on the spot, setting the new dialogue in the script. The newly scripted scenes are printed and handed immediately to the actors to film. This frightens actors who are suddenly filming a scene that may have changed radically. Stay focused and breathe. Yes, you will be thinking about the new lines in your head, but don't worry, the audience will see you having interesting thoughts; it will look fine. Be aware that the new dialogue and blocking must stay the same through the takes for editing and continuity purposes.

A TYPICAL FILM SHOOT

After blocking, the lighting is set. Unless it's a low budget film, stand-ins will take the place of the actors during this phase. After the lights are set, the actors are called back for a technical rehearsal. This rehearsal usually stops and starts or runs cue-to-cue. A full dress rehearsal follows. The director gives final adjustments to the actors. The director of photography makes final adjustments to the lighting. Then the scene is shot. Depending on time, budget, and director's preference, there may be just a few takes, or there may be many.

Recently, an actress worked as a main character on a film where there was no table read. The actors all met on the first day of shooting. To combat nerves, the director had the actors improvise moments from the film to loosen them up. This actress pointed out that in film, as opposed to television, there is more time to work your character. Directors usually shoot many takes. There is also time to develop your character choices with the other actors or to work on your scenes in your trailer between camera set-ups.

REHEARSING FOR TELEVISION

NIGHTTIME DRAMA

In nighttime television drama, most rehearsals are done on-set, and it is fast, fast, fast. You must do your homework before a shoot, especially since you may be handed rewrites. Know your choices, your substitutions, and your lines. Bring in a fully fleshed out character. Don't leave it to chance. If you work consistently this way, directors will request you for roles. They will want you on set, because you make their job easier.

BLOCKING FOR TELEVISION

Your blocking rehearsal is your primary rehearsal. This rehearsal is done on-set with the crew watching. You must learn to handle this pressure quickly. You are expected to learn your blocking on the spot. And, above all, hit your mark every time.

A DAY ON-SET

A day on the set can vary depending on whether the scenes to be shot that day are interior or exterior, on location or in the studio, in daylight or nighttime. The day will typically be around 12 hours depending on the number of scenes and set-ups (camera shots) filmed that day. One of my actors working on a drama filmed in New York describes the process, which might go something like this: A typical scene may require three to five camera set-ups. For each new scene repeat steps 2-6. For each new camera set-up repeat steps 4-6

1. The actor reports to hair and makeup around 6:30 am. Costuming has been done ahead of time—the actor has already reported for their fittings on previous days.

2. The actors, which may only include the series regulars, do a read-through and focus on working off each other. (Many shows don't have a read-through).

3. Next, the actor is called to the set for blocking rehearsal. The director and the DP block the scene and set the camera shots. The lighting, sound, hair and makeup crews observe to see what special requirements there are for the scene.

4. The actors are sent back to their dressing rooms to wait. The second team (stand-ins) replace the actors while the lighting is set and the camera shots are fine-tuned.

5. Toward the end of this process, this particular actor goes to the "video village" (the group of monitors for playback). The actor watches the stand-ins move through the final camera shots to see how the scene will look—making notes of any blocking changes, and creating choices to motivate the movements when they are called on-set.

6. After the lighting is completed, the actors are called to the set for dress rehearsal. Hair and makeup perform "last looks" and the scene is shot.

This actor stressed that you must know your blocking! Develop a good sense of peripheral vision and spatial relationships so you know exactly where you are in relation to the camera and the other actors. There is a lot of pressure to know your marks. You are expected to be able to hit your mark every time; otherwise your eye line may not match shot-to-shot causing a huge continuity problem.

CHALLENGES

Some dramas shoot with two cameras. Perhaps one camera films a medium shot and another films a close-up. As both cameras are filming at once, it's essential that you hit your mark exactly so that both camera shots are aligned.

The actress also worked on a drama where "guerilla" filming was utilized and explained that as you're running, the handheld camera is running with you. On this show, the actors have "the luxury" of rehearsing with the director for about 10 to 15 minutes. This actress prepared the night before by going through her structure, script analysis, finding the "emotional blend," working her substitutions. Her work paid off. She had fifteen takes filming an emotional crying scene, and the director told her she did it so well that even her "tears had continuity."

Filming on location often involves long waits in the trailer, which you can use to work on your character choices. Four to five takes can be filmed on each camera angle in every scene, also with two cameras filming simultaneously. Again, you must know your technical aspects and bring in a prepared character before you step on-set.

THE DAY PLAYER EXPERIENCE

As a Day Player or recurring character, an actor will have only one or two takes to get the scene down. An actress was cast on a popular nighttime drama, where the set was extremely well organized. The director worked more with the series regulars, who had three to four takes. On this show, the director blocks and rehearses on-set. The second team of stand-ins arrive for lighting while the principals depart for hair and makeup. Then the actors come back to shoot the scene. The director may rehearse the actors again for smoothness. Then it's last looks and the scene is shot.

A TYPICAL TV DRAMA SHOOT

An actor can shoot for 12 to 15 hours a day on a drama. That takes stamina. For most television drama you go to hair and makeup, perhaps run-through the script with the other actors, mark the blocking and rehearse, leave for hair and makeup while the scene is lit, and come back and shoot, many times with two cameras. The more you are prepared and ready to go, the easier it will be.

SOAP OPERA

Soap opera filming has drastically changed in the past few years. It used to be that you would have ample rehearsal time before shooting. Just like everything else, soap opera has sped up tremendously.

A DAY ON A SOAP

On a soap opera set, the process goes like this for someone with a morning shoot schedule:

- The actor will call the studio prior to the shoot to check for call times and to see if there are rewrites.
- The actor then reports in before call time, picking up any rewrites. There could be last minute rewrites on-set.
- The actor knows their lines "cold" and has made all of their choices. The first couple of scenes might be dry-blocked in the green room, and then the actors are sent to hair and makeup.
- The actors then report to the set and run through the blocking while the cameras rehearse their shots. Dress/camera blocking rehearsal is where you should typically look for your shots.

There are usually visible monitors on-set so you can check that you're squared to your camera and not blocking other actors. There are last looks for hair and makeup and then the scene is shot. Re-shooting generally only happens for technical problems, or to re-shoot the climax of a high emotional scene. This process varies, so this is a general idea.

Depending on the director, there can be anything from having no dry blocking to working with the director more extensively. You may end up dry blocking as the cameras are moved from one set to another. If you are scheduled for an afternoon shoot, you may have time to rehearse your scenes in the morning, while the morning group is working on the set. This actor said to definitely bring your lunch—there's no time to go to the commissary! The work is fast, fast, fast. The advantage is more personal time for the actor, but the actor has to prepare more on their own.

Soap operas usually block and shoot set-by-set in order of the script. For instance, all the diner scenes are shot at the same time, before moving on to shoot the living room scenes. Some shows used to shoot the script in order, but it's much faster to shoot set-by-set.

DIPS

"Dips" are particular to soap operas. A "dip" is where the film is continuously running in the cameras while the actors pause in the scene. Usually a dip is done so that an actor can take time to bring up emotion needed for the scene.

SITCOM

Traditional sitcoms operate in a five-day process. This offers the actor more time to develop their character.

There is a table read on the first day with the series regulars and guest stars. The director blocks and works the scenes for the next three days; also finding the timing and rhythms that are key in comedy. The actors may have to cope with rewrites every day, including on filming day.

The sitcom is filmed on the fifth day, generally in front of a live audience. You are expected to learn any script changes on the spot. Working in front of a live audience can be daunting, but there is also a feeling of theatre in the performance. You may have to do take after take, but the energy of the audience can fuel your work and make filming the sitcom a fun experience.

TURNING DIRECTORS' TERMS INTO ACTORS' TERMS

Generally the director hires the actor, so it concerns me when actors come for coaching and say things like, "I don't like what the director is doing and I'm going to do my own thing. I'm going to ignore the director." Your job is to make the director's vision come alive, not to change the director's concept.

"I'm more prone to go with them (the director) than my own (concept)… otherwise it's going to become predictably my work." —Jack Nicholson, in the documentary about making *The Shining."*

I team with the actor to try to find out how the actor has been directed, and feel out what the director's vision is for the scene. If the actor's not sure, I'll ask, "What has the director been saying to you and what do you think they are going for?" Sometimes it's just a matter of deciphering the director's language.

"CAN YOU MAKE THIS FUNNIER?"

In comedy, all your internal lights have to be on, like a Christmas tree. Even if you're an enigmatic character, you have to have a twinkle inside. Stephen Colbert is a great example. He's so droll, but he always has that inner sparkle. George Clooney is another example. It's an important part of the actor's work to turn on those lights, especially for comedy. Christmas tree lights twinkling all over the place!

So if a director asks you for "funnier" the solution can often be found in the style and a lighter, brighter energy. Try going back to the drawing board with your Core and Driving Question. If a comedic character's Core is truth and it's not working, perhaps you should change your Core to security. Or freedom. See what changing the Core does to your character.

In a drama, you can have a light scene, but eventually you're going to go to a darker, more intense energy. In comedy, it can be tragic, but it has a different quality of energy. In the Coen brothers' film *Fargo,* kidnappers chase the pregnant wife, who is wrapped in a shower curtain, and then falls down the stairs. Because it's black comedy, it's funny. However, a realistic drama about a pregnant woman falling down a flight of stairs would receive a very different reaction. There really is an energy difference between comedy and drama.

"NO, NO, YOU'RE NOT DOING WHAT I WANT!"

What can you do when a director says, "No, no, you're not doing what I want," but they can't communicate what they do want? It's easy to get frustrated— some directors simply don't know what they want! So if they don't know, you choose. Always think of other possible ideas for your character as part of your homework. Pick another Core. Pick another rhythm. Play with different actions and tactics. Show the director a different choice, and see what happens. Observe the director as they work with others. Get a sense of what they want without having to ask them questions. If the director is extremely vague and you're not getting anywhere with them, contact a good coach who can give you a fresh perspective.

"FASTER!" OR *"PICK UP THE PACE!"*

I watched an actor I'd coached on a complex on camera scene drop all the choices we had worked on during filming. When he came off set I asked him, "What happened?" He said, "The director wanted it faster." `

When a director says "faster," don't think about making it physically faster. Instead of speeding up your movements and dialogue, try picking up the impulses and cues. That's the difference. If you're waiting to react, react as you're saying the line and as lines are being said to you—on the line instead of after the line.

Another essential tool to speed up your reactions and cues is to remove all the punctuation in the script. I see actors perform material pausing for every comma and period. Take that all out. Let your impulses to pause arise naturally. We don't speak in clear punctuated sentences in real life, so don't pause for every comma and period on the page.

You can also add an adjustment, such as: you will miss your train, or your daughter's ballet recital, or you have an assignment due for work shortly.

"I REALLY LIKE WHAT YOU'RE DOING."
"I'M NOT WORRIED ABOUT YOU."

Be happy if this is the only note you get! What a director is saying is, "I have to worry about other actors who are the weak links." Due to pressure and time constraints, when you're talented and dependable, you may not get much feedback or direction. In addition to working with the actors, the director is responsible for many other aspects of the production. They must be concerned with setting up the shot, working with lighting, or focusing on another actor who is having trouble.

When your work is exceptional, it can be exasperating to get little attention from the director. It's also the biggest compliment in the world. When you feel you're not getting enough notes or direction, work with a coach to help you work more deeply on the character.

"I NEED MORE/LESS INTENSITY HERE!"
"I NEED YOU TO SHOW MORE LOVE, MORE ANGER, ETC."

Beef up your emotional response before the scene by using improvisation and substitutions. If the director wants you to show more love, for example, but your line is "I hate you," improvise saying "I'm crazy about you!" or "I adore you!" in your own words substituting someone you love from your real life. Then say the line "I hate you" while thinking, "I adore you!" under the line.

"TRY SOMETHING DIFFERENT."

Be prepared in case the director asks you for another choice. Before going to rehearsals or filming, think ahead. Always have other ideas up your sleeve so that you aren't stuck trying to come up with a choice right on the spot.

An actress filming a feature film was receiving new rewrites from the director every day, when she would arrive on set. The night before her next day's scenes, she would rehearse all the different emotional choices that she could think of. It wasn't an ideal situation, but at least she had rehearsed all the possible feelings for her character. On-set the next day, she was able to connect with one of her fully rehearsed choices on the spot when she was handed a new rewrite.

WHAT TO DO IF YOU'RE OFF-TRACK AND THE DIRECTOR CAN'T HELP

Do not wait to get help if you are into the rehearsal process and feel you don't have a handle on your character. Sometimes when you are intently working on a role, you do not have the perspective to step outside of yourself and know if you're going in the right direction. The director may be stressed, busy, or may not know why a scene is not working and how to communicate. Don't take a chance on being replaced. This is the time to connect with someone whose artistic wisdom and instincts you trust.

You want to have relationships with reliable experts before you start working on an important job. That way, if you run into a wall or the director isn't getting what they need from you; contact that person and say, "help!" It might take only one adjustment for all the pieces to fall into place. Or perhaps you're on the right track, but need that trusted person to reassure you.

Develop relationships with an expert before working. Avoid meeting a coach for the first time while you're on the job. Since they have never met you before, that coach will be trying to figure you out as a person at the same time they are trying to help you with your character. Sometimes another actor can be an eye for you, but in general, try to go to a pro.

Being a Working Actor

Professionalism vs. Ego

If you want to work consistently, leave your ego at the door.

The more you work in the business, the more important the people you work with, the more chance ego has to rear its ugly head. An actress described the difference between two stars she worked with on a feature film. Both are considered great actors. One comes in, stirs everything up, making everybody crazy on-set, and even hurts the project. The other comes in, keeps her head down, and just does her work. That's being a professional vs. being a huge ego.

You can't just claim to be an artist and say, "I work in an artist's way." You have to understand how to translate your craft into being a working artist. Learn to keep your artistry within the reality of using it in the real world, knowing what you can and can't change.

STAY TRUE TO YOURSELF

Stay grounded. Surround yourself with people who are healthy and down-to-earth, a group of people you trust. It's hard to always get a straight answer from people in this business. A leading actress was starring in a pilot and frustrated because she didn't feel she getting truthful feedback from anyone. Her inner voice was telling her it wasn't working. Everyone from the director to the crew told her, "Oh you're wonderful! It's great! It's going to be such a hit!" Her instincts were right and the pilot was never picked up. Trust your instincts.

LA vs. NYC

A person going to the opposite coast can feel like a fish out of water. The environments of the business are vastly different. LA and NYC have contrasting energies and ways of doing business. In LA, you have to drive everywhere and distances can be far. The sheer numbers of actors competing for roles far outstrips NYC, and the focus is often more on the "young and beautiful" actor. However, because there are so many actors to choose from, casting directors and agents are more open to finding the next new "it" actor.

In NYC, you have to be prepared to work within a much smaller pool of people, all who have heard of or know each other. It can be competitive and can make you crazy. Also, because it's a smaller group of actors, those who are known to casting directors and agents are called in repeatedly, leaving a new or returning actor at a disadvantage

BE THE EXAMPLE TO FOLLOW ON-SET:

An actress filming a movie had a leading man who was difficult, but because she knew her craft, she tactfully did what she needed to do. Everyone else followed her lead. His lack of professionalism didn't bother her at all. In his insecurity he was trying to take over, but he had no concept of what he was doing. Soon the director was working exclusively with the actress on what was needed in their scenes. This is an example of an insecure actor trying to muddy things on the set. The actress knew she had to come in, do her job and not get involved with the off-screen drama. This made the project work. Her work ethic also made her more attractive to the director and producers.

"Failure and its accompanying misery is for the artist his most vital source of creative energy." —Montgomery Clift

"YOU'RE NOBODY IN THIS BUSINESS UNTIL YOU'VE BEEN FIRED"

Great actors have all been fired from some kind of acting work during their careers. One day, you may be fired from an acting job. It's a tough lesson, but an important one—if you learn from it! If you know the reason and it's a weakness in your technique or training– don't wait. Fix it! Go to a coach or class and take care of it right away. You don't want it to repeat itself again. If it was a clash of personalities, or there doesn't seem to be a logical reason– you just can't figure it out, just go on like some of following wonderful actors:

Actors Burt Reynolds and Clint Eastwood were fired after co-starring in the television series, *Riverboat*. Burt recalled, *"They said I had no talent and Clint's Adam's apple was too big."*

Meanwhile, actor Billy Crudup said that getting fired from a job at the beginning of his career was what ultimately changed his career:

> It was my first big job. I went and worked on it for two days, and I got a call from the casting director saying that I was fired. The Daily Transom wondered why? I think I sucked, that was the main problem, replied Crudup. But a week later I got the call for Tom Stoppard's Arcadia at Lincoln Center, which changed my career for sure. It was a devastating and exhilarating couple of weeks.

OWNING YOUR WORK & SENDING IT OUT INTO THE WORLD

WRITE IT!

Writing is part of the process of owning your work. When you write, even if it's just for yourself, you start to understand what comprises good writing. You begin to comprehend your acting process better, because it's coming off of the structural writing process. You will have insights into your acting practice inspired, in part, by your own writing.

When you work on creations, they're part of you. They can often be used later in your work, like a character you create for yourself, or a one-man show. Many famous characters or well-known one-person shows came about because an actor wondered, "If I could play any role, what would I want that to be?"

I ask my students to write the beginning scene for their own one-person shows. At first, they're terrified. However, as they see other actors bringing material in, they get inspired and bravely start. As the actors continue on this journey, their writing begins to have meaning. They start to realize their worth. They aren't dependent on a script. They aren't dependent on an agent or a manager. They have the power within themselves. The energy of the actors starts to change. Their unique personalities come out in their work as they accept who they are—creators. They have tapped into the pure gold that comes from within themselves.

PRODUCE IT!

Take charge of your projects. Send your work into the world. One actress created a monologue about her life and filmed it in the restaurant where she worked. It was so well-received that she created more scenes, all taking place in her little restaurant, and finally produced it as a play. As she discovered this talent, her energy began to change. When she started writing all of these pieces, she stopped worrying about everyone else. She just started doing her thing and realized it had worth. When she met a manager, she wasn't worried about what the manager wanted to hear. She knew what she was about and what was special about her. Now three of her plays have been produced and she's continuing to write.

Another actor works as a moving man during the day. He wrote a play that he loved, and said, "You know what? I'm going to produce it." So he and his wife wrote the grants, got the funding, and got the show up. Both he and the show were wonderful! He's taking responsibility for bringing himself forward in his own artistry.

CHOOSING PROJECTS

WHAT IS RIGHT FOR YOUR CAREER?

Successful actors don't just fall into their careers. They make carefully considered choices that shape where they want their careers to go. Russell Crowe talked about waiting a year after filming *The Quick and the Dead*. It was painful to turn down projects, but he did so because he didn't want to diminish his mission of finding a worthy and inspiring artistic project. Then he was offered *L.A. Confidential*.

Initially you have to get work, but there comes a point when you have to take charge of shaping your future. An actor who'd played a supporting lead in a feature film was offered a frat boy comedy. He hadn't worked in a while and wanted to accept the role. His manager felt his client's career was a step ahead of this kind of work. The manager wanted the actor to wait for roles that would advance his career. The actor passed on the project and sure enough, a better role came along.

Knowing when to accept a project is important. Here are the three criteria I used to guide me:

- Great director
- Great material
- Great cast

Two out of three and I would take the role. Be selective. Don't take just anything, and don't let your agent and/or manager pressure you to take projects you know you don't want.

LEAVING A PRODUCTION

If it's a non-union production and you see the project's not coming together, the other actors are not up to par, or the script is really badly written, get out. If not, you'll be miserable and your work will suffer. It's not fair to everybody else in the production. An actress used to have "relatives" that got sick if she needed to leave a show. Don't be a martyr. If you decide to leave a production, it's important that you notify the director. Don't just disappear! Be professional and give notice immediately, so you can be replaced promptly.

You can't quit a union production. You are working under a contract and are expected to honor the terms of the contract. Be a professional and make it work. You never know who might be in that audience.

A friend and seasoned Broadway actress, Virginia Sandifur, shared with me that:

> Sometimes you just need to acknowledge that you need the money and have to take a job. Also, sometimes it works in your favor. I once did a terrible off-Broadway show, but Frank Rich showed up from the NY Times. He hated the show, but he singled me out, and gave me a rave review. In fact, half of the review was about me. That led to me being hired on another Broadway show. So you never know.

THE ONGOING CHALLENGE OF ARTISTRY

As they become successful, some actors start to let go of their skills. They work hard to master their craft, but when they start being cast in projects and have more auditions, they stop working on what got them the work in the first place. This is the pet peeve that I mentioned in Chapter 1. Mastering auditions is not being an artist. You may become really good at auditioning, but once they give you the role, what are you going to do?

BEING IN CHARACTER 24/7

Some actors choose to be a character 24/7 for months on end. They will walk around in a role for however it takes to feel like the character. I went to see a production of a well-known play with a great star as the mother character. At an awards ceremony, when she went up to get her statuette, she was still in character. She was even wearing a gown that her character would have worn. It was bizarre.

Few people can organize their lives, relationships, and finances to make those kinds of choices. Just because you work hard doesn't make you better or smarter than the next actor. Expertise and consistency are about knowing "how" to go there.

BE IN CONTROL OF THE UNCONTROLLABLE

Part of the professionalism of acting is learning to manage your inner world so you can use it and consistently apply it to your craft. Stay healthy with it. Be in control of the uncontrollable. You wouldn't ask somebody who just lost a close family member to relive that over and over, yet actors do that to themselves. They'll go for that event they haven't worked through and get lost in it.

DOING YOUR OWN THING

A young actor had to put a monologue on tape for a sitcom audition, and his performance was all over the place. I recommended setting choices. "I never set choices," he said. I asked, "Do you watch Jon Stewart or Stephen Colbert?" "I love them!" he said. I told him, "They are so clear and effortless because at some point they set their dialogue and choices. That's how you want to be." Unfortunately, this actor wanted to do his thing instead. He couldn't take any suggestions or direction. Do that at an audition and you definitely won't get the job. Do that on-set and you could be fired.

HOW TO DEAL WITH ABUSE AND PREJUDICE

CONTACT THE UNION

I coached an actress who was performing with a professional company. The director stepped over the line and physically abused her by directing the other actors to kick this actress in scenes of the play. She wound up in the hospital. I counseled her to leave the production and contact the police and the union immediately. If you're in an abusive situation, protect yourself.

DON'T BE AFRAID TO REPORT ABUSE, PREJUDICE OR DISCRIMINATION

Without the resources of a union behind you, it can be a challenge for non-union actors to know just who to turn to when they encounter abuse, prejudice, or discrimination. So what should you do? First, if you are physically abused, report it to the police. This is very serious. You're not going to work with this person again anyway, so don't be afraid to protect yourself by filing a police report. With prejudice, ageism, sexism, etc. contact the American Civil Liberties Union or your State Attorney General's Office. They will be able to inform you of your rights and let you know your options to protect yourself. Every human being deserves respect. No job is worth being abused.

WHAT TO DO IN CASES OF SEXUAL HARASSMENT

It's tough to know how to deal with directors, producers, or other show business professionals who make sexual advances toward actors, male or female. They can threaten not to hire you or fire you if you don't get involved with them. Be as diplomatic as possible, and give all the clues that you don't want to be involved. Put your foot down in a nice way. One actor believes if you use humor and tact, you can handle almost any situation. A director wanted an actress to go to a nightclub with him and she said, "Oh, my husband and I would love it!" He said, "Oh…let me get back to you." If the director doesn't take a hint, leave the project. This is where the excuse of a "sick" relative can come into play.

No role is worth sleeping with a director, producer, or casting director. An actress rebuffed an important producer, who began to stalk her. When he finally stopped, she was dropped from the movie. She said, "What this has taught me is to work on being the best actor I can be. I'm going to do this business my way, and that's a better way."

EMPOWER YOURSELF

Handle the situations you encounter in a way that makes sense to you. This is your life. You decide what to do. Don't give your power to someone else.

STAYING SANE IN AN INSANE BUSINESS

Understand these points:

- This business is cyclical! Good times are followed by bad times are followed by good times, etc. This applies to every actor, including stars.

- This business is filled with negativity. Don't listen to insecure, pessimistic actors. All this will do is destroy your confidence and take your energy and focus off the ball. "Those who say you can't do it should stay out of the way of those who are doing it."

- Develop interests and hobbies that are outside the entertainment business. So in those times when your acting goals are not where you want, you have a life and a greater perspective on that life.

- Be a part of a supportive system. There will always be those telling you you're not good enough. Get support from people you trust. Work with a coach or be in a class where you are always moving forward in your artistry.

- Unprofessional and nasty people are not your problem. If you are working with a director or actor who is personally putting you through hell because of their own insecurity or craziness, remember this— it's the other person's problem. Don't get involved. Do your best work and don't let it get you down. Sometimes you will be on the short end of the stick, but other times your integrity and professionalism will really be appreciated and lead to something wonderful.

- Have a sense of humor. If you're going through a horrible experience, keep reminding yourself of what a great story it will make! Actors love to tell war stories. Many actors share the challenges and battles they've endured on a job. I learn a lot by asking, "What did you do about it?"

IN CONCLUSION

As you close the cover of this book, I hope I have opened your eyes to the truth of a larger, more realistic picture.

My goals are ongoing: to bring the craft into the present reality of the nature of our business today and to search for the tools that put actors on a higher path to artistry within that reality. This can be through adjusting techniques to make them vibrantly alive again or honestly examining the truth about the professional world. Fair or not, our job is to understand that truth and take control of our craft not just by doing, but by knowing what we're doing.

We are at the forefront of an exciting new century, not unlike the Industrial Age. We can't just yearn for what has been—we must evolve into what will be. We can put our heads in the sand and hope that computers, the Internet and electronics will pass over, or we can hop on board, take the reins and find the craft of the 21st century. Past artists have found how to marry the older techniques of the craft of acting with the newer demands of television and film acting. We may be looking at acting on chips implanted in our brains someday, but hopefully the craft will have evolved so the words remain true, vital and will stir our hearts no matter what the medium might become.

The main core of this book has come from the collective effort of the many actors who have made their acting-home here in our studio. You are welcome to e-mail me with your thoughts and comments, and to join in sharing your knowledge to help us all to continue to grow in the craft.

Penny Templeton

pts158@pennytempletonstudio.com

APPENDIX A EMOTIONS / FEELINGS

JOY
Amused
Anointed
Beautiful
Cherished
Complete
Elated
Encouraged
Excited
Free
Giggly
Gleeful
Happy
Healed
Honored
Inspired
Joyous
Pretty
Purged
Rejuvenated
Relieved
Respected
Revived
Silly
Spiritual
Thrilled
Tickled
Wanted
LOVE/SEX
Adoring
Aroused
Cuddled
Cute
Drunk with
    love

Enticed
Flirty
Horny
Hot
Hugged
Kinky
Loved
Loving
Maternal
Mesmerized
Needed
Nurturing
Paternal
Puppy love
Romantic
Seduced
Seductive
Sexy
Sparked
Stripped
Tempted
Tickled
Tingly
Titillated
Touched
Wanted
Warmed
**ANGER/
HATE**
Angry
Appalled
Boiling
Castrated
Defensive
Enraged

Envious
Furious
Hateful
Irritable
Jealous
Livid
Mad
Loathsome
Murderous
Pissed
Prejudiced
Steamed
Vengeful
SAD
Abandoned
Abused
Confused
Crushed
Damaged
Depressed
Drained
Dumped
Empty
Grief - stricken
Guilty
Hurt
Lonely
Lost
Mourning
Punished
Ratted out
Rejected
Rock-bottom
Sad
Shaken

Sullen
Tormented
Worthless
**POWER/
CONTROL**
Avenged
Balanced
Calm
Cemented
Charged
Clear
Cool
Determined
Devilish
Dirty
Dominant
Driven
Focused
Godly
Heroic
Ignited
In control
Intelligent
I've got you
Magical
On Fire
Possessive
Regal
Reinforced
Smooth
Sparked
Steady
Strong
Super-natural
Triumphant

Unhinged
United
Victorious
Wicked
ANXIOUS
Alarmed
Alerted
Amazed
Baited
Bothered
Breathless
Caged
Concerned
Curious
Distracted
Examined
Flipped
Frantic
Frozen
Guarded
Haunted
Hopeless
Infected
Intimidated
Itchy
Longing
Lurid
Melted
'Oh shit'
Out of control
Paranoid
Pressured
Protected
Sympathetic
WEAK
Bent
Bored
Challenged

Burdened
Confused
Cornered
Crucified
Crushed
Depleted
Derailed
Desperate
Diffused
Engulfed
Exposed
Unwrapped
Embarrassed
Exhausted
Freaked out
Frustrated
Fucked
Gawky
Humiliated
Insecure
On the edge
Paraded
Pulverized
Punched
Rattled
Respectful
Ripped
Scared
Scarred
Sheltered
Shielded
Small
Smeared
Smothered
Speechless
Stupid
Submissive
Swayed

Swatted
Terrified
Tested
Tortured
Toyed with
Vulnerable
Wasted
Weak
Wimpy

APPENDIX B SECRET INNER ACTION VERBS

DEFLECT/
WITHDRAW
Abandon
Abstain
Back off
Bite the bullet
Bluff
Bolt
Bypass
Coast
Concede
Cover
Deflect
Disengage
Disguise
Dump
Escape
Give up
Grieve
Head butt
Pull back
Purge
Push back
Recover
Regroup
Release
Say uncle
Sidestep
Smokescreen
Steady
Surrender
Take the hit
Throw off scent
Wall out
DESTROY/
OPPRESS
Ambush
Annihilate

Asphyxiate
Atomize
Avenge
Banish
Betray
Bitch slap
Bleed
Castrate
Condemn
Crucify
Crush
Cut down
Deceive
Demolish
Detonate
Douse
Embarrass
Exterminate
Flay
Haunt
Humiliate
Infantize
Nail
Neutralize
Pave
Pin
Pulverize
Punish
Rattle
Rip
Shrink
Smear
Smother
Squash
Stalk
Terrorize
Torture
Whip

EXAMINE/
EXPOSE
Absorb
Alert
Audition
Burst
Decipher
Digest
Dissect
Dive into
Examine
Extract
Feel out
Flush
Focus
Gauge
Hone in
Laser
Measure
Process
Replay
Retrace
Scan
Scope
Score
Search
Snitch
Spy
Strip
Target
Test
Uncover
Unravel
Unwrap
Weed
X-ray

Zero in

BUILD/
PROTECT
Affirm
Anchor
Anoint
Balance
Barricade
Bond
Buck up
Cherish
Comfort
Commit
Crown
Defend
Encourage
End the pain
Enfold
Fix
Gather myself
Guard
Heal
Hold
Honor
Hug
Mend
Merge
Plug
Protect
Rebuild
Reinforce
Revive
Salvage
Save
Share
Shield

Shelter
Unite

**LEAD/
CONTROL**
Align
Ambush
Arm
Bend
Block
Bonfire
Capture
Catch
Cement
Challenge
Collar
Concoct
Confuse
Conspire
Corner
Corral
Correct
Crucify
Cut through
Derail
Disarm
Drive
Engulf
Flip
Force out
Freeze
F**k with
Govern
Grab attention
Guide
Guiltify
Hide
Hypnotize
Inspire

Instruct
Intimidate
Intrigue
Launch
Leash
Maneuver
Mobilize
Parade
Plant
Plot
Provoke
Push
Put down
Redirect
Reign
Reject
Remind
Scold
Separate
Share a secret
Shove
Shut down
Snag
Snare
Spur
Squelch
Stamp
Stir
Tag
Take charge
Take stage
Toy with
Train
Trap
Turn around
Twist
**SELL/
SEDUCE**
Amuse
Appeal
Arouse
Bait

Bargain
Beguile
Bewitch
Bonfire
Bribe
Camouflage
Carrot
Captivate
Charm
Close the deal
Coax
Come on
Deal
Decoy
Dissuade
Enchant
Enlist
Enthrall
Entice
Entwine
Fascinate
Foreplay
Gain entry
Hook
Hustle
Hypnotize
Ignite
Infect
Lure
Magnetize
Manipulate
Melt
Mermaid
Mesmerize
Mousetrap
Pitch
Placate
Seduce
Showboat
Slide in
Smooth
Snare

Spark
Steer
String along
Suck in
Sway
Sweep off feet
Tempt
Trap
Web
Wheedle

APPENDIX C   OUTER TACTIC VERB LIST

DESTROY/ OPPRESS
Abandoning
Annihilating
Avalanching
Biting
Blasting
Bolting
Bombing
Bruising
Chopping
Clamping
Clasping
Clenching
Clobbering
Corking
Crucifying
Devouring
Dropping
Grinding
Hammering
Harpooning
Headbutting
Jabbing
Mocking
Nail-gunning
Pummeling
Ridiculing
Ripping
Scalding
Searing
Shoving
Slamming
Slicing

Smearing
Sniping
Spitting
Stampeding
Steamrolling
Stinging
Stomping
Strangling
Stuffing
Throttling
Trampling
Trapping
Whipping

EXAMINE/ EXPOSE
Absorbing
Alerting
Analyzing
Announcing
Bumping
Carving
Challenging
Charging
Chipping
Daring
Digging
Dissecting
Drilling
Dueling
Exploring
Filtering
Gauging
Gawking
Glaring

Grilling
Groping
Interrogating
Kneading
Lasering
Measuring
Nailing
Negotiating
Opening
Patting
Peeling
Peering
Pinning
Poking
Popping
Probing
Processing
Prodding
Prowling
Replaying
Rooting
Scraping
Searching
Sifting
Sneaking
Sniffing
Spying
Stalking
Tapping
Trolling
Weighing
X-raying

LEAD/ MANIPULATE
Torquing

Buttering
Coaching
Collaring
Commanding
Commiserating
Counseling
Cranking
Diving into
Entwining
Ferreting
Flipping
Gossiping
Grabbing
Gripping
Injecting
Luring
Nabbing
Ordering
Plunging
Pontificating
Pushing
Queening
Rallying
Refereeing
Reminding
Shoving
Shuffling
Snagging
Soldiering
Spelling out
Spurring
Stacking
Teaching

ACTING LIONS

Thumping
Toying
Trumping
Twisting

**DEFLECT/
WITHDRAW**

Amnesia-ing
Backing off
Begging
Blanketing
Bracing
Breezing
Burrowing
Caving in
Cocooning
Cringing
Crumpling
Dashing
Deadpanning
Despairing
Detaching
Dismissing
Drifting
Dummying
Dusting
Festering
Fogging
Freezing
Frosting
Gawking
Glossing
Grieving
Groaning
Groping
Guarding
Holding
Lambing

Lurching
Marinating
Monotone-ing
Mourning
Pasting
Pleading
Plodding
Pouring
Recoiling
Scampering
Scanicking
   (scan/panic)
Scratching
Sighing
Slipping
Spackling
Swallowing
Sweeping
Swimming
Tap dancing
Tip-toeing
Tossing off
Walling out

**BUILD/
PROTECT**

Adorning
Affirming
Applauding
Awarding
Bracing
Breathing
Cherishing
Confiding
Enfolding
Feeding
Fortressing
Fueling

Healing
Honoring
Hugging
Inhaling
Knighting
Lambing
Mommy-ing
Patting
Praying
Perking
Proclaiming
Sailing
Savoring
Shielding
Soaring
Sparking
Stitching
Superhero-ing
Vowing
Warning

**SELL/
SEDUCE**

Bargaining
Bathing
Buddha-ing
Befriending
Boasting
Bragging
Charming
Cheering
Chirping
Come-hithering
Coochi-cooing
Dancing
Daring
Dreaming
Drooling

Enticing
Flirting
Gleaming
Gushing
Hypnotizing
Inspiring
Leering
Licking
Marveling
Massaging
Oiling
Peacocking
Purring
Rubbing
Sliding In
Slithering
Smoldering
Smoothing
Sprinkling
Sparkling
Spell-casting
Spinning
Spooning
Stripping
Strutting
Sugarcoating
Teasing
Tempting

Appendix D
Sample Outline for a Character Bio

Character's name/nickname:
    Reason for nickname:

Birthplace:

Present living circumstances:

Present political and social environment:

Character's innate intelligence:

Physical appearance:

    Actual age:
    How old does the character look?
    Type of body/build:
    Distinguishing marks:
    Healthy? If not, Why?

Interests, activities, favorites:

    Color:
    Music:
    Time of day:
    Food:
    Literature:
    Sayings:
    Swear words:
    Mannerisms:
    Hobby:
    Inspirations, including other people:

Background:
    What was the character's childhood like?
    Religious background:
    Education:

Relationship with mother:
Relationship with father:
Relationship with siblings, if any:
Birth order, if any:
Other important family relationships:
Economic status:
Social status:

Point of View:

When is the character most comfortable?
Least comfortable?
Philosophy of life:
Self-worth:
Views on politics:
Optimist or pessimist?
Introvert or extrovert?
Greatest vulnerability:
Biggest regret:
Greatest accomplishment to date:
Darkest secret:
Does anyone know?

What one word would the character use to describe self?
Maturity level:
Sense of humor:

Interpersonal relationships:

Important current relationship:
Past important relationships:
Married? Single, Divorced?
Children?
Dependent on others?
Independent?
Friends?
Describe their social life:
Attitude toward sexuality:

Life goals:

> Immediate goals:
> Long-range goals:
> Has this character accomplished goals in the past?
> Will they accomplish goals now?

Crises and conflict:

> How does this character react to crises?
> Coping skills:
> Types of repeating problems in life:
> Patterns of behavior:
> Reaction to conflict:

GLOSSARY OF ACTING TERMS

Actions/Intentions: The action verbs the actor uses to fulfill the Objective/Driving Question. i.e. to possess.

Activity: A specific physical task that may or may not be connected to an action, such as a character loading a gun or packing a suitcase.

Ad-Lib: Spoken words (sometimes witty comments) said out loud that are not in the script. They can also be given "off the cuff" when another actor forgets a line.

Adjustment: A direction or modification an actor makes in the playing of material. They are often instructions given by the director.

Affective memory: (Or "Remembered emotion") Memory that involves the actor personally, so that deeply rooted emotional experiences begin to respond. His instrument begins to awaken and he becomes capable of the kind of living on stage which is essentially reliving.

Animal work: Sensory and body work based on the observation of animals, birds and reptiles.

Apron: The area of the stage in front of the proscenium arch.

Arena: A type of stage where the audience is seated on three sides (also referred to as Thrust).

Aside: A character's comment or observation, often delivered directly to the audience or themselves.

Beat: 1. A component of spoken material with a single action. A new beat occurs when the character changes what he is doing to attain his objective. **2.** In blocking, holding for 1 second=1 beat.

Blocking: To set the movements of actors on a stage or set. Also, any given movement that enhances the scene, such as a specific character gesture.

Central conflict: The oppositional force between characters that directly affects or motivates the action of the plot.

Characterization: The actor using their craft to explore and develop the specific qualities of a character.

Cheating or Opening Out: Angling or squaring the body out toward the audience or camera, while still partly facing the other actor/character.

Cold Reading: Unfamiliar material, such as a scene or audition sides. An audition in which you are asked to read from copy you are not familiar with, generally with little or no time to prepare.

Composition: The arrangement of the staging and design elements to create a visual picture.

Conflict: An essential and vital element of acting that involves the obstacles and struggles (inner and outer) that a character must overcome to reach their objective.

Countering: A blocking movement by an actor to rebalance the stage in reaction to another actor's movement, or change of position.

Cue: The action, line, or phrase of dialogue that signals your character to move or speak.

Cue-to-Cue: A tech rehearsal where to save time, action and text is cut out between cues.

Dialogue: The written words spoken by the actors/characters.

Downstage: The front of the stage or the part closest to the audience.

Dramaturge: A profession in theatre that deals mainly with the research and development of plays. The dramaturge often assists the director in the preparation of a production.

Driving Question: Always beginning with "How can I...?" It is the rephrasing of the actor's objective in the active and very specific form of a question that needs to be answered in the scene, i.e. "How can I rip the blinders from her eyes?"

Dry tech: The rehearsal and setting of lighting, scenery, and sound cues, in preparation for the full technical rehearsal with actors.

Emotion: The agitation of feelings such as: sadness, power, fear, love, hate and joy. These can be followed by responses such as: rapid heartbeat, crying or shaking.

Emotional Recall: (or Emotional Memory) The emotions from an actor's memory (long or short term) of personal experiences that are used to connect the actor to the character, and meet the emotional needs of the situation in the play or film.

Endowment: To give physical or emotional attributes to your character, to create more reality and meaning to further the needs of the story. Objects can also be endowed with physical, emotional or historical attributes: shaving without a blade, removing wet clothing when it's not wet, drinking water as if it's vodka.

Fourth wall: The imaginary wall which separates the actors from the audience, and the audience from the stage. The actor uses it to create the reality in the scene, and keep one's mind in the world of the film or play.

Framing: Crafting and sculpting individual moments for the purpose of highlighting them.

Given circumstances: The background and current circumstances of a character, ranging from who you are, where you are, and why you are doing it. The costumes, sets and lighting—all the circumstances that are given to the actor to take into account as they create their role.

Group Theatre: Founded by Harold Clurman, Cheryl Crawford and Lee Strasberg in the 1930's, the Group Theatre based its acting on the innovative teachings of Constantin Stanislavsky. A renowned American theatrical company whose members included: Lee Strasberg, Stella Adler, Bobby Lewis, Sandford Meisner and Harold Clurman. The company was based on an ensemble approach to acting as first seen in the Moscow Art Theater, and changed the course of American theatre forever. They created new American plays with a vision that spoke to and reflected the common man and to change the troubled times. The traditions of the Group Theatre are continued to this day.

Happiness: (also called The Super Objective) The character's long term objective or "big dream" in life. The "happiness" does not necessarily apply directly to any single scene but has an effect on every scene. It also helps in providing conflict and dimension to every scene.

Improvisation: Setting out to do a scene with no pre-planned or written idea. A process leading to spontaneous discovery that allows the actor to find real, organic impulses within themselves.

Impulse: A natural response that an actor responds to in the moment.

Indicating: Showing what your character is feeling or doing without really feeling or doing, leading to a false and shallow performance.

Inner Action: A physical action verb chosen by the actor in the pursuit of an objective. It always begins with the word "to" i.e. to attack, to soothe, to tickle.

Inner Life/Inner Monologue: A character's active, imaginative inner thoughts while the actor is playing a role.

Instinct: A compelling or powerful impulse.

Instrument: The actor's collective working of the body, voice, mind, and imagination.

Intention: Another word for an acting objective, or action, that an actor pursues while onstage.

Line Cue: The last portion of the last line before your cue begins.

Magic if/What if ? : Created by Stanislavsky, the actor tries to answer the question, *"If this were real, how would I react?"*

Meisner Technique: An acting program that uses (among other things) repetitive and in-the-moment exercises first devised by Sanford Meisner of the Group Theatre. The technique emphasizes "moment-to-moment" spontaneity through communication with other actors to generate behavior that is "truthful under imaginary circumstances."

Meisner also emphasized using the actor's imagination to create emotional reality—the creative "as-if"— over the personal, emotional experience philosophy championed by fellow Group Theatre member Lee Strasberg.

Method, The: A generic term used to describe the acting philosophy of using personal emotional experiences in acting, as first introduced to the Western world by Stanislavsky and furthered by members of America's Group Theatre in the 1930's. When used today, "The Method" most often refers to the deeply personal emotional work taught by followers of Lee Strasberg, one of the Group Theatre members, and can be summed up as: "Training the subconscious to behave spontaneously."

Moment-to-moment: The acting process concentrating on the present, not what's going to happen in the future.

Monologue: An uninterrupted speech by a character in a performance. The monologue may be to another character or the audience.

Moscow Art Theatre: Co-founded in 1897 by Constantin Stanislavsky with Vladimir Nemirovich-Danchenko. The theatre was conceived as a venue for naturalistic theatre, as opposed to the melodramatic style which was popular in Russia at the time.

Motivation: The Why? The reason a character pursues a particular objective or super objective.

Objects: Physical items used by the actor to enhance and add give more reality to a character.

Objective: A character's pursuit of a specific goal in a scene. Also referred to as the intention or driving question.

Obstacle: The conflict and stumbling blocks to a character's struggle in pursuit of an action or objective.

Organic: A natural response that comes (organically) from deep within the character/actor.

Outer Tactics: The method or "how" an actor/character goes about doing their action in a beat. An active verb form preceded with "by" always ending in "ing." Each beat has both an Inner Action and an Outer Tactic: To gain entry (Inner Action)/By honeying (Outer Tactic.)

Pace: The speed at which you pick up your cue and deliver the next line of your dialogue. Pace can also be the speed that creates a style for the piece.

Pantomime: An art form related to the dance; not to be confused with "silent scenes" or a "scene without words."

Physical gesture: A specific movement or physical action of a character that expresses the psychology, feelings and desires incorporated into one gesture. It is often used by the actor to awaken the essence of his character.

Particularization: The process Uta Hagen taught, making each event, person and place (down to the smallest physical object) as exact as possible. These details are explored in great detail to discover how they are relevant to the character.

Physicalization: To express with the body. Showing as opposed to telling. Externals of a character, such as how they eat, walk and talk.

Presentational: An actor's awareness of the audience through direct address to the audience, by looks, signs or gestures.

Private Moment: A well-known technique developed by Lee Strasberg, based on Stanislavsky's theory that the challenge of the actor is to "act privately in public." An individual acting exercise (performed in front of others) in which the actor does an intensely personal activity while alone, while giving the effect of "being private in public."

Psychological gesture: If we define gesture to mean a movement that has intention, we could say that the Psychological Gesture is a movement that expresses the psychology of the character.

Props: All objects on a theatrical or film set, used by the actors. **Hand Props:** often small and hand-carried objects used by actors during performance, i.e. glasses, wallet, handkerchief. **Practical Props:** props that actually have to work during performance, i.e. cigarette lighter, flashlight.

Representational: Represents "realism." Characters in their real lives that are not aware the audience is there.

Run: 1. A series of brief lines building to a speech or key moment. **2.** The number of performances a show does.

Script Analysis: The close study of a play or screenplay. This incorporates all of the dialogue and stage directions to find the answers necessary to create a full and rich character and to craft a performance that serves the script. The exploration of the script may include the questions of theme, story, character, and overall elements of the play and characters.

Sensory: Connecting the character to the body and mind through the senses; to taste, hear, feel, see, think, perceive; to know through the physical inner self, as opposed to the instinctive.

Sense memory: (emotional recall) The basis for Lee Strasberg's Method Acting. "Sense memory" is used to refer to the recall of physical sensations: sight, touch, taste, smell, and sound. These physical sensations surround an emotional event, instead of the emotions themselves.

Sides: A portion of a script (pages) selected for an audition that highlights a specific character.

Soliloquy: A speech given directly to the audience, ordinarily with no one else on stage. Usually played as a direct address to the audience, sometimes played as a character thinking aloud in the audience's presence.

Speed-through: A rehearsal with actors going through the lines of the play as quickly as possible, picking up the cues. Sometimes called a "glib thru."

Spontaneity: A free unplanned impulsive moment.

Stage Business: A stage activity used to accent, intensify, or heighten the manner in which one uses an object on stage.

Stage Directions: The writer's insertions of blocking, reactions, gestures, or use of props to clarify the action.

Staging: The final results of blocking—Alternatively called blocking.

Stage Left: In a proscenium theatre, the actor's left, while facing the audience.

Stage Right: In a proscenium theatre, the actor's right, while facing the audience.

Stakes: The heightened consequences for each character of achieving or failing to achieve their objectives.

Stanislavsky, Constantin (1863-1938): Russian theatre director, actor, and teacher most responsible for the manner and technique in which the craft of acting is taught. Co-founder/director of the Moscow Art Theatre in 1897 with Vladimir Nemirovich-Danchenko. He developed a "system" or "method" by which actors could consistently produce superior work by tapping into themselves and their real feelings, to create naturalistic acting as opposed to the representational acting style popular at the time.

Strasberg, Lee (1901-1982): Acting teacher, artistic director of the Actor's Studio, and developer of what came to be known as "Method Acting," an approach based on early writings of Stanislavsky. His teaching method was based on Stanislavsky; but, among other things, Strasberg intensely focused on actors exploring past memories to use real emotions to connect them to their character.

Subtext: The character's complex thoughts, feelings, motives, etc. created and layered under the actual words and actions of the character by the actor.

Substitution: The recasting of people, objects, and events in the script that the character must react act to, with real people, objects and events that the actor has known or experienced in their own life.

Super objective: Stanislavsky developed the concept of the *super-objective* (referred to here as The Happiness) that would carry the 'through line of action,' mapped out for the character through the entire play.

Tactics: "How" a character goes about achieving their goal. Also, specifically the way a character "masks" their inner action or intention, on the outside: i.e. to alarm (inner action) by freaking out (outer tactic).

Tasks: Pieces of work or functions that need to be done, the total of which comprises an overall activity.

Tempo; pace; rhythm: The level of speed with which the scene or play is acted out. The general effect creates a specific mood or tone to the work.

Three-Quarters (Actually ¼): A stage position in a proscenium theatre, where the actor is facing half-way toward the actor to their side and half-way toward the audience. Thus the audience is essentially seeing a three-quarter view of the actor.

Through line of action or continuity: Stanislavsky's concept of the inner line of effort that guides the actors from the beginning to the end of the play. (An Actor Prepares)

Transference: Uta Hagen's term for the actor's process of making transferences from their own experiences to those in the play until they become synonymous with them.

Trigger: An emotional or physical signal that signals or sparks a bonfire of emotion to break through to the surface.

Upstage: The opposite of downstage; the back part of stage in a proscenium theatre; the farthest part from the audience. Derives from the eighteenth century, when the stage was slanted, or "raked" toward the audience, with the rear of the stage higher than the front.

Upstaging: To go upstage of an actor with whom you are sharing a scene. This causes the other actor to be in the downstage, weakened position of having to face upstage to maintain the illusion of eye contact.

Upping the stakes: Increasing and upping the importance on a scene or moment to heighten the dramatic tension of the character or scene.

World of the play: What happens. Where it happens. When it happens. The circumstances affected by the society, economics, culture and politics of the time. What we learn from the setting of the play.

FILM & TELEVISION

ADR: (Automatic Dialogue Replacemrnt) see looping.

Cinematographer: The expert responsible for capturing, recording or photographing images for a film, through the selection of visual recording devices, camera angles, film stock, lenses, framing, and arrangement of lighting.

CU: Close up.

Double: A person doubling for a principal actor usually for stunts (dangerous shots).

DP: Director of photography, the head cinematographer.

Eye Line: Eye line is the direction an actor should look off-screen to match a reverse angle or a P.O.V. (point of view) shot. It is best to give the actor an actual thing or spot to look at rather than a blank spot on an empty wall or an empty space in mid air.

Extras: Actors hired for non-specific, non-speaking roles, to add background atmosphere and reality.

First AD: The First Assistant Director. This is the director's right hand man, who basically stage manages the entire set.

Holding: The area or bus set aside for extras to wait between scenes.

Key 2nd AD: The senior 2nd AD is responsible for having extras on set at the right time, blocking extras into crowd scenes, cueing of extras etc.

Looping: The recording or re-recording of dialogue for a previously for filmed scene.

M.O.S: A shot, a sequence, or a film that is shot without sound, which is added later. M.O.S. stands for "With Out Sound," and derives from German director (Otto Preminger) asking for a shot to be filmed "Mit out sound," which was written "M.O.S." on the slate.

OC: Off camera.

Off: 1. A scene starting with a shot of one actor and opening to the scene. 2. A cue to an actor to take their cue off of the reaction of another actor. (see reaction shot)

OS: Off stage.

Over the Shoulder: A camera shot of the scene shot from behind or "over the shoulder" of a principal actor, revealing what they are seeing from their point of view.

Pick Up: Reshooting a section of a scene from a specific point. i.e. "We'll pick it up from here."

Piggy Back: A camera shot with both actors involved, facing the camera one behind the other. The "piggyback" allows both characters to have their private thoughts about each other, while allowing the audience to see what both characters are thinking.

POV: A shot that shows the scene through the character's eyes. We see the world from their point of view.

Reaction Shot: The camera shooting a character's emotional or physical response or reaction to something that is happening in the scene.

Reverse: A camera shot set up to shoot the reverse 180° view of the previous shot.

Second AD: Second Assistant Director. On most sets there are many 2nd AD's responsible for everything from crowd control, extras, parking, traffic control, security, cueing, and actors on camera.

Second Team: Stand-ins for the principals involved in a specific scene. You will hear an AD yell "Second Team!" calling stand-ins on set to stand where the principals were, while the DP lights the scene and the camera operators rehearse their moves and focus.

Spreading the Shot: One actor stands too far from the other, which "spreads the shot out."

Stand-in: An extra hired for size and coloring to double for a principal actor for lighting and camera set ups.

Take: A reaction shot of an actor. i.e. "take Stabler."

Video Village: The area where all of the camera shots are fed into video monitors, allowing the director to get an accurate view of every shot.

VO (Voice Over): A recording that will either be added later or played back while shooting the scene.

BOOKS

ACTING THEORY AND TECHNIQUE:

Adler, Stella. *The Art of Acting*. New York: Applause Theatre and Cinema Book Publishers, 2000.

Adler, Stella. *The Technique of Acting*. New York: Bantam Books, 1988.

Boleslavsky, Richard. *Acting: The First Six Lessons*. London: Routledge, 1970.

Chekhov, Michael. *To The Actor: On the Technique of Acting*. London and New York: Routledge, 2002.

Chubback, Ivana. *The Power Of The Actor*. New York: Gotham Books, 2004.

Cohen, Lola (Ed.) *The Lee Strasberg Notes*. New York: Routledge, 2010.

Easty, Edward Dwight. *On Method Acting*. New York: Ivy Books, 1989.

Esper, William and Damion Di Marco. *The Actor's Art and Craft*. New York: Anchor Books, 2008.

Hagen, Uta. *A Challenge for the Actor*. New York: Scribner, 1991.

Hagen, Uta. *Respect For Acting*. New York: Wiley, 1973.

Elizabeth Hapgood (Ed.) Stanislavski, Constantin. *An Actor's Handbook.*. Theatre Arts Books, 1963.

Katselas, Milton. *Acting Class, Take a Seat*. Los Angeles: Phoenix Books, 2008.

Meisner, Sanford and Dennis Longwell. *On Acting*. New York: Random House, 1987.

Moss, Larry. *The Intent to Live*. New York: Bantam Books, 2005.

Rotté, Joanna. *Acting with Adler*. New York: Limelight Editions, 2004.

Schreiber, Terry. *Acting: Advanced Techniques for the Actor, Director and Teacher*. New York: Allworth Press, 2005.

Shurtliff, Michael. *Audition*. New York: Random House, 1981.

Silverberg, Larry. *The Sanford Meisner Approach, Volume I: An Actor's Workbook*. New Hampshire: Smith and Kraus, 1994.

Stanislavsky, Constantin. *An Actor Prepares*. New York: Theatre Arts Books, 1989.

Stanislavsky, Constantin. *Building A Character*. New York: Theatre Arts Books, 1961.

Stanislavsky, Constantin. *Creating A Role*. New York: Theatre Arts Books, 1961.

Strasberg, Lee. *A Dream of Passion: A Development of Method, Reissue Ed*. New York: Plume Books, 1990.

Strasberg, Lee and Robert H. Hethmon (Ed.). *Strasberg at the Actors Studio: Tape-Recorded Sessions*. New York: Viking Press, 1965.

Wangh, Stephen. *The Acrobat of The Heart: A Physical Approach to Acting Inspired by the Work of Jerzy Grotowski*. New York: Vintage Books, 2000.

AUTOBIOGRAPHY AND BIOGRAPHY:

Bragg, Melvyn. *Richard Burton: A Life*. London: Little, Brown and Company, 1988.

Eliot, Marc. *Cary Grant: A Biography*. New York: Harmony Books, 2004.

Poitier, Sidney. *The Measure of a Man*. San Francisco: HarperSanFrancisco, 2000.

Walker, Alexander. *Vivien: The Life of Vivien Leigh*. New York: Grove Press, 1987.

BUSINESS OF ACTING:

Alterman, Glenn. *Promoting Your Acting Career: A Step by Step Guide to Opening The Right Doors.* New York: Allworth Press, 2004.

Becker, Leslie. *7 Roles Every Actor Must Play: How to Take on the Business Side of Acting and Flourish in the Part.* New York: Triple Threat Ventures, 2007.
http://www.organizedactor.com/

Becker. Leslie. *The Organized Actor, 4th Ed.* New York: Lulu, 2006.

Colvin, Geoff. *Talent Is Overrated: What Really Separates World Class Performers From Everybody Else.* New York: Penguin, 2008.

Emory, Margaret. *Ask An Agent: Everything Actors Need to Know About Agents.* New York: Back Stage Books, 2005.

Gillespie, Bonnie. *Self Management For Actors: Getting Down to (Show) Business, 3rd Ed.* Los Angeles: Cricket Feet Publishing, 2009.

Henry, Mari Lyn and Lynne Rogers. *How to Be A Working Actor, 5th Ed.* New York: Back Stage Books, 2007.

DIRECTING ACTORS:

Badham, John and Craig Modderno. *I'll Be in My Trailer: The Creative Wars Between Directors And Actors.* Los Angeles: Michael Wiese Productions, 2006.

Ball, William. *A Sense of Direction.* New York: Drama Book Publishers, 1984.

Bogart, Anne. *A Director Prepares: Seven Essays on Art and Theatre.* London: Routledge, 2001.

Lumet, Sidney. *Making Movies.* New York: Vintage Books, 1996.

HISTORY AND REFERENCES:

Clurman, Harold. *The Fervent Years.* New York: Knopf, 1945.

Rand, Ronald and Luigi Scorcia. *Acting Teachers Of America: A Vital Tradition.* New York: Allworth Press, 2007.

Smith, Wendy. *Real Life Drama: The Group Theatre and America 1931-1940.* New York: Alfred A. Knopf, 1990.

Stanislavsky, Constantin. *My Life In Art.* New York: Theatre Arts Books, 1961.

MONOLOGUES AND SCENE RESOURCES:

Hooks, Ed. *Ultimate Scene and Monologue Book. An Actor's Reference to over 1,000 Monologues and Scenes from More Than 300 Contemporary Plays.* New York: Crown, 2007.

Terkel, Studs. *Coming of Age: Growing Up in the Twentieth Century.* New York: The New Press, 2007.

Terkel, Studs. *Working.* New York: The New Press. 1997.

ON CAMERA ACTING:

Barr, Tony. *Acting For the Camera, Rev. Ed.* New York: Perennial Currents, 1997.

Brestoff, Richard. *The Camera Smart Actor.* Hanover, NH: Smith and Kraus, 1994.

Caine, Michael. *Acting In Film: An Actor's Take on Movie Making, Rev. Ed.* New York: Applause Books, 1997.

VOICE:

Linklater, Kristin. *Freeing Shakespeare's Voice. Rev. Ed.* New York: Drama Publishers, 2006.

Chwat, Sam. The SpeakUp! Self Study Program for Eliminating American Regional Accents;

Eliminating Spanish Accents;

Eliminating Asian, Middle Eastern and Pacific Accents (includes Russian, Slavic, Arabic, Hebrew, Indian/Pakistani/Hindi/Urdu, Japanese, Chinese, Cambodian, Vietnamese, Filipino/Tagalog Accents).

All include 4 CDs with a 272-page manual of exercises.

WRITING AND PERFORMING:

Cameron, Julia. *The Artist's Way: A Spiritual Path to Higher Creativity.* New York: Jeremy P. Tarcher/Putnam, 1992.

Catron, Louis E. *The Power of One: The Solo Play for Playwrights, Actors and Directors.* Portsmouth, NH: Heinemann, 2000.

Kearns, Michael. *The Solo Performer's Journey: From the Page to the Stage.* Portsmouth, NH: Heinemann, 2005.

McKee, Robert. *Story: Substance, Structure, Style and The Principles of Screenwriting.* New York: HarperCollins, 1997.

Merson, Susan. *Your Name Here: An Actor's/Writer's Guide to Solo Performance.* Nevada: Star Publish, 2004.

Polti, Georges. *The Thirty-Six Dramatic Situations.* Ridgewood, NJ: The Editor Company, 1917.

Tobias, Ronald. *20 Master Plots: And How to Build Them.* Cincinnati, OH: Writer's Digest Books, 1993.

DVDs

Caine, Michael. *Acting In Film: An Actor's Take on Movie Making.* BBC, 1989.

Hagen, Uta. *Uta Hagen's Acting Class: The DVDs.* Applause Books, 2004.

Kubrick, Stanley. *The Shining (Two-Disc Special Edition).* Warner Home Video, 2007. (Specifically *The Making of the Shining* documentary with optional commentary by Vivian Kubrick.)

Lipton, James. *Inside the Actors Studio.* Shout!Factory, 1994-current.

McKellan, Ian. *Acting Shakespeare (1982).* E1 Entertainment, 2010.

Meisner, Sanford. *Sanford Meisner Master Class.* Sanford Meisner Estate, 2007.

ONLINE COLUMNS

For in-depth exploration of the business of acting, auditions, etc.:

Gillespie, Bonnie. *The Actor's Voice.* Actors Access, www.actorsaccess.com/content/columns.cfm

Sikes, Mark. *The Casting Corner.* www.actorsaccess.com/content/columns.cfm

ESSENTIAL WEBSITES

UNIONS

www.sag.org
www.actorsequity.org
www.aftra.org

VOICE, ACCENTS AND DIALECTS:

http://www.nyspeech.com
http://www.kristinlinklater.com
http://web.ku.edu/~idea/

FREE SCRIPTS:

www.script-o-rama.com
www.simplyscripts.com
www.imsdb.com
www.showfax.com
www.joblo.com/moviescripts.php
http://sfy.ru/scripts.html
www.weeklyscript.com

FREE MONOLOGUES:

www.whysanity.net/monos
www.shakespeare-monologues.org
www.notmyshoes.net/monologues

CASTING SITES:

Actors Access - www.actorsaccess.com
LA Casting - www.lacasting.com
Backstage/Backstage West - www.backstage.com
NY Castings - www.nycastings.com
Nowcasting - www.nowcasting.com
Sag Indie - www.sagindie.org
Casting Networks - www.nycasting.com
Playbill - www.playbill.com
IMDbPro - http://pro.imdb.com
Equity Association -
http://www.actorsequity.org/CastingCall/castingcallhome.asp

Go to www.PennyTempletonStudio.com
for updates to On-Line Resources

REFERENCES

Abbott & Costello, The Baseball Almanac. *Who's on First.* Abbott & Costello transcript. Retrieved from www.baseball-almanac.com (pg.124)

Adler, S. & Kissel, H. (Ed.). (2000). *The Art of Acting.* Canada: Applause Books. (pg. 22) "When you stand…listen."-Stella Adler. (pg. 29)

Adler, S. & Kissel, H. (Ed.). (2000). *The Art of Acting.* Canada: Applause Books. (pg.65) "You have to…experiences."-Stella Adler. (pg. 26)

Aleksander, I. (2008). At Fete for Ethan Hawke, Actors Justin Long and Billy Crudup Recall What It's Like to Be Laid Off. *The New York Observer.* Retrieved from www.observer.com. "It's was my…weeks."-Billy Crudup (pg. 273)

Bosworth, P. (2007). *Montgomery Clift: A Biography.* United States: Proscenium Publishers. (pg.147) "Failure and its…energy." - Montgomery Clift (pg. 272)

Bragg, M. (1988). *Richard Burton: A Life.* United State: Little, Brown, and Company. (pg.33) "He didn't adopt…him." -Richard Burton (pg. 2)

Bragg, M. (1988). *Richard Burton: A Life.* United State: Little, Brown, and Company. (pg. 84) "say the chorus…mattered." -Richard Burton (pg. 3)

Buckley, M. (2004). Stage to Screen: A Chat with Theresa Rebeck; Remembering Uta Hagen. Retrieved from www.playbill.com. "Working with Brando…together."- Uta Hagen (pg.149)

Caine, M. (1997). *Acting in Film.* New York, NY: Applause Theatre Cinema Books. (pg. 61) "Blinking makes your…across." – Michael Caine (pg.174)

Dafoe, W. (2011) CBS Entertainment. *Willem Dafoe Trivia and Quotes.* Retrieved from www.tv.com. "One of the …learned." – Willem Dafoe (pg. 60)

Depp, J. (2011). The Internet Movie Database. *Johnny Depp.* Retrieved from www.imdb.com. "with any part… lying." -Johnny Depp (pg. 101)

Depp, J. (2011). The Internet Movie Database. *Johnny Depp*. Retrieved from www.imdb.com. "Brando wanted me…can." -Johnny Depp (pg. 180)

Freeman, M. (2011). The Internet Movie Database. *Morgan Freeman*. Retrieved from www.imdb.com. "That was a…one." -Morgan Freeman (pg. 255)

Hagen, U. & Frankel, H. (2008). *Respect for Acting*. United States: John Wiley & Sons. (pg. 31) "Talent is an …seen." -Uta Hagen (pg. 31)

Hagen, U. (1991). *A Challenge for the Actor*. New York: Scribner (pg. 134) "the 6 step"-Uta Hagen (pg.33)

Hagen, U. (1991). *A Challenge for the Actor*. New York: Scribner (pg. 170) "Endowing the objects…will." -Uta Hagen (pg. 34)

Hagen, U. (1991). *A Challenge for the Actor*. New York: Scribner (pg. 66) "The making of…specific." -Uta Hagen (pg. 34)

Hagen, U. & Frankel, H. (2008). *Respect for Acting*. United States: John Wiley & Sons. (pg. 8) "In 1947, I…doing." -Uta Hagen (pg. 59)

Harris. E. HBO Box Office. (2011). *Interview with Ed Harris*. Retrieved from www.hbo.com. "I like working…doing."-Ed Harris (pg. 251)

Hasday, J.L., (2004). *Agnes de Mille*. United States: Chelsea House Publishers. (pg. 57) "There's a vitality…open."-Martha Graham (pg. 9)

Healy, P. (2010). Better Acting Through Chemistry. *New York Times*. "We talked until…fire."-Viola Davis (pg.115)

Healy, P. (2010). Better Acting Through Chemistry. *New York Times*. "Seem inseparable in…work."-Kenny Leon (pg. 115)

Honthaner, E.L., (2005). *Hollywood Drive: What it Takes to Break in, Hang in & Make it in the Industry*. Oxford: UK: Focal Press. (pg. 141) "You've gotta be…for?"-Bernadette Peters (pg. 11)

Jaehne, K. (1995). *"Convento, O" (The Convent) Press Conference at the 1995 New York Film Festival*. Retrieved from www.filmscouts.com. "who invite you…being."-Catherine Deneuve (pg.114)

Jung, C.G. (1933). *Modern Man in Search of a Soul.* Great Britain: Routledge. (pg.49-50) "The meeting of...transformed." -Carl Gustav Jung (pg. 112)

Kanfer, S. (2008). *Somebody: The Reckless Life and Remarkable Career of Marlon Brando.* United States: Vintage Books. (Intro xi) "Never confuse the...talent." -Marlon Brando (pg. 1)

Kaplan, J. (2009). I had to Start All Over Again. *Parade Magazine,4-5.* "Not beautiful enough ... enough." -Naomi Watts (pg. 211)

Kaplan, J. (2009). I had to Start All Over Again. *Parade Magazine,4-5.* "You get to ... truth."- Naomi Watts (pg. 211)

Kubrick, Vivian. (1999) *The Making of the Shining Documentary.* Warner Bros. "I'm more prone...work." Jack Nicholson. (267)

LeBlanc, R.D. (1985). Potholes Aplenty on the Road to Success. *The Deseret News.* (pg. 3) "They said I...big."-Burt Reynolds (pg. 272)

McKellan, I. (1982). Tears in Bratislava. *The Sunday Telegraph Magazine.* Retrieved from www.mckellan.com/writings. "when it came...past." -Sir Ian McKellan (pg. 60)

Malden, K. (2004). SAG Magazine. *SAG Awards* (Volume 45/1). "The biggest lesson...be." -Karl Malden (pg. 10)

Malden, K. (2004). SAG Magazine. *SAG Awards* (Volume 45/1). "The whole idea...onstsage." -Karl Malden(pg. 41)

Meisner, S. & Longwell, D. (1987). *Sanford Meisner on Acting.* New York: Vintage. (pg.178) "Acting is living... circumstances.""-Sanford Meisner (pg. 25)

Meisner, S. & Longwell, D. (1987). *Sanford Meisner on Acting.* New York: Vintage. (pg. 128) "Don't be an...circumstances." -Sanford Meisner(pg. 25)

Mora, J. (2004). Interview: Michael Hurst on Macbeth. *National Radio.* Retrieved from www.michaelhurstnow.com. "When you're a...part."-Laurence Olivier (pg. 179)

Ms London Magazine. (2005). *Acting is a Tough Business.* "Acting is a...physically" -Juliette Binoche (pg. 11)

Nemiroff, P. (2010). *Interview: Little Focker's Robert De Niro and Ben Stiller.* Retrieved from www.cinemablend.com. "Sometimes a scene...going."-Ben Stiller (pg. 149)

O'Toole, L. (2008). Why Morgan Freeman Doesn't Fear Death at All. *Belefast Telegraph*. Retrieved from www.belfasttelegraph.co.uk. "Upon getting work...go." -Morgan Freeman (pg. 209)

Ozon, Francois.(2011). *Interview About Time to Leave. Interview with Jeanne Moreau*. Retrieved from www.francois-ozon.com. "When I'm acting...fear." -Jeanne Moreau (pg. 163)

Raindance. (2009). *Actors on Acting*. Retrieved from www.raindance.co.uk "You jot down...work."-Chris Cooper (pg. 89)

Rombauer, I., Becker Rombauer, M. & Becker, E. (1997). *Joy of Cooking*. New York: Scribner. (pg. 923) "Baking a cake...heavenly." -Joy of Cooking (pg. 57)

Rose, C. (1997). *A Rebroadcast of a Conversation with Janet McTeer*. [Television Broadcast] Charlie Rose Inc. "the whole point...acting."-Janet McTeer (pg. 82)

Scott, W. (2008). Personality Parade. *Parade Magazine*. Retrieved from www.parade.com. ""Dick (Wolf) had me...witness."-Linus Roache (pg. 224)

Stanislavsky, C. (2004). *An Actors Handbook*. New York: Routledge. (pg. 126) "The actor must...truth." -Constantin Stanislavsky (pg. 18)

Stanislavsky, C. (2003). *An Actor Prepares*. New York: Routledge. (pg. 16) "Plan your role...experienced." -Constantin Stanislavsky. (pg. 21)

Stanislavsky, C. (2003). *An Actor Prepares*. New York: Routledge. (pg. 54) "If is the...other."- Constantin Stanislavsky. (pg. 19)

Stanislavsky, C. (2003). *An Actor Prepares*. New York: Routledge. (pg.126)"What is the...exist?" Constantin Stanislavsky. (pg.19)

Strasberg, L. & Hethmon R.H. (1965). *Strasberg at the Actors Studio: Tape-Recorded Sessions*. New York: Viking Press. (pg. 209) "The Actor creates...describe." -Lee Strasberg (pg. 21)

Strasberg, L. & Hethmon R.H. (1965). *Strasberg at the Actors Studio: Tape-Recorded Sessions*. New York: Viking Press. (pg. 88) "When there is...feel." -Lee Strasberg (pg. 22)

Strasberg, L. & Hethmon R.H. (1965). *Strasberg at the Actors Studio: Tape-Recorded Sessions*. New York: Viking Press. (pg. 90) "Wherever the actor...naturally." -Lee Strasberg (pg. 22)

Strasberg, L. & Hethmon R.H. (1965). *Strasberg at the Actors Studio: Tape-Recorded Sessions.* New York: Viking Press. (pgs. 115-119) "While reading Stanislavsky...them.'" -Lee Strasberg (pg. 23)

Tapley, K., (2009). *Interview: Jeff Bridges.* Retrieved from www.incontention.com. "They had no...great." -Jeff Bridges (pg. 256)

Washington, D. *Don't Call me Mr. Biography.* Retrieved from www.iofilm.co.uk "I mean, he... training." -Denzel Washington (pg. 71)

Wolff, M. (2006). *In Sweet Company: Conversations with Extraordinary Women about Living a Spiritual Life.* United States: John Wiley & Sons. (pg. 83). " I constantly play...them." -Olympia Dukakis (pg. 175)

PHOTOGRAPH CREDITS

Photograph Credits

Adler, Stella (1991). *LA Times* interview. Photo by Stella Adler Studio (pg. 28)

Barrington, Eva (1880). Billy Rose Theatre Division, The New York Public Library for the Performing Arts, Lenox and Tilden Foundations. Photograph B-file (pg.x)

Barrington, Eva (1906). Photo by J. Willis Sayre. University of Washington Libraries, Special Collections, UW28009z (pg.x)

Davis, Viola & l Washington, Denze (2010). photo by Sara Krulwich, NY Times/ Redux 2010. Interview, Better Acting Through Chemistry. (pg114)

Hagen, Uta (1973). *Respect for Acting,* New York. Photo by Jack Mitchell (pg. 31)

Meisner, Sandford (1987). Courtesy of The Sanford Meisner Center. "Sanford Meisner on Acting" by Sandford Meisner & Dennis Longwell (pg.25)

Stanislavsky, Constantin - (date of photo unknown) German Federal Archive (pg.18)

Strasberg, Lee (Date unavailable) Photo by Ken Regan, Camera 5 www.kenregan.com (pg. 21)

INDEX

PENNY TEMPLETON

Penny Templeton's artistry is the culmination of four generations of theatre actresses. Although Penny was warned by her family not to go on the Stage, she embraced her legacy and began performing and studying under such masters as Paul Sorvino and Wynn Handman. Highlights of her career include starring in Joyce Carol Oates' *I Stand Before You Naked* at the American Place Theatre, and as Paul Sorvino's wife in *All The King's Men*.

Her unique teaching methods and techniques have garnered awareness and recognition from industry peers, including articles in national magazines, and as a finalist Judge for the New York Film Festival, Daytime Emmys and Cable Ace Awards. She started teaching in the early 1990's, and opened the Penny Templeton Studio in Manhattan in 1994. Ms. Templeton was selected by Columbia University's School of the Arts, and Catholic University in Washington, D.C. to teach 'Acting for the Camera' to third year MFA students.

Her directorial credits include the Off Broadway show, *The Rise of Dorothy Hale,* as well as the one man shows: *F Train*, and *Idiot's Guide to Life.*

She is profiled in Ronald Rand's acclaimed *Acting Teachers of America,* and Glenn Alterman's book, *Promoting Your Acting Career.* She was featured in, "The Group Theatre & How It Transformed American Culture" at the Martin E. Segal Theatre Center, The Graduate Center, City University of NY. She has also been a sought after contributor to ABC News, NBC, and radio stations, national and around the world.

Ms. Templeton works and Skypes regularly with actors in theatre, film and television in New York City, Los Angeles, throughout the United States, and all over the world.

HANK SCHOB – Contributor

Chapters: *Where to Start – Script Analysis*
Blocking and Technical Aspects.

Mr. Schob is co-owner and teacher at the Penny Templeton Studio. A graduate of the American Academy of Dramatic Arts, his years of theatre experience include Off Broadway, Regional Theatre and National Tours, Film and Television. He has worked with many notable actors, including Jose' Ferrer in *A Song For Cyrano*, and John Raitt in *Shenandoah* and *Camelot*, and the Group Theatre actors, Morris Carnovsky and Will Lee, in the 40th anniversary production of *Awake and Sing*. He was the casting director for the Independent feature film *Paragon Cortex*.

ACTING LIONS

www.ActingLions.com